Acclaim for Jane Smiley's

A YEAR AT THE RACES

"Poetic and deeply humane. . . . Smiley turns a lot of precepts about animal behavior upside down, and . . . provides essential information for observers of the human zoo."   —*Newsday*

"Those who have a love affair with horses should race out and buy this winner."   —*Boston Herald*

"Fascinating. . . . Smiley's style is a pleasure: clean, calm and plain . . . spiced up with some wry humor. . . . *A Year at the Races* has the charm of a colt and the grace of a thoroughbred."
—*The Atlanta Journal-Constitution*

"Sometimes amusing, sometimes sobering, always informative. . . . Jane Smiley is a wonderful writer."   —*Chicago Sun-Times*

"[Smiley] knows how to . . . capture the atmosphere of the track and to play out deft scenes with often wacky characters. . . . Endearing and eccentric—sort of like horses themselves."
—*The Wall Street Journal*

"For lifetime horse lovers, this book will give you new rational constructs for approaching the training and care of your creatures. For animal lovers in general, here's a marvelously reasoned argument for ethical animal ownership."
—*St. Louis Post-Dispatch*

JANE SMILEY

A YEAR AT THE RACES

Jane Smiley is the Pulitzer Prize–winning author of *A Thousand Acres* and more than ten other works of fiction, including *Horse Heaven*, *Moo*, and *The Greenlanders*, as well as a critically acclaimed biography of Charles Dickens. In 2001 she was inducted into the American Academy of Arts and Letters. She owns several horses and lives in northern California.

ALSO BY JANE SMILEY

FICTION

Good Faith

Horse Heaven

The All-True Travels and Adventures of Lidie Newton

Moo

A Thousand Acres

Ordinary Love & Good Will

The Greenlanders

The Age of Grief

Duplicate Keys

At Paradise Gate

Barn Blind

NONFICTION

Charles Dickens

Catskill Crafts

A YEAR
AT THE RACES

A YEAR AT

ANCHOR BOOKS

A DIVISION OF RANDOM HOUSE, INC.

NEW YORK

★ JANE SMILEY ★

THE RACES

Reflections on Horses,
Humans, Love, Money,
and Luck

FIRST ANCHOR BOOKS EDITION, APRIL 2005

Copyright © 2004 by Jane Smiley

All rights reserved under International and Pan-American Copyright Conventions. Published in the United States by Anchor Books, a division of Random House, Inc., New York, and simultaneously in Canada by Random House of Canada Limited, Toronto. Originally published in hardcover in the United States by Alfred A. Knopf, a division of Random House, Inc., New York, in 2004.

Anchor Books and colophon are registered trademarks of Random House, Inc.

Grateful acknowledgment is made to Souvenir Press Ltd. for permission to reprint excerpts from *Talking with Horses* by Henry Blake. Published originally by Souvenir Press Ltd. London and in the United States by Trafalgar House. Copyright © by Henry Blake. Reprinted by permission of Souvenir Press Ltd.

The Library of Congress has cataloged the Knopf edition as follows:
Smiley, Jane.
A year at the races : reflections on horses, humans, love, money & luck / Jane Smiley.—1st ed.
p.   cm.
1. Horse racing—United States.   2. Race horses—United States.
3. Human-animal relationships.   4. Smiley, Jane.   I. Title.
SF335.5.S56 2004
798.4'00973—dc22
2003065655

Anchor ISBN: 1-4000-3317-9

Book design by Cassandra Pappas

www.anchorbooks.com

Printed in the United States of America
10 9 8 7 6 5 4 3 2

All crazy opinions expressed in this book belong solely to the author and are not to be attributed to any friend, teacher, or other associate.

CONTENTS

ACKNOWLEDGMENTS

Thanks to everyone, human and equine, named in this book, which is dedicated to Casey, Sterling, Amber, and Fallon, who always have to take a backseat.

A YEAR
AT THE RACES

Introduction

A LOVE STORY, at least a convincing one, requires three elements—the lover, the beloved, and the adventures they have together. If the lover isn't ardent, then the story isn't a love story. If the beloved isn't appealing, then the lover just seems idiosyncratic, or even crazy; and if they have no adventures, then their love is too easy, and they have no way of learning anything important about themselves and one another. Without going into detail, I will say that two of my favorite love stories are *Pride and Prejudice* and *The Big Sleep*. All three of these elements are distinctly present in both of them—Darcy and Elizabeth, Bogart and Bacall—the lovers are ardent and appealing, the events dramatic and revealing, and the ultimate connection, the witness feels, is both lasting and exemplary.

I mention this because every horse story is a love story. In the following volume I will make the case that it is often a story of mutual love (or, to be cooler about it, mutual attachment). In every horse story the lover (customarily the human) is ardent for something, maybe only winning, but often something more intangible and altruistic, and in every story the human and the horse do many things together, some of them wonderful, many of them foolish, and some of them simply mysterious. But the element often missing, as far as the outside witness is concerned, is the appeal of the beloved, the horse himself, herself, and so the love story fails to convince and becomes only a testament to skill or obsession or life-style on the part of the human. But horses are individuals, and humans do have an authentic response to their individuality that offers as many revelations as any other kind of love.

E. M. Forster once pointed out that characters in novels spend far more time thinking about love than people do, or at least than English people that he knew did. No doubt this is because love is a riddle that has to be solved over and over—we read and write about characters solving this riddle in order not only to enjoy it with them, but also to generalize from their situations to our own. For this reason, the love story I am about to tell is first particular and then general. Though I esteem and admire horses in general and Thoroughbred horses in particular, my love is for my own horses. Love has moved me to observe them and to ponder what I have observed, to relate what I've observed to others, and to try to make something of each incident, or at least fit it into a pattern. My hope is that the incidents are interesting or entertaining enough to engage the reader, but also that what I have made of them will give the reader something larger to think about than the doings of Jane Smiley's horses. Most horse books are manuals—compendia of techniques for getting along with horses, staying safe, taking care of their needs, and getting them to perform. The greatest of these—for example, Alois Podhajsky's *My Horses, My Teachers*—add a philosophical view to the practicalities, and are not only useful but profound. Other horse books attempt, through pictures and anecdotes, to evoke in the reader the admiration and pleasure the author feels for horses as a species—a herd thundering past, two beautiful stallions rearing, a mare and foal galloping in a green pasture. The pictures are representative of horseness. What I am hoping to do is somewhat different—not to evoke horseness, but to evoke horse individuality; to do what a novelist naturally does, which is to limn idiosyncrasy and character, and thereby to shade in some things about identity.

I readily admit that it is easy to make of horses what we will. Silent, in some ways reserved, they allow us to train them, and to project our ideas upon them; to ride and drive them, and to make them symbolic, perhaps to a greater degree than any other species. For this reason, every horseman is convinced that his horse, and horses in general, are possessed of certain qualities. These qualities may be largely useful and mechanical, or they may be largely athletic, or they may be largely grand and spiritual, or they may be largely emotional. A trainer I knew told me that a woman she knew had said that she was having trouble with her horse because the horse wanted to have sex with her. My trainer and I found this hard to believe—we suspected that the horse simply wanted to dominate the woman. But this idea was no more unbelievable to another horseman I know than that I think that some of my horses feel affection for me. When I expressed the opinion that my horse's bumping me gently with his head was a sign of affection, he said, "Affection? I never think of horses as having affections." The fact is that, with horses as with everything else, we see what we are predisposed to see, and then we mold them, consciously and unconsciously, to fit in with our predispositions. Nevertheless, it is always a worthy exercise to attempt to transcend subjectivity, to let the action speak for itself, and to let the reader judge.

The sentiments of horsemen exist in uneasy relationship

(sometimes in the same breast) with the beliefs of behaviorists. This is analogous to reading about love in a novel and reading about love in a treatise on "attachment behaviors," with the difference that romantic ideas of love are the norm for people, and scientific theories of attachment behaviors are considered evidence of an unsavory degree of coldheartedness on the part of scientists. The opposite obtains in the horse world—horsemen, and especially horsewomen, are repeatedly warned not to sentimentalize or anthropomorphize their animals, and so they keep their attitudes private. They kiss their horses or hug them or baby-talk them only when the expert isn't around. They feed treats rather surreptitiously, or try not to tell cute stories in general company. But I am going to tell cute stories anyway, in the hope that an accumulation of cute stories will someday change the widespread human perception of horses as Cartesian machines, or lower beings, or unpredictable beasts, or selfish and insensate items of bulky furniture. What science has discovered about the minds of horses would make a short book—in fact has made a short book, *The World According to Horses,* by science writer Stephen Budiansky, ninety pages. Like the anecdotes of lovers and parents, the anecdotes of horsemen form a larger body of information than the findings of science. In this book, I will make the case that horses are more like people than they are like machines, and that the insights of psychology into the human mind have productive applications to the equine mind. The study of human psychology has two branches—scientific findings and anecdotal evidence. Both Freud and Piaget observed their subjects in detail and drew conclusions that were later supported or disproved by more rigorously conceived studies. Observation came first, because detailed observation inspires the imagination to go further, to be more systematic, and to ask more particular questions.

Certainly, my ignorance will be showing. If novels and stories are bulletins from the progressive states of ignorance a writer passes through over the years, observations and opinions about horses are all the more so, since horses are more mysterious than life and harder to understand. Like all mysteries, horses tempt the horseman to have theories. Theories of horses are lenses, taken up for a while and then discarded, for organizing and perceiving the mystery. Their value is in their usefulness—does a particular theory promote improved cooperation between horse and human? If so, it is a good theory for a time. This book is full of theories.

There is a sociology of horses, as well as a psychology. It is most evident in the world of horse racing, where many horses are gathered together, where year after year, decade after decade, they do the same, rather simple thing—run in races and try to win. Records have been kept about the racing and breeding of Thoroughbred horses for almost three hundred years, especially in England, where the *General Studbook* is not unlike *Burke's Peerage*. Every horse at every Thoroughbred track in the world is a statistical unit. His parentage for at least sixty-two generations (since the publication of the first volume of the *General Studbook* in 1791) is known. His performance in every race, and even in every training work, is recorded somewhere. Some proportion of the horses alive and racing today will win great races and lots of money, will earn high stud fees and produce the great racehorses of the future. Others will be worthless, and others will be modestly useful. The phenotypes will slot into their niches in the history of the genotype. As long as racing lasts, this is an incontrovertible sociological truth. But for the owner, the trainer, the jockey, and the bettor, the eternal conundrum is, which one? Statistics tell many truths, but they are silent on that one, and so racing, too, abounds in theories, only some of them psychological. When my horse goes to the racetrack (an expensive place), I enter into a conflict of interest. My pure fascination with how his mind works, what his idiosyncrasies mean, yields in part to my desire for him to win big, or win small, or at least earn his keep.

And to me, the racetrack is an inherently amazing place, rich in language and personality, sometimes beautiful and sometimes sordid, always unpredictable. Racing is a business, an art, an athletic contest, a moral and a spiritual test. Every day, racing poses a choice for its aficionados: Is life a tragedy? Is life a comedy? Is life a utilitarian task? At the racetrack, I am just another hopeful owner, having many passing thoughts that are a varying blend of wishes, theories, and justifications, what psychologists would call "magical thinking," which is not quite like anything else in my life.

We have emerged once and for all from the era of purely mechanical horseflesh, and horses have benefited from their new role as companion animals. Most horses alive today are treated well and are better loved, better cared for medically, better housed, better fed, and better understood than horses of previous eras. Episodes such as the scene in Feodor Dostoevsky's *Crime and Punishment,* where a cart horse is beaten to death by its owner in the streets of St. Petersburg, are as out of date as Russian serfdom. No horse lives like Black Beauty anymore. Now we no longer ask only, What are they good for? We also ask, What is good for them? We may also ask, if we wish to, What do they have to tell us about themselves once we start listening to them?

ONE

Two Gals, a Horse, and the Baby Jesus

I WAS RIDING in a Manhattan cab downtown, from 48th Street to Hudson Street, and I was talking on my cell phone to my racehorse trainer at Santa Anita. I was not unaware that this was a rather worldly thing to be doing, but we weren't kvelling or counting our millions. We were autopsying the race of the day before, my four-year-old maiden's first race back after a long layoff. He had trembled in the gate ("McCarron said he was shaking like a leaf," said Alexis, not a good sign). "Then, when they came to him, he folded." He had finished second to last; I hadn't seen it, because, after the sixth or seventh race, races from Santa Anita weren't broadcast in OTB parlors in Manhattan. I had listened the night before to Alexis's glum report of the race in another cab—heading uptown—alone in the dark, all dolled up for a fund-raiser. Now she said, "The Baby Jesus thinks McCarron's the wrong jockey for him."

"He does? Why?"

"He doesn't push them. If they want to run, he encourages them, but if they don't want to, he doesn't motivate them."

I said, "Who does the Baby Jesus think would be better?"

"Oh, he didn't say. They never do."

I reflected on Chris McCarron, a great jockey, and just the sort of kind, sensitive, tactful rider I wanted my maiden to do best with. I reflected on the Baby Jesus. I said, "Well, ask him, just to see. Just tell the Baby Jesus to close his eyes, put the heel of his hand on his third eye, and come up with a name."

"I'll try it," said Alexis.

"Has the Baby Jesus ever ridden him?"

"Oh, sure. He loves him."

"Well, I think we should just ask the Baby Jesus. Just once."

"Well, anyway," said Alexis, "he came out of the race fine. Ate up every oat and looked for more. His legs are cool and tight. No problems. I just worry about that trembling thing. We'll see. You know, that horse we had, Golden Post, he shook like mad before every race. He was psyching himself up because he didn't have much talent. He really wanted to win. We tried for years to relax him, and the only time he ever went to the post relaxed, he ran last. He won five hundred thousand dollars all in all. You never know with these horses."

I agreed. After all, she had decades of experience, and if she never knew, well, I certainly never, never knew. I thanked her and hung up. We had just turned onto Varick Street. The cab-driver spoke. He had a mellow baritone voice and a rich Middle Eastern accent. He said, "This Baby Jesus you were talking about. Is he the Baby Jesus in the Bible?"

It took me a moment to recall my attention from the sunny environs of Arcadia, California, where I imagined the horses and their riders wafting among the green shedrow barns with their well-tended rose gardens and their horse bandages swaying in the breeze. The weather was pleasant enough in Manhattan, but it was February, and not warm. I envisioned Alexis and Andy and Barry, and, of course, the Baby Jesus, standing in a circle in the golden sunlight, shaking their heads over my maiden's sad performance. I said, "Oh, no. The Baby Jesus is a little Irish exercise rider at a racetrack. He's so little and darling that they nicknamed him the Baby Jesus." As I said this, I wondered if the cabdriver was of a religious persuasion that would cause him to be offended at this idea. I offered, "It's an Irish thing, I think."

The cabdriver looked at me for a moment, then said, "I have a funny name, too." He pointed to his cabbie's license, displayed on the dashboard. It said that his name, his first name, was "Soccer." We laughed together, and I got out of the cab.

To the cabdriver, I may have sounded like I knew something, but in fact I had been racing my horse, whose registered name was "Hornblower," for less than two years, and for ten months of that he had vacationed at a farm in the country, recovering from an injury that was tiny but might have gotten serious without several months off. The horse was a gray colt of humble breeding but much beauty and grace, with a big, fluid stride. The adjective often used to describe him was "promising." He was my first horse to get to the track.

He lived at Santa Anita, in a stall in a moss-green shedrow barn. The barns at Santa Anita are board-and-batten, old, but roomy and well kept. The paths are raked neatly every day. By the end of morning exercise, everything is so quiet, balmy, and neat that you wouldn't even know that horses live there, except for their heads peering over stall doors, or their hay nets hanging within easy reach. Citation lived here once, as did Seabiscuit. Tiznow, who won the Breeders' Cup twice, lived here until a few months ago. Silver Charm, Real Quiet,

Fusaichi Pegasus, and Charismatic walked to the track just as Hornblower does every day. Like these great horses, my horse is perfectly cared for and perfectly fit. It is possible that every day, somewhere on the backside or on the track, Hornblower encounters the horse that will win this year's Kentucky Derby. He himself is too old for the Derby, since he is four, but, like him, all the horses are incognito—what their futures hold, what they can do and will do, is secret from their trainers and riders, though perhaps not quite so secret to the horses themselves.

The "backside" of a racetrack is where the horses are maintained. At Santa Anita, it is really the "leftside"—hidden behind high hedges to the left of the main parking lot (at Hollywood Park and Del Mar, it is more traditionally located across the track from the grandstand; and at Bay Meadows, outside of San Francisco, it was recently relocated to the infield of the track, after the land was sold off to condo developers). The backside is a world apart within the larger world apart of horse racing. It is where trainers, assistant trainers, exercise riders, jockeys, veterinarians, and farriers work every day, sometimes for forty or fifty years, and it is where grooms and hot-walkers live as well as work. Passions may run high on the backside, as they do in any workplace, but the atmosphere is tranquil because of the horses, who like routine and reassurance. Trainers like their horses to be happy and relaxed. But horsemen have secrets, too. If, as psychologists like to assert, human society is primarily a vast set of overlapping and interlocking stories, then backside society is a concentrated version, where almost all conversation is the telling of tales, the keeping and divining of secrets.

Hornblower was a "maiden," a horse that has never won a race. Like "backside," this word is a typical horse-lore double entendre, and a perfect example of the covert sexuality of the

Hornblower at five days, investigating the water tank.

English of horse racing and of the horse world in general.* A maiden is a modern representative of untried youth, a *maghu* in Indo-European. And of course he is a virgin, and of course, as a stallion, he is a little bit suspect. Male horses at the racetrack don't get to stay stallions for long if they don't win races. And so I was beginning to feel rather protective of my maiden's *cojones.* Now that he had started again after his layoff, and had done

---

*I always think of the language of horses, in English, as an especially rich and pure stream running into our world from Middle English, Anglo-Saxon, proto-Germanic, and even proto–Indo-European. All of the terms for a horse's parts are archaic, from his poll (the top of his head) to his withers (the highest part of his topline, arising just at the base of his neck, from an obsolete Middle-English word meaning "against"), to his haunches (his hips and buttocks, from Old Germanic *hanka,* totally obscure), to his fetlocks (the angular joint just above his hooves, from *fet,* meaning "foot," and *lock,* meaning a lock of hair, going straight back to the Indo-European roots *ped,* foot, and *leug,* turn, or something that curls).

poorly, and had trembled, and had not responded to the master hand of Chris McCarron, the inevitable pressure to castrate was going to build. One English term, not current in America, for a tool used to castrate horses is "scrungers."* I had to admit I recoiled from the idea of having my maiden scrunged.

There were two reasons not to cut him. One was that he always behaved perfectly. He didn't bite or strike or squeal or act aggressive around fillies (a word for young female horses, which, appropriately, comes from the French). The other was that he was breathtakingly beautiful. My maiden had excellent conformation. He was built to stand and to move stably and efficiently. All horses have conformation, which is not beauty but mechanical usefulness: Are the horse's parts put together so that they will function and last? Do his legs have the proper angles? Does his head meet his neck in a manner that promotes balance and flexibility? Is his front end (chest, shoulders) balanced in size and power with his back end (hips and buttocks)? And so forth. Horse conformation is as much about architecture or engineering as aesthetics. But in addition to this, he was put together with exceptional grace. His shape, his lines, his demeanor all came together in unnecessarily gorgeous ways—the curve of his ears, the lift of his tail, his color of dark, dappled gray, the large size of his eye, and the classic etched refinement of his profile. A man I know, not only an experienced horseman but also a skeptical one, told me, "You are to be commended for breeding such a specimen." And the horse had been a beautiful specimen since the day he was born. He came out of the womb with muscle tone, presence of mind, and

---

*Any word in English that begins with a three-consonant cluster (like "string," from *strenk*) is extremely archaic. "Scrungers" comes from the same root—meaning "to cut"—as "scratch" and "inscribe."

self-confidence. I didn't want to cut him because I wanted to breed him to my own mares, to upgrade their imperfections, not merely because I had a studbook fantasy, which I of course also had.

I was exhibiting distinct signs of owneritis, the disease of loving your worthy but, let's admit it, mediocre horse too much. However, there is the universal recognition that scrunging (more commonly known as gelding*) is an irreversible operation, and even its most resolute proponents are subject to a degree of visceral hesitation, which I was exploiting to the full. Alexis wasn't yet insisting on gelding him, she was only floating the idea from time to time, because every gelding works out differently—often the new gelding concentrates less on fillies and more on racing, and so betters his record and wins more money, but sometimes the new gelding loses the competitive edge altogether. Much depended on what sort of theory we came up with to account for the trembling.

Counterbalancing the trembling was the appetite. If the race had been so traumatic for him, he wouldn't have eaten so heartily right afterward. The trembling was maybe excitement rather than nerves? We could use lots of phrases—keyed up, charged up, psyched up—that made the trembling into something strong rather than weak. On the other hand, the acknowledged expert, McCarron, intuitively understood the trembling as fear.

I was blue. Alexis was blue. No infusion of funds, no fulfillment of fantasy, no relief from the burden of supporting the horse at the track, which costs about as much as a Harvard education. The horse continued his daily routine as if he had never exerted himself—he was sound and enthusiastic and well

*"Gelding" goes back to the Indo-European root *ghel,* also meaning "to cut."

behaved. He began to seem a little enigmatic. I consulted a horse-astrology site online.

In the catalogue of superstitious rituals that racing people resort to in order to come up with a winner, I personally think that consulting a horse-astrology site is practically mainstream, which did not mean that I confided what I learned in those around me. The site was Australian, which was once again interesting—Aussies are hard-nosed and sunburnt and forthright, but there is an ill-concealed vein of romantic fervor there, especially when it comes to horses. They preserve the skeleton of Phar Lap, for example, the greatest racehorse of the Southern Hemisphere, in one place, and his hide in another. They preserve the notion that he was murdered by the Americans, though probably he only died of colic. This is not to say that I am unsympathetic to Australian ideas about horses—rather, that I am relieved that there is a horse-astrology Web site, and that I'm not surprised that it is Australian.

The news under "Pisces" was not encouraging. The operative words were "sensitive, impressionable, and a dreamer." Additionally, there was "very gentle nature." Normally, successful racehorses are not known for gentle natures. Alexis, in fact, has a picture in her office of one of the best horses she has ever trained (or helped train—at the time she was the assistant trainer for Eddie Gregson). His name was Super Diamond (changed at Eddie's insistence from "Super Chicken"). In the picture, he is pinning his ears and trying to bite the passerby with cobralike viciousness and speed. Whenever I happened to ask her about Super Diamond, who won over a million dollars, she would laugh affectionately and say, "Oh, he was a son of a bitch! He'd do anything to get you! He was great!"

There was more in the astrological description about Pisces horses taking a larger, more evolved perspective on things. I felt that my maiden could ill afford to take a larger perspective before he had won a few races. I thought about alternative careers that might require a larger perspective, though I couldn't come up with one other than his being a stud and commanding a small band of mares, patrolling the perimeter, planting the seeds of future generations, etc. The bar to a larger perspective in the future remained learning how to take a smaller, more focused perspective now.

He was my only Pisces, and I didn't like what I read, so I was tempted to discount the astrologer's opinion, except that the descriptions under the other signs *did* ring true. My Aries horse was active, bossy, dominating. My Taurus horses were comfortable in the herd, steady, very food-oriented, tending to be balky sometimes. My Gemini horse was unusually friendly. If I came to the gate when she was eating her hay, she would nicker and walk over to me every time, even when the others kept feeding.

Perhaps my maiden's problem was to be found, literally, in his conception. When I sent his dam to his sire, I wasn't interested in racing, I was interested in three-day eventing. I had hoped to produce a tough, good staying-and-jumping horse for my own use. It was only after he was born, when I was working on my novel *Horse Heaven*, that I'd seen what a fine specimen he was and considered sending him to the track. It was not only his muscle tone, mysteriously well developed for a newborn foal, so that he was up and cantering around his stall within a half an hour of birth, even though one of his feet was bent from his position in the womb and he could touch only the toe of that foot to the ground. It was not only his stride, which was long and liquid from the first. It was more the look on his face, which was serious.

Racehorse people always talk about "the look of eagles," but

I can't honestly say that I know what they mean. Horses do have characteristic expressions, though, and Hornblower had a distinct characteristic expression of total seriousness. My older colt, the only other foal I'd known, my number-one son, Jackie, did not have this expression. He was far more inquisitive and alert. If there was something going on, he had to know about it and, if he could, get involved and do something about it. Hornblower gazed at you in a steady, sober way, for a long moment, then turned his head calmly and gazed at something else. Then he would look back at you, approach (he was friendly), offer himself to be petted. Then he might gallop away, seriously, musically, fluidly. Unlike most young horses, unlike even the cherished Jackie, he never had an unlovely moment, never had an unlovely movement. Looking back from the perspective of four years and five lost races, perhaps I would have said that if he was lacking something maybe he was lacking fire, zip, pizzazz, chutzpah, but his sheer effortless grace was so dazzling that when you saw him gallop across a field it did not occur to you that he was lacking in anything.

MANY A THOROUGHBRED has never gotten to the races, many a Thoroughbred has never won a race, many a Thoroughbred has chosen to throw in the towel in the middle of a race—or "spit the bit," as they say. Alexis and I did not discuss the idea that our pretty boy was one of these. Two days after the race, she was much more hopeful. It was a bad race, she admitted. And he trembled and got all sweated up in the paddock, but, after all, it was his first race after almost a year. Whatever he had learned as a two-year-old had possibly not been retained. It was like starting all over again. And the fractional times were very fast—twenty-one seconds for the first two furlongs,* forty-five seconds for the first half-mile. We had put a stayer (a "plodder") in with the sprinters,† at six furlongs, a sprinter's natural distance. He was more like a forty-eight-second-half horse (and there's nothing wrong with that—a horse that can put together three forty-eights can win the Belmont Stakes in record time. Of course, the only horse ever to put together three forty-eights in the Belmont was Secretariat, and he won by thirty-one lengths, or two and a fifth seconds). Actually, thinking we were sticking him in a safe spot, we had betrayed him. We were not to be discouraged, she said. She had several ideas. I gave up discouragement. At least we could rest assured that, given his performance, he could run in cheap claiming races‡ and learn his business with no danger that we would lose him to another owner and trainer. Horse racing is full of the simultaneous giveth and taketh away.

In the next couple of weeks, Hornblower worked well in the mornings. He was breezing five furlongs in 1:01 or even 1:00, and he had two ego-boosting adventures. Once, while he was breezing, he came up beside two other colts, one a stakes winner, and dug in and passed them. Another time, his rider agreed to help a friend with a misbehaving horse by breaking with him from the gate. The naughty horse in question was a little Irish turf horse, just imported, who had won several stakes in Europe. Hornblower went out in front of him by several lengths.

---

*Furlong, going back to the Anglo-Saxon, is the length of a furrow in a ten-acre field.

†Possibly from the Scandinavian, "sprinter" is akin to a Swedish word meaning "to jump."

‡Claiming races are a staple of tracks all over the world. A horse in a claiming race (a "selling race" in England) may be bought by any trainer or owner for a set price, in cash, which the claiming party deposits in the racing secretary's office before the race. The price is set in the published conditions of the race. As soon as the claimed horse goes into the starting gate, he belongs to the new owner no matter what happens in the race. Any winnings go to the previous owner.

Thus we got to our next race, a mile and a sixteenth, much encouraged. But we didn't dare approach McCarron again. Alexis said, "You know, P Val is back."

"Who is that?"

"Patrick Valenzuela. Some people think he's the best. He wasn't riding, but now he's back. He won a couple yesterday."

She sounded as if she had been struck by a revelation. That's what I trust. No weighing and pondering or sifting through the evidence. Hornblower had been bred by revelation—I'd seen his sire and said, "Who's that? I want one of those."

I said, "Go for it."

This time I got to the simulcast at the Monterey Fairgrounds. As usual, I had my nine-year-old along and I had to pretend that I didn't know that children weren't allowed in, or even to wander around outside the simulcast facility, and I had to depend on the kindness of the ticket lady and promise not to bring him again. As usual, we were almost late, and got there in time only to watch the end of the post parade. As usual, I meant to buy my *Daily Racing Form* and study it carefully to see how my horse fit statistically with the others in the race, and maybe place an exotic bet, but instead, mesmerized, I just watched my horse, who was the color of a brilliantly shiny gray flannel suit. His feet, on TV, seemed to spring from the ground. He went into the gate nicely.

At the clang of the bell, he sprang from the gate, much the way he had as a two-year-old, going straight to the rail and straight to the front. Valenzuela was neither urging him nor holding him back, but riding him kindly, letting him choose the pace. But within seconds, the fanciest horse in the race, a horse that had cost $250,000 as a yearling, now rummaging down among the riffraff, shot in front of him and kept going. Very quickly, the two of them were alone on the lead, the rest of the horses two or three lengths back. At the half-mile pole, the time was forty-six. I said, "Uh-oh."

And "Uh-oh" was right. The expensive horse was too fast for him, but Hornblower pressed the pace. After three-quarters of a mile, they were still one-two, in a time of 1:11, but then they both faded, and the horses that had broken fourth, seventh, and eighth came up first, second, and third. Hornblower and the fancy horse ran fifth and fourth. It was the usual story, horse-racing-wise—the rabbits wore themselves out, and the stalkers came up to take the lead. Hornblower's race plan seemed to be to get out on the lead early and try not to get overtaken. It was a good plan for a sensitive horse who didn't like to be held in and didn't like to get dirt kicked in his face or be bumped. It was a plan I liked, too—less chance of injury and accident. But it was a difficult plan for a horse with no speed if he wanted to win.

P Val said to Alexis, "I had to make up my mind. I couldn't let that horse get too far out in front and run away with the race. I was the only one pressing him. This is a good horse."

Alexis said to me, "He ran a good race. Much braver than last time. And he didn't tremble so *much* in the gate. I'm happy with that. I think he's willing to ride him again, too."

I was able to look on an even brighter side than either of them. I exclaimed, "You mean we'll get a little check for this? Anyway, fitness is his friend, Alexis! He's sound and tough. He was bred to plod forever, and my dream race is the San Juan Capistrano!"

Nobody's dream race is the San Juan Capistrano. The San Juan Capistrano is a mile and three-quarters on the grass. It's usually won by a European horse, but Hornblower's sire ran second in it in 1994, and his dam's sire ran second in it in 1973. If he wasn't bred to win it, well, then, he was bred to place. Just getting there would be good enough for me.

We also got the advice of another expert. As Alexis and Jose, the groom, were leading the horse under the stands after the race, one of the railbirds shouted out, "Why don't you run that horse on the grass?"

Why not, indeed? I felt vindicated already.

Neurosis

MOST HORSES, especially riding horses, come to their owners from the unknown. Horse dealers are conventionally supposed to be dishonest, worse than used-car dealers, but in fact it would be impossible for them to represent their animals honestly, since likely as not they have no idea about either the horse's nature—his pedigree and the individual personalities of his forebears, or his nurture—the sort of mother he had, her life in the mare herd, the sort of early training and feeding he had, how he was gelded and backed and taught to work under a rider. A horse is like a used car insofar as he is what he is when he appears on the lot and the dealer has to make the best of it by buying low and selling as high as possible.

Good judges of horseflesh are smart at discerning the logical connections between all the things a horse does and what might plausibly have caused such habits to arise. A horse who flinches when a hand nears his head may have been beaten or roughly treated about the head by a previous owner. A horse who constantly pulls on the bit, or has a "hard mouth," has never been taught to carry himself in the proper way, and his mouth has become desensitized by some rider's heavy hands. Other causes and effects are more subtle. Most professional horsemen spend a great deal of time teasing out the connections in the horse's mind between what might have gone before and how the horse behaves now, in an effort to resolve problems and make the horse a useful companion and mount.

When, however, you are privileged to breed and raise your own horses, a lot of these connections are obvious. If you have seen a particular horse every day, you may not know how to make him perfect, or to ride him expertly, but you are extremely familiar with his habitual choices. My best example of this is the horse I've known the longest, my mare Persey. Persey's history convinces me that horses' mental states are uncannily like human mental states, and that horses' crazinesses can be ameliorated but continue to exist even after years of training and maturing, as a formative base, or maybe a default option, for the horses' behavior.

I could not stop thinking of Persey when I read *A General Theory of Love,* by Thomas Lewis, Fari Amini, and Richard Lannon, psychiatrists at the medical school of the University of California, San Francisco. Persey, aka Persephone, was the dark-gray daughter of a mare named Lucy that I had purchased with a friend. She was born in 1996—my eldest "daughter," as it were. I started training and then riding her in the spring of 1998, when she was two.

When Persey began her training, it at first seemed that things would go easily—the trainer reported that she didn't buck much the first time he put the saddle on her, and soon began trotting calmly around the round corral, first to the right, then to the left. Things went well for two or three lessons; then the filly began to act strangely. It was not, at this point, that she was rebellious or resistant. It was more that she was nonresponsive. Once she had begun trotting around the trainer, she would continue to do so, ignoring, or, I think now, not perceiving the signals he was giving her to come in to him, move away from him, stop, or whatever. She was strangely machinelike—that is, she couldn't relate to the trainer or the training as other horses did, by seeking to figure out what the trainer wanted and then supplying that response. After about ten sessions, when her behavior didn't improve, he declined to work with her anymore, telling me that he considered her dangerous.

I then put her with another trainer, a traditional event-horse trainer, who used European rather than cowboy methods. He, too, began by thinking that she would be easy to work with. He lunged her around in a circle on a long line, with and without side-reins running from the bit in her mouth to loops attached to a band around her body where a saddle would normally be. After that, he ground-drove her, walking behind her, using two long lines as if she were a carriage horse without a carriage, teaching her to turn right and left, to stop and go, and respond to his voice. As long as he did this on my property, where she felt at home, she was fine, but he decided she needed a larger and more stimulating venue to get used to, so I moved her to a local stable where there was a lot going on. Within a week, this trainer, too, had declined to work with her, because her response to every stimulus (and there were plenty of those every day) was to rear up. And when she reared up, she did so with conviction— once, the trainer's wife, also an experienced and accomplished equestrienne, put a German noseband on her that was designed to apply pressure to the bridge of her nose if she reared. She reared so high and so resolutely with this noseband on that she stayed in the air for ninety seconds, while the trainer tried to pull her down with all her strength. After that, we were intimidated—not just by the horse's rearing, which was scary enough, but also by what methods might be required to gain her submission. The first trainer had suggested that I invest no more in her, just get rid of her. But what did that mean? If she was untrainable, as dangerous as these two experienced trainers said, wouldn't it be safest—not just for us, but for all future owners— to euthanize her?

The trouble, I came to realize, was not only that she was fearful, but that she had a constitutional conviction that her fears were justified. She was like some people I have known who would do anything to persuade me that something terrible was about to happen, putting as much energy into trying to prove to me that the very thing that they were terrified of was inevitable as they would have if they actually wanted the terrible outcome to take place. That is what I call neurotic. On the one hand, I admired Persey's conviction—ears up, eyes alert, body still as a statue, or, indeed, up in the air on her hind legs, she conveyed a certain beauty that more cooperative horses did not. On the other hand, the skills she required were way beyond me. So I took her to the bravest guy in town, Ray Berta. He worked with her, and after the first day he said, "This should be easy."

My heart sank.

A General Theory of Love proposes that it is possible to understand human intimate relationships by investigating the connections between brain structure (emotions arise in the limbic brain, which is possessed by all mammals but not by reptiles), brain chemistry (various chemicals that the brain discharges or disposes of are felt as emotions), and early relationships between the mammal mother and her offspring. The doctors propose that, for mammals, consistent maternal nurturing is essential for the healthy growth of the infant brain, which is only partially developed at birth. A badly mothered infant actually grows up with damaged connections in the brain, preventing it from developing both good reproductive relationships ("Leben") and good life skills ("Arbeit").* No studies cited in the book are of horses, but there are many of other mammals, particularly chimps and monkeys. The doctors state categorically: "Mammals form close-knit, mutually nurturant social groups—families—in which members spend time touching and caring for one another. Parents nourish and safeguard their young and each other from the hostile world outside their group. A mammal will risk and sometimes lose its life to protect a child or mate from attack" (pp. 25–26). The ways in which Lucy had not been a good mom to Persey were legion—she was anxious, so she ran along the fence line, back and forth, hardly pausing to allow Persey to suckle. When Persey was near her, she was often inattentive, but when Persey wandered away, she whinnied after her with a desperate note in her voice. And there were no other mares and foals for company and reassurance.

In an experiment that might have been constructed with Persey's foalhood as a model, researchers constructed a situation in which monkey mothers were intermittently deprived of access to food, so that they sometimes felt at ease and sometimes were distracted—their nurturing relationships with their offspring were randomly interrupted by worry. The infants grew up to be clingy, subordinate, and clumsy in relationships. Researchers found that the neurotransmitter systems in their brains were permanently damaged. And numerous observations of human infants over the last fifty or sixty years have shown,

---

*An additional study, presented by Michael Meaney of McGill University in June 2003, showed that the degree of maternal licking of newborn rats predicted the infants' ability to deal with stress as adults by influencing the expression of a gene that dictated the development of cortisol receptors in the brain. The effect of the licking worked equally well with all rat babies, whatever their innate temperament.

according to the authors, that, "because human physiology is (at least in part) an open-loop arrangement, an individual does not direct all of his functions. A second person transmits regulatory information that can alter hormone levels, cardiovascular function, sleep rhythms, immune function, and more—inside the body of the first. The reciprocal process occurs simultaneously: the first person regulates the second even as he himself is regulated" (p. 85). Bad mothering provides bad regulation of the infant's physiological processes. "An isolated monkey becomes a grotesque caricature because because the mammalian nervous system cannot self-assemble" (p. 88).

Unlike monkeys, rats, dogs, and cats, horses are never used for experiments whose results are intended to apply to humans (though some results of studies and procedures on joints and tendons are transferred from horse to man, because horses have large joints and tendons, and suffer some of the same sorts of athletic-induced injury and deterioration). Nor is the psychology of the horse much investigated, simply because research funds are short and their richest source is from the horse racing industry, which prefers to finance studies that keep horses racing and earning money rather than those that just want find out how the animals develop and function. Most of what we believe about horses comes from observation: Equines certainly have families and herds, and mares certainly guide and nurture their young and form protective groups with one another. Horses also spend their whole lives forming affiliative relationships with other horses—perfect strangers that they encounter for a few hours or a few weeks. It's a rare horse who cannot make friends with other horses, who can't come to be part of a group, whether high or low in the pecking order.

Thus we may say that horses have emotions as other mammals and people do. If the source of human mental suffering is

*Ray Berta and Persey (age three) in a characteristic pose in a round pen
nestled in the hills of California. She looks cooperative, but it is only a pose.*

often in the limbic brain, and horses have limbic brains, then
perhaps some of the things that go wrong with horses are analogous to some of the things that go wrong with humans, both in
their origin and in their amelioration.

ON HER SECOND DAY with Ray Berta, a little more familiar
with her new situation, and therefore more self-confident, she
displayed every facet of what you might call her self-image. I
remember looking at her chin. Horses' chins are expressive; a
trainer wants the horse to carry his chin, not dangling it, but also
not tightening it. Persey's chin was pressed against her lower jaw,
creased with determination. Ray, who is tall, muscular, and slen-

der, strong as a bundle of wires lashed together, was sitting on another horse, holding Persey on a long line. He asked her to step forward by tugging lightly on his end of the rope. She looked so alert and intent that I thought she had stepped forward, but she hadn't. He asked her again, tugging a little harder. This time, she made her refusal a little more clear, as if maybe Ray had made a mistake in interpreting her body language: she declined to step forward. There would be no stepping forward as far as she was concerned. What she was afraid of, I don't know, possibly just the novelty of the situation. She stepped backward, but Ray stopped her with the rope. He was equally resolute that there would be no stepping backward. The horse he was sitting on soon began to tremble all over and flap his lips together, the clear sign that he felt himself to be between a rock and a hard place—the rock being a strong trainer and the hard place being a determined female. Ray dismounted him and let him go out of the round corral. He then worked with Persey on foot. It took twenty-five minutes of rearing, backing up, falling down, avoiding in every way the idea of stepping forward, before the mare stepped forward one step, and then two. He sometimes shook the rope in her face, but he never resorted to unkind or impatient means—no whip, no waving arms, no anger, just the absolute conviction that at some point she would realize that it was easier to step forward than to not step forward. That was the basic principle of his training method—make it easy for the horse to choose the right thing, and hard for her to choose the wrong thing. When I asked for a diagnosis after a few days, he said, in his usual relaxed and smiling way, that she was in the habit of making wrong choices that worked for her to a degree. Habitual wrong choices? Isn't that neurosis?

As her year with Ray progressed, there were further diagnoses, the most important one that all of her bad behavior came out of her habit of bracing her right hind leg. How horses think manifests in how they move. As soon as she got a chance to brace that right hind, she would stop going forward and get ready to rear up. The key was to never allow her even the beginnings of a brace. An acupuncturist who worked with her said, independently, that her right ovary was painful and that she was probably protecting herself on the right hind in some way. This analysis was borne out by the fact that she was always harder to handle when she was in season. One time, she was very much in season, and when I asked her to turn to the right at a canter, she bucked me off right there and continued to the left. My interpretation of the PMS theory was that the coursing of hormones enhanced her conviction that whatever she perceived was true and right and had to be acted upon.

Persey has proved to be the most difficult of my many horses to train—not because she is unintelligent or unathletic, but because she is always prone to anxiety, which sometimes renders her impervious to reassurance or direction. All young horses, of course, are fearful. Most horse training progresses by means of habituation—the horse is gradually introduced to new objects and scenes, and allowed to get used to them, sometimes very slowly, but he is never allowed to flee them. Flight confirms the horse's idea that the object that had seemed fearful was indeed threatening. The horse's fear and unwillingness are like a spreading pool of water—continually expanding or contracting. The trainer's job is to make the pool contract as much as possible. If he or she does not, then the fears and reluctances can expand to include almost everything outside the horse's stall.

Always the question was, how much force to apply. Certain trainers, all men, felt that her problem was a lack of respect, which would be resolved by the use of strong driving aids, including the whip. Usually this was a course they advised me to take, not actually volunteering to take it themselves. They felt she had to be made to submit. But Persey's response to harshness was to rear rather than to go forward. Women trainers advised me not to accommodate her but to circumvent her—find a way around her resistance (her braced right hind leg) and then get her to move forward slowly, in a way that allowed her to reassure herself that there was nothing really to be afraid of. They gave more weight to the fact that she was a mare, which meant that she was likely to put up a fight that perhaps I was not able to handle.

Persey's behavior, I think, bears out the idea that horses have a world-view, and that they filter experience through it. The normal horse has a world-view sufficiently close to reality that it seems transparent—his obedience and his reactions are what trainers expect them to be, and as reasonable as if he had no world-view at all. He responds steadily to habituation, getting more and more used to whatever humans require of him, only spooking at the obvious—flapping tarps, sudden half-hidden movements, other things that are clearly startling. Experienced racehorses learn to tolerate quite a bit of activity at the racetrack, and even to enjoy it, since it puts them in the mood to run. Obviously, show horses, rodeo horses, endurance horses, police horses, and circus horses do the same (at Cheval-Théâtre, a Canadian horse-circus, the audience, sitting in the dark, is asked only to refrain from taking photographs with flashbulbs, which is just the sort of thing that would happen too irregularly for the horses to habituate to). But Persey's habituation process was very slow. She would hesitate about the same things over and over, stare off into the same distances day after day, wonder about the same mysteries that she had already investigated the day before or even the hour before. I didn't feel that she was exhibiting a lack of intelligence as much as an inability to allow experience to change her mind.

Ray had to move the horses from one ranch, where the landscape was an open bowl in the middle of equally open hills, where threats could at least be seen from afar, to another, where the buildings and arenas and roads were surrounded with trees. This was Persey's worst nightmare. It seemed as though she was experiencing the normal disappearances and reappearances of people and animals as they went among the trees as ghosts in a horror movie, jumping unexpectedly out of dark corners.

Federico Tesio, the great Italian horse breeder, wrote after watching his horses go through the Second World War that horses never look up, because he never saw them raise their eyes to the sky, no matter how many planes went over or bombs dropped. Persey would have shown him a thing or two. She looked up most of the time—at the high ridgeline above the arena, at the tops of the hills across the valley, at the horses in the upper arena from the lower arena. She was always on the alert, but she hardly showed it. As with her earliest training, her nervousness rendered her impervious rather than visibly disturbed. Within a day after her arrival at the new ranch, she did a strange thing that seemed more and more logical as we got to know her better.

Ray had taken two fillies—Persey, aged four, and another four-year-old—down to the big arena, where he removed their halters and sent them to the far end. They trotted around while he stood in the middle watching them. Then Persey suddenly turned and ran toward him at full speed. He lifted his arm and his rope to wave her off, but she kept coming and knocked him flat with her chest. He woke up stretched out in the sand sometime later. When I asked him if she had seen him, he said, "Not more than a second before she ran over me." The reason he didn't step out of the way was that her behavior was unusual, even unique. Horses in general will do anything to avoid running over a person—I once saw an eighteen-hand jumper literally twist himself in air to avoid landing on his rider, who had fallen facedown on the far side of the fence. But Persey, like other neurotics, wasn't looking outward. She was attentive only to her inner world—whatever had scared her made her temporarily unreachable.

We made some progress at the new place, though not as much as I would have liked. I began to quiz Ray about whether Persey was his worst student ever, the one who had been there longest. He reassured me. But it wasn't until I rode her every day for twenty-one days that she began to settle down. With daily discipline and no breaks for contemplating her fears, she began to be somewhat reliable, somewhat relaxed. She was four. She started to learn to jump, which she liked, and to go out on trails. I considered the battle mostly won. I moved her to yet another ranch, closer to my house, where the country was open. She stopped surveying the periphery and lulled me into complacency.

Just after Christmas, when I thought I had everything worked out with Persey, we were leaving the arena at our new barn—a barn where the landscape was open and not obviously threatening—and, lo and behold, there was a Chevy Suburban in the wrong spot. It was crossing a small wooden bridge that cars never (in Persey's knowledge) crossed, and it made a noise. She took one look, spun on that right hind, and tried to bolt for the barn. She meant it, too. She didn't jump a couple of steps and come to a halt; she ran like hell for a hundred yards before I could pull her up.

We were at the end of our ride, and so I brought her back to the spot where she had bolted and walked her around there for a bit. She wasn't perfectly calm, but she was calm enough, so I allowed her to go up the hill and out to the pasture, and didn't think much of it until the next day, when she absolutely refused to go down the hill even one step, though in the previous four months she had marched down the hill a hundred times. I was amazed. Her refusal to go down the hill, to go past the spot where she had witnessed the Suburban, even to turn toward that spot if she was approaching the area from a different direction, was adamant. She would back up, throw her shoulders, rear. More force on my part met with greater resistance on her part. No respecter of persons, she gave Ray the same treatment. We worked with her daily. Her area of fear might diminish in size after we had ridden her over the same ground time and again, but if we allowed the least fear to take hold again, the area would literally expand in size from a few square feet to a half-acre or more in a day, and we would have to start all over. Sometimes, her fear expanded to the whole ranch, to any car that was parked anywhere outside of the parking lot. The only consolation was that she remained willing to work once she was in an enclosed space. In spite of the chaos, her training progressed, and then, sometime in May, she came back to normal. I realized that, in fact, sometimes the only thing that reassured her, the only thing that she was interested enough in to forget her fears, was jumping. It was as if that very particular task of cantering toward a series of obstacles, jumping them, and cantering on was reassuring to her, because it was limited and understandable, not like having to decide whether there was something in the trees, or whether the number of times she had safely crossed a certain piece of ground outnumbered the number of times she had been afraid of crossing that piece of ground. In fact, she was like a neurotic person who does a good job at work because the job is defined.

The thing I would like to emphasize here is that nothing bad ever happened to her—no animal ever jumped out at her, no pain ever was inflicted upon her. She was not afraid of a spot because she remembered being hurt there, she was afraid of it because she remembered being afraid there. Her mental process made me think of obsessive-compulsive disorder in humans, which is defined as unwanted, intrusive thoughts that prevent the sufferer from understanding objective reality. One of the meliorating treatments for OCD is habituation—if the person gives in to his fears and engages in more and more rituals, the fears expand; if he habituates himself to the things he is fearful of, the fears contract. The similarity in both the symptoms and the treatment between horse and human seem to me to indicate that the problem of excessive fear is a general mammalian brain problem, not specifically a human psychological problem.

At any rate, after Persey became a good horse again, she remained so for about a year, until I began asking more of her by taking her to clinics and horse shows. At that point, she reacted to separation from her herd by having extreme moods— at one show, she was extremely resentful; at another, she was extremely nervous. On another occasion, when she required two weeks of medication that involved being separated from her herd and put in an individual corral, she did not act at all as most horses do, which is to whinny for her friends for at most twenty-four hours, then to settle in, enjoy the plentiful rations, and make friends with the horses around her. Instead, she kept up what Lewis, Amini, and Lannon term "searching and calling behavior"—that is, pacing her corral, straining her eyes and ears for the sight and sound of her herd-mates, and whinnying constantly. She searched and called frantically for over a week, and even after that, she was jumpy and hyper-alert. Everyone at the barn was glad when the course of medication was completed and she could return to the herd. One young woman mentioned in *A General Theory of Love* could not leave an abusive relationship because she found abuse easier to tolerate than isolation. That reminded me of Persey. Many horses, if not most, can go off on a trail ride with only the rider and no other horses, or can adapt fairly easily to a new living situation. Persey, neurotic in ways that echo the neuroses of humans, could not, it appeared, be taught to do these things.

As of this writing, it still isn't clear whether we can control her mental condition and keep her reliable in new situations. Lucy, her mother, also had a lot of difficulty with unstructured activity. In the arena, doing exercises, circles, changes of gait, she was like a machine—going forward, staying on the bit, doing whatever was asked of her—but she could not under any circumstances go on a trail ride, even with other horses. Is Persey's problem owing to nature or nurture? Did Lucy pass on her nervousness through her genes or through her behavior toward the foal? Drs. Lewis, Amini, and Lannon would say, perhaps, nurture becomes nature, and nature becomes nurture.

It is a well-known fact among racehorse breeders that really good mares produce winner after winner. Normally, this is considered a facet of pedigree—somehow these mares have genes that combine or "nick" especially well with those of particular stallions, or their genes are especially good no matter who the stallion is. A truism of breeding is that the best broodmares are out of the same dam as great racemares. But, judging from Lucy and Persey, it could as easily be true that some manner in which the mares raise the foals also predicts success at the racetrack. One horse agent in California did an informal study on his own—he observed all the offspring of a certain stallion at a large studfarm. The offspring of mares who lived in stable herds on the farm did far better at the track than the offspring of mares who came for the birth, were bred again, and then sent back to their home farms. Possibly the stress of finding or gaining status in a new herd was so taxing to the imported mares that it had both a biochemical and a behavioral effect on the mares and their foals, like that of the monkeys whose mothers were intermittently deprived of food.

My next foal after Persey, the first I bred on my own, was Jackie. I found the mare and researched the stallion, and planned the mating. I even went for a look at the mare's own sire, Big Spruce, who was pensioned at Gainesway Farm in Kentucky. The mare was named Biosymmetree. I bought her on Valentine's Day, 1996, because she looked bright and perky trotting around the round corral, and then, when her owner put her back in her stall, the mare turned as she stepped past me, put her chin on my shoulder, and looked me in the eye for a long minute. Her gaze was inquisitive, trusting, and kind.

She got pregnant right away, and as her pregnancy progressed she became more and more affectionate. She would stand as close to me as she could and put her head right next to me, down, quiet, inviting pats but never pushing me. I joked that she wanted to sit in my lap. Jackie was friendly and beautiful from the day he was born. I have a picture of him and Biosymmetree, exercising in their field. She is trotting with her ears pricked and he is trotting also, but seeming to hang back. His head is up and pressed a bit into her side, as if he is seeking comfort or reassurance. Though they lived an hour from me, I was enamored of them, and went to see them once or twice every week. Each time, I petted and brushed the foal and mare from top to bottom. I couldn't get over how perfect I thought the colt was.

Exactly a month to the day after the birth, I arrived at the ranch to discover the vet just leaving. He came to my car window and said, "I was trying to get hold of you. Your husband said you were on the way."

"Is there a problem?"

"I had to put your mare down. I didn't see any way to save her. I'm sure there was a twist, but I couldn't reach it, and I never felt it." He meant a twist in her intestine, blocking the passage of food through her gut.

The mare's body was in the field where I had last seen her grazing with her group of mares and foals, stretched out on her right side. She had colicked sometime in the night, and had rolled around in such pain that she had rubbed hair off her head. When they found her, during feeding at 6 a.m., she was already in shock. By the time the vet arrived, she was close to death from widespread septicemia. But here was the really heartbreaking part. After he diagnosed her, after he decided that he couldn't save her, she struggled, on her own, to get to her feet so that Jackie, who had been nosing her udder, could nurse. She had managed to stand for a few minutes, long enough for him to get a few mouthfuls, and then she had staggered to her knees and collapsed. Thoroughbred people are always talking about heart. That's what I call heart.

The manager of the ranch had had an orphan foal before, so they knew how to take care of him. They gave him a mini-horse companion for a couple of months, and fed him a suitable milk mixture from a bowl until he learned to get nutrition from grass and hay. I was too naive to worry. I so adored him that I figured that even such a setback surely couldn't have a terribly lasting effect. I continued to visit him as often as possible, and every time, I brushed him and petted him from top to toe. He was receptive and quiet, never skittish the way many foals are, and so it went on, him being my number-one son and me being— what? Impossible to say. His great and good friend, maybe.

When he was three months old, he was put in with a four-month-old filly who had recently been weaned. His subsequent behavior illustrates some different principles of emotional growth. Whereas Jackie is quiet and reliable to ride and his manners with humans are excellent (he is interested in what humans do—if I approach him with something in my hand, he always wants to investigate it; he will allow the vet to perform any procedure if the vet just lets him sniff the equipment), his relationships with other horses would have to be called grandiose and domineering. When he was living in the typical fashion, relating to other horses only through the bars of a stall or over a fence, he watched their doings constantly, and reacted to whatever they did by whinnying, rearing, galloping, calling. Stall living came to an end when a groom was leading him from the paddock to his stall and he reared up because a horse in another paddock was running around, pulled away from the groom, and galloped down a paved road, only to slip and fall, giving himself a bad wound in the forearm as he slid along the concrete. As soon as he was healed, he went to live with other horses. His first companion was another of my geldings (born in 1999, number seven), a gray named Cheerful. Cheerful is actually quite submissive. Nevertheless, when I turned Jackie out in a rather small but long corral with Cheerful, everyone was in for a surprise.

Cheerful was standing eating hay toward the top of the corral, up a slope. As soon as I opened the gate, Jackie lifted his head, puffed his chest, and set out at a run to establish his authority over the younger horse. His arched neck and swelled chest indicated that he was planning to push Cheerful away from the hay, ordering him to yield his space. Without even lifting his head from eating, Cheerful let fly with both hind legs, kicking Jackie in the flank. Then he did it again. Jackie turned around and trotted back down the hill, where he stood for a good twenty minutes, staring at the other horse. It was clear from his facial expression, as well as his subsequent behavior, that he was altering his views of himself. Nevertheless, in his five-horse herd, Jackie is boss. When he turns his head toward another horse and puts back his ears, the other horse always moves away. He is jealous about carrots and treats, and he always has a pile of hay to himself. Usually, in a mixed herd of mares and geldings, a mare is in charge, but Jackie, who was gelded at nine months old, I think, perceives himself as a stallion. He is amorous, protective, and domineering. Maybe his most unusual behavior is as my enforcer with other horses—if in Jackie's presence I happen to command a horse, say, to move away from the gate, especially a horse that is not in his band, he will attack that horse quite energetically, usually biting it on the rump (biting is a stallion behavior; mares prefer to kick) and sending it off. I have to be very careful with other people's horses when Jackie is in the vicinity.

But where has he gotten those attitudes? Chances are that the death of his mother when he was a month old prevented him from certain colt experiences—most colts begin attempting to mount their mothers or otherwise push them around when they are about two months old. The dams put up with some of this, but not all of it. If the colt gets too aggressive, the mare disciplines him by pinning her ears, squealing, nipping, and administering small kicks. Since Jackie missed out on a certain period of foalhood—not the period where the foal requires complete nurture, but the period when he requires discipline—he grew up grandiose and impulsive but able to form relationships (a good horse relationship consists of being able to connect to another horse and live in a herd, but also to go away from the other horses calmly and do a job). Other horses have, to some extent, been able to discipline him, especially Hornblower's sister Kiss Me, who had the benefit of many months with a firm and directive mother, but Jackie is the boss. Although *A General Theory of Love* doesn't address later aspects of infant growth, perhaps we can extrapolate and surmise that Jackie's excitability—the way that, even though he is a gelding, he is aggressive with other horses and has evident signs of energy surges that come from adrenaline, as well as other stallionlike behaviors—shows that a mare's discipline of her colt modifies his body chemistry as well. When he tries to push her around and she reprimands him, she is not only changing his behavior, but also regulating his testosterone production.

Not all my foals are neurotic; most of them fit into their herds and cooperate willingly with humans. The fact is, I can trace each "normal"—that is, steady, willing, and happy—foal to a vigorous, attentive, and directive dam whose relationships with humans are friendly. I still don't understand the exact balance between nurture, inherited predilections, brain structure, and brain chemistry, but I recognize that there is one for horses as for every other mammal.

THREE

Trainer and Owner

ALEXIS'S COMPETITIVE SPIRIT emerged early. In kindergarten, on a field trip, another girl mentioned that she loved horses, and without really thinking about it, Alexis informed the girl that she loved horses more. By the age of eight, she was hanging around a local barn, grooming the ponies and the rent horses, and saving her money for the occasional ride. Or she would sit next to the donkey at Fairyland, in Oakland, petting it endlessly. She threw tantrums and fits to try to persuade her parents to buy her a horse, but they thought, of course, that she would outgrow it.

When she was thirteen, she met every girl's dream friend—an older Englishwoman of great elegance and superb education who lived at the barn, drove an old beat-up truck and trailer, and took on little girls. Marie, tall and beautiful and well spoken, gave the girls lessons in dressage* and jumping—for free—and

---

*Dressage is the training of horse and rider in traditional, highly prescribed movements at walk, trot, and canter. The training was developed in European cavalry schools such

Alexis in sunglasses. Everyone at the racetrack wears sunglasses. Sunglasses, vitality, and charm are what enable Alexis to survive life on the backside.

carried them off to shows, where they rode and won, beating the enviable girls with horses their parents had bought for them. After a couple of years, Marie decided to move to Australia.

Alexis's first acquisition, when she was fifteen years old, was a quarter-horse gelding named Dicky's Agogo, who sometimes

---

as the French cavalry school at Saumur, and was originally used to prepare warhorses. The word comes from French, *dresser.* The meaning is more like "prepare" than "dress." The closest analogue in English is to "dress" a turkey.

reared up and flipped over. Not unlike me at the same age, Alexis was pretty much undaunted, which was good, but not much of a horse-psychologist, which was bad. Our horses put up with us because we didn't know that their bad behaviors were symptoms of fear or distress—we thought they were just fixed elements of their personalities. And we put up with them because we had waited so long, with such frustrated yearning.

Dicky's Agogo was going to be Alexis's last horse as well as her first. She was twenty-three, and by that time had done a lot with horses, including caring for Charlie O, the mule that served as the mascot for the Oakland Athletics ("Now, *he* was affectionate," she says), but right before she was going to wash her hands of the whole thing, she happened to go to her doctor one day, and there was the receptionist, and the receptionist had a friend who knew someone, and pretty soon Alexis found herself in Simi Valley with her truck and single-horse trailer, taking possession of a beautiful gray stallion, a son of a good Thoroughbred racehorse sire named Poker. Shortly after that, she got another stallion, and then there was a yearling filly, and she found herself hanging around Golden Gate Fields, trying to learn about racing so she could get her filly to the races. But the filly never got to the races, and it seemed reasonable to turn her out in the arena with the beautiful son of Poker, and the foal that arrived on George Washington's birthday the following year was the first of seventeen that Alexis got from that original mare, most of them winners.

Horse racing used to be an entirely male world, and on a scale of one to ten, its masculinity quotient remains about an eight. In the 1970s, when Alexis began hanging out at the track, women first entered the ranks of trainers, jockeys, grooms, and, especially, exercise riders, but the dominant culture remains competitive, secretive, individualistic, and focused on money.

Women who work at the track may or may not find this culture congenial—often they merely accept it in exchange for the pleasure of working with the horses. There is, emphatically, no feminist theory to help them understand their social situation or to bolster personal feelings of friendship or female solidarity. Somehow, though, Alexis has not only gotten along at the racetrack over the years (twenty-seven), but has even enjoyed it. I think her pivotal quality, in this regard, is charm. She is straightforward, with a ready smile and a bright laugh. She is enthusiastic about the horses she trains and more than ready to listen to her owners' opinions, theories, wishes, dreams, and notions, no matter how cockamamie they may be. She is friendly. She is kind to the animals. She is kind in general. But maybe the best thing going for Alexis at the racetrack is that she knows how to keep her mouth shut—whatever dirty story, dirty joke, outrageous behavior, outrageous talk is going around, she keeps her opinion to herself. She has women friends and well-wishers. She has men friends and well-wishers. In the years I've know her, I haven't met anyone who doesn't wish her well. Alexis is Greek. Her parents immigrated to Oakland from Kalamata and Turkey in the forties. She has that sturdy and vibrant Zorba-the-Greek look, an upbeat demeanor even when she is discouraged or upset.

We are nearly the same age—her horse-obsessed adolescence in the Oakland hills above Berkeley, California, pretty much overlapped my horse-obsessed adolescence in St. Louis, Missouri. Our self-assigned job was to ride as much as we could manage and envy the girls whose parents were horsey themselves or who had the money and inclination to fully support their daughters' passions. My parents, like hers, thought I would get over it. Our parents should have been right, but they were wrong. Someday, we would have boyfriends, husbands, children, careers—that's what the horses are a substitute for, according to adult theorists. But what truly horsey girls discover in the end is that boyfriends, husbands, children, and careers are the substitute—for horses.

Over the years, Alexis worked for some famous trainers—Jack Utley, Bill Spawr, Tommy Doyle, Neil Drysdale, and, for almost twenty years, Eddie Gregson—not because she wanted to be a trainer herself, but because she couldn't afford to send her horses to a trainer, and she wanted to get them to the races. She groomed, she rode, she watched and listened. When she talks about it now, she has a certain tone, a sort of surprised and pleased tone—the horse won, she had some luck, it was fun, good things unexpectedly happened. Once we were talking about life and death, the way you do when you are about fifty, and she said, "Oh, if anything ever happens to me, just patch me back together and put me out on the road again." She laughed. "It's too much fun to stop just because everything doesn't work perfectly." Alexis is not only enthusiastic and inventive, she's got vitality. Is it a racetrack thing? But many at the track, some of the most famous and successful ones, take a darker and more fatalistic view.

FASCINATION WITH HORSES predated every other single thing I knew. Before I was a mother, before I was a writer, before I knew the facts of life, before I was a schoolgirl, before I learned to read, I wanted a horse. If the specifics of desire are what differentiate one personality from another, then my yearning for a horse is one of the founding characteristics of my being. Horses came to me by television (*Fury, My Friend Flicka, Roy Rogers*) and by the pony rides that once occupied a corner at the intersection of Manchester Road and Brentwood Boulevard in St. Louis

County, Missouri. The ponies wore Western saddles with horns. The helper hoisted me onto the pony, then strapped me into the saddle, using a leather strap that wrapped around the horn. Then the pony was led out, and it trotted around a three- or four-corridor maze—out into the twilight, back into the light— maybe twice, but certainly never as many times as I wished. In retrospect, the best thing about it was that the ponies trotted. If I wanted to ride, then I had to do it the hardest, bounciest way, but the strap held me in. It was an excellent beginning and removed all fears of going fast. But there was no relating to the ponies. I was lucky if I found out their names, if I could give them a little pat before I got on or after I got off. But it was okay; it was enough. The times we drove past and I got a long look at the ponies tied to their hitching post under the lights were almost as satisfying as the times we stopped.

After that, there were summer horse camps. At the first of these, Playschool on the Farm, the saddles were old U.S. Cavalry saddles, the kind with a high, curved pommel in the front, a matching cantle in the back, and a mysterious fissure down the middle. They were big and impossible to sit in (and, indeed, how did men arrange their genitals against injury in these contraptions?). The next camp, in Wisconsin, had a sad string of eight horses and a small riding ring—you had to hike through the woods to get to the barn. The first-class activities at that camp were canoeing and sailing. When I was thirteen, I found Teela-Wooket, a bona-fide horse camp in Vermont, where there were a huge barn, several arenas, many horses, and many levels of riding. Campers were not allowed in the barn, but we could request our favorite horses and imagine ourselves in relationships with them. The head of the equestrian activities was an old man who wore what looked like a uniform and was called Cappy. On the wall of the barn was a row of pictures of Cappy as a young man, performing dressage movements—looking back, I am guessing piaffe or passage—on an Andalusian or a Lusitano. In the winter, Cappy and the horses worked at a boarding school in Massachusetts. The riders were ranked. The most experienced of them (I was not one) went to the two horse-shows of the summer. Other enthusiasts (I was one) got to go along as spectators. Two girls brought their own horses. I seemed like a permanent member of the envious class.

When I was fourteen, I fell in love with a big brown Thoroughbred mare who lived at a club that my parents joined. Somehow, her owners were persuaded to let me ride her, but in the winter they moved her to their own house, and they allowed me to come over and clean her stall and ride her up and down the road. That spring, I broke my arm in PE class, but I kept cleaning that stall with one hand, and at the beginning of the summer, my parents decided to buy the horse. She cost $1,000, and $65 to board at the club. In the fall, because of the long drive, we moved her to a show barn in town. Her board cost $90. To put this into perspective, the mortgage payment on our very sleek six-bedroom, five-bath house on three acres in the best suburb of St. Louis was something like $250 per month, and the tuition at my famous private school was $1,600 per year. The horse was not cheap.

I was allowed to foxhunt with her that Thanksgiving, and she fell in slippery footing and broke her leg. She could not be saved and was euthanized two days later, out at the hunt kennels, and fed to the hounds. I was numb with shock, but so driven that I kept riding at the barn where I had boarded her. They didn't give regular lessons, but there were always horses around that needed exercise. Most of that winter, I rode horses taking time off from the racetracks in Illinois, who were undergoing their yearly blistering and pin-firing. (Those were primitive days in veterinary medicine. At the end of the racing season, the various soft-tissue ills accrued at the track were thought to benefit from a type of wholesale burning or wounding of the horse's forelegs that encouraged increased circulation to the limbs and supposedly tightened the tissues. Such procedures are extremely rare these days.) As the horses recovered, the girls hanging around the barn were thrown up on them, to walk, trot, and eventually gallop them in preparation for the spring season.

I talked my parents into another horse, this one only three hundred dollars. He lasted through the summer, but he came down with an asthmalike allergy called "the heaves," caused by the choice the barn owner made to stop the yearly effort of painting his barn white, and try covering every surface with creosote (today a known carcinogen). One day in October, the horse had a heart attack underneath me. I tried again the following year, but that horse proved unsound shortly after she came to me and was sent back to her previous owner. The second and third horses (though not the first) could have been cured of their ailments in 2002, but not in 1966. Although having a horse of my own seemed a Jobian endeavor, demanding reservoirs of emotional endurance and resilience that I can't remember having summoned up, I didn't give up until I went to college, where I took up my substitute life at last and my mother breathed a sigh of relief.

I went back to horses in 1993, just because I was driving down a road with my nine-month-old baby, looking for a lady who sold Discovery toys. Instead, I found a barnful of hunters and jumpers and a pleasant young couple who owned and ran the barn. I remember standing with the baby on my hip, talking to the woman, whose name was Tina. She was holding a horse. A wire ran between us that I wasn't paying attention to. We made arrangements for me to have a lesson. I reached forward to pat the horse on the forehead. My son's big toe touched the wire. The baby got a shock and cried. The horse got a shock and jumped back. I got a shock and said, "Well, there go a thousand brain cells." If it was an omen, I didn't pay any attention to it.

Two weeks later, I owned a horse, the fabulous Mr. T., a skinny white Thoroughbred gelding of unknown origins, but tall enough and kind enough for a returning middle-aged equestrienne. I remember that I was excited, but very worried about the expense. I intended to try it all out, just to see if I still liked it.

Instead, I went whole-hog. Mr. T. needed many things. A place to live, a bridle, a saddle, a halter, some wraps and horse-boots. I needed a helmet, some magazine subscriptions, some expert advice. More trainers. Soon, the things we needed got bigger—a horse blanket, saddles and bridles, a tack trunk, a trailer, a truck. A trip to Texas in the winter. To North Carolina. To California. A farm. A companion horse. A mare. The mare needed a foal. The foal needed a facility. And more expert advice. I don't think "whole-hog" even begins to describe it. Maybe "I went crazy" is how my friends saw it, but "I found my destiny" was how I saw it. More and more expert advice was what I really needed, from trainers and books, from breeders and the Internet, from veterinarians and farriers and acupuncturists and horse communicators and denizens of the racetrack, from other owners, from judges and videos and clinics and demonstrations and horse races. From the horses themselves. I cannot say I became an expert—even a faux expert. Becoming an expert on horses, even in a single discipline, takes much longer than ten years. I remain an eager amateur. I would rather take a riding lesson than eat lunch. Given the choice between a vacation in Hawaii and a vacation in Arcadia, I would take Arcadia any day. I would rather talk to Alexis about horses than meet any Nobel Prize winner you could name, and whenever I am asked to sit on a panel with some literary light or other, I always suggest that we adjourn to the track afterward. They always think I'm joking, but I'm not.

ALEXIS AND I met when I sent Jackie to be trained by Eddie Gregson, who was a respected fancy trainer, well known for taking perfect care of his string. Alexis was his assistant trainer. She took care of the barn and rode several horses each morning. She was quiet and friendly and stayed in the background. I was always staring at Eddie, waiting for him to tell me that my horse was going to win the Triple Crown. Jackie lasted three days before he injured himself, but I got to be friends with Eddie, and the next year I sent him Hornblower. This would have been May of 2000. In June, Eddie died, and Alexis became my trainer. Hornblower was two. I was fifty. Alexis was forty-eight. Mr. T. had died the year before, at twenty. Jackie was three. Persey was four. Alexis and I began being friends. In the fall of 2000, Hornblower had a few starts, but early in 2001, Alexis noticed a hard bump on his pastern, down by the hoof. The vet said that if we continued to run him he would get hurt, but if we turned him out for five months, the hard bump would calcify and be stronger than ever, so we turned him out. He came back as the vet predicted at the end of 2001, three now, soon to be four.

Alexis was trying to get a horse to the races, too: the beautiful Pangloss, who was also a maiden, and a year older than my maiden. He was big and round, dark bay, and glossy. Alexis knew he was fast, but he had trouble with his shins—every time she brought him to the track, his shins got sore after a while and she had to turn him out again. A majority of racehorses "buck"* their shins when first in training—it is a process of bone remodeling through stress that seems to result in denser, tougher bone—but Pangloss, who sometimes worked with Hornblower, couldn't seem to do what other horses do—get sore and get over it in a week or two. He had bucked his shins every year for three years.

HORNBLOWER CONTINUED to behave with perfect decorum around the barn and in his morning works, but in preparation for his first race on the grass, Alexis started taking him to the saddling enclosure and the paddock every day, to attempt to forestall the trembling and the sweating. "Oh, they know when it's a race!" she said. "You can't fool them after the second start or so. Different time of day, more people around, got to go through the test barn. It's not like they're stupid. A race is just different from a work."

Our ability to reproduce the conditions of the test, in other words, was limited. Nevertheless, since a fifth of a second equals a length, and a nose or a head or a neck or a half-length can equal a win, any energy saved in the saddling enclosure can be earned back with interest at the end of a race. These were practical considerations. Other than that, it was now March. The weather around Pasadena was even better than it had been, and it had been perfect. The grass of the Santa Anita turf course was startlingly green and thick. I thought Hornblower would look marvelous on the grass, the dappled gray against the green.

*Short for "buckle," from Old French via Middle English.

IT WOULD SEEM as though it is but a short step down the yellow brick road of magical thinking from a horse-astrology site to an animal communicator. But in fact, I had been chatting with Mr. T. through Hali, the gorgeous blond animal-communicator, for several years. Horse communicators are controversial among horsemen, but popular. Probably, opinions run from "interesting and worth a try" at one end of the spectrum through "harmless insanity" to "fraud" at the other. By the time I met Hali, I had read a couple of articles on the subject in the equestrian press and heard a few things through the grapevine. And many horsemen are familiar with a book written in the seventies by English horseman Henry Blake, called *Talking with Horses,* in which Blake described his own experiences in what he called ESP, which was the transfer of an emotional state from horse to horse or horse to human, and "telepathy," which was the transfer of specific mental pictures. Blake, however, did not work through a third person; he explored his own ability to communicate with his animals.

I had asked Hali all the usual questions in the beginning, in 1996, when I first moved to California with Mr. T.: Does he like me? Is he happy? Does he want anything? Where did he come from? The answers were, respectively, "Yes, yes, twenty pounds of carrots every day, and the south of France, someplace where the sky was blue and the buildings were very white." Was there something he especially did not like? Was there anything he was afraid of? Did he realize that my husband had left? The answers to these questions were "Men who spoke German, me falling off over a jump and getting hurt (thereby endangering his security), and, yes, he had made every effort to drive him away."

Hali always maintained that Mr. T. was an especially talkative horse, who said of himself that he was trilingual, and whose opinions had a certain maturity of outlook. Over the years, I got into the habit of talking to him without either believing or disbelieving that we were actually communicating, but accepting it as a productive conceit, in much the same way that a reader accepts the reality of a work of fiction. And it had an effect upon me similar to that of a work of fiction—I was moved and delighted by what the horse had to say, and I learned from it to treat him with respect. I stopped barking one-word commands at him as if he were a dog, and began taking him into my confidence. We became very relaxed and trusting around one another. But communication was a game that we had played together once in a while; after Mr. T. died, I rather forgot about it. It hadn't really occurred to me to talk to Hornblower, who was far away. His state of mind was Alexis's business, and she didn't seem like the animal-communication type. Anyway, I didn't know enough about him for my knowledge to serve as a check upon what Hali might say.

One evening, though, we called him up. This involved Hali's closing her eyes and letting him come into her mind. She had seen him once or twice as a foal, and she knew what he looked like. She said that he was quite ready to talk. I stared at the ceiling and got a little more comfortable.

Did he like his situation?

Yes, he did. He considered himself more or less the lord of all he surveyed.

Did he like racing?

Yes, he did.

Then what was the trembling about?

He didn't respond to this question.

Did he think he could win?

He did win. (Hali got a picture of another horse dropping back and Hornblower beating him.) I said, "I wonder if he realizes that you have to beat the whole field in order to win." She said, "He doesn't understand that idea."

How did he see himself in relation to the horses around him?

He was the best. Most beautiful, most talented.

Then why didn't he run faster than all of them?

He hadn't made up his mind to do so yet. Though he could certainly do it, he hadn't decided that it was necessary.

Now I was fully into it. I said, "He hasn't made a commitment. You know, we all sensed that. He comes back as fresh as when he goes out, and eats his dinner right up. He doesn't seem to have really exerted himself." I thought for a minute. "Ask him if he knows what a gelding is."

He didn't.

"Ask him if he knows the difference between himself and Pangloss."

Into Hali's mind came the picture of a rounded, dark, glossy horse. Hali had never seen Pangloss, or heard of him, but when she described what she was seeing, I said, "That's Pangloss."

Hornblower didn't understand the difference between himself and Pangloss. I said, "Ask him if he knows what a filly is."

His response indicated that he was mostly indifferent to fillies. That's what his behavior, as reported by Alexis, indicated, too.

Did he want to win?

He didn't know yet.

I felt this was a typical Pisces sort of conversation.

When I later reported it to Alexis, I softened her up first by describing the picture of Pangloss that had entered Hali's mind.

She was more receptive than I expected, and right away we came up with what I felt was a reasonable analysis, though admittedly in such a context "reasonable" has a fairly technical meaning. We agreed that the horse sounded like an adolescent boy, say a thirteen-year-old, full of bravado but not really in possession of the big picture. Puberty hadn't kicked in yet (and around the barn, he really didn't pay any more attention to fillies than to male horses. That he thought it was enough to focus on one other horse—a single rival—was interesting in the context of what we knew about racing. When a horse and jockey are coming up on another horse and jockey in a race, the horses are more likely to dig in and run harder for the win if they "hook on"—that is, see each other. Pictures of Silver Charm and Freehouse, two grays who raced against each other frequently in the late nineties, show this clearly—the eye of the horse in front is rolling back toward the approaching horse. By the same token, a horse going wide can sometimes sneak up on the front-runner, who doesn't put out any extra effort because he doesn't see him. It made perfect sense that a horse with an immature understanding of his task would decide that some horse he was racing right next to was his real rival, and if he showed up that one, that was good enough. I said to Alexis, "He hasn't realized that it's fun to win. He just thinks it's an effort." I could only blame myself; he sounded exactly like what I had bred him to be—a late bloomer.

And this was his seventh start already—four as a two-year-old and two since coming back.

I called around for reassurance. My friend Jim, in Kentucky, said, "Cigar didn't break his maiden until his eleventh start." That was reassurance indeed. Cigar had won the most money of any horse ever, was not especially well bred, and equaled Citation's record for the most consecutive wins. But, then, here was my problem exactly: I could make that mental leap from my trembling, uncommitted, inexperienced four-year-old colt to the greatest money-winner ever in a heartbeat. And feel a surge of confidence! On the magical-thinking scale, horse communication seemed sane by comparison. That is the way they routinely talk at the racetrack, though, citing a list of examples (and there are examples of every phenomenon) to prove that no bolt of good luck is unprecedented (and no bolt of bad luck, either). If it happened once, it can happen again. If they had talked to Cigar after his sixth start, what would he have said?

When Hornblower went in his much-anticipated (by me) first turf race, the *Daily Racing Form* said, "Bred to run all day." I took this as a compliment, but really it was just a descriptor, like "plodder."

His company in the race was of a distinctly higher level than usual, which is typical of races on the grass in southern California. The program was a roster of famous classic sires, but with a worldly, European feel. Nureyev, Sadlers Wells, that sort of thing. Sires with stud fees of a hundred thousand dollars. Hornblower was well enough bred, in a sense—his sire was by the sire of Winning Colors, who won the Kentucky Derby wire to wire in 1988, one of three fillies in history to do so, and of Cozzene, one of the most productive sires in Kentucky. His dam's sire was a contemporary of Secretariat, and when he died, they wrote a little article about him in the *Thoroughbred Times*. But the most notable characteristics of all of Hornblower's progenitors were beauty, soundness, and sanity, not speed. He was a little out of his class in this race, and the handicappers noted this; he went off at ninety to one.

This time, Alexis tried a few things before the race—she hosed him off back at the barn, to cool him off and prevent him from going into a sweat, and she girthed him up before heading to the saddling enclosure, because putting the saddle on in the paddock seemed to agitate him.

I was once again out of range of a simulcast, reduced to listening to Alexis report the race to me over the phone. He broke in the middle of the pack, not good, and stayed there, fourth out of the gate, fifth most of the way around, then eighth of nine at the finish. The horse who came in last had gone off at fourteen to one, so at least we had shown up the handicappers in a single small detail—he had beaten a horse that was supposed to be six times better than he was.

Alexis was not dissatisfied. Hornblower had kept running, though the other horses were bunched around him rather tightly. She said, "That's one of the problems with grass races. They run closer together, maybe because they don't get any dirt kicked in their faces. The jockey said the horse tried a couple of times"—instead of trembling and throwing in the towel when the other horses bunched around him, he had dug in. "I'm not discouraged," said Alexis. "I think it was a good race."

He contacted Hali about a week later. She woke up early one morning with him in her mind, and he was eager to discuss a particular issue, which was his name. "Hornblower" was simply too difficult to overcome. Its vibrational qualities were negative—it started low and went lower. A racehorse, he said, needed a name full of high vibrations to be a winner. It was a herd-status thing. All the other horses around the backside knew your name and judged you by it.

I was dismayed, and also a little insulted. I had thought that "Hornblower" was perfect for him—son of Grand Flotilla, out of Rapid Response. Obviously a name with a naval theme would be just the ticket. And there was that classy hint of the literary, too. But no. The next time Hali came for a session, we told the horse that his name couldn't be changed—once he had raced as Hornblower, that was it. He then requested that the people in Alexis's barn be instructed to call him "Wowie," the nickname we had given him as a foal. If he were addressed as Wowie, which had a higher vibration, he might be able to overcome the disadvantages of "Hornblower." Since he had offered what you might call a critique of names, we asked him to analyze other racehorse names: "Forego"—medium vibration. "Native Dancer"—very high. "Secretariat"—very high. "John Henry"—medium to low. I ran through the list of names I had given my other racehorses. He didn't like them, and suggested that I consult him before naming anyone else. Then I asked him about several of his stablemates. "Mpenzi"—good name but she won't win, anyway (and she didn't). "So Wistfullee" (Alexis's best stakes horse). He said, "That's a good name, but she's going to be injured."

Hali and I looked at each other.

The next day, I spoke to Alexis about the names. She agreed to call him Wowie. We laughed at the maiden's literary self-confidence, and also at this further evidence that the horses at the racetrack lived in a social system parallel to the human social system. I didn't mention So Wistfullee, because I didn't want to put any bad ideas in Alexis's head. Then I forgot about it. Four days later, I called Alexis and she said, "You know, I am so upset. So Wistfullee ran in that race, and she came out of it with a condylar fracture behind. She's okay, but I don't think she can run again. She was my best horse."

I said, "Alexis, what I am about to tell you is going to freak you out."

And it did.

FOUR

Love

IN HIS BOOK *Guns, Germs, and Steel,* Jared Diamond considers the characteristics of the "big five" domesticated animals–the sheep, the goat, the pig, the cow, and the horse. Successful domestication of these animals, for work, fiber, and food, was dependent upon three factors inherent in the way the wild populations organized their groups. All of the big five species have social herds, overlapping ranges among the herds, and a well-defined dominance hierarchy within the herd. They are also quick to mature, easy to confine, neither vicious nor panicky, and willing to mate at the convenience of humans. Among the big five, horses have served more functions and answered to more uses than any of the others.

Diamond remarks: "Domestic horses of a pack line follow the human leader as they would normally follow the top-ranking female. . . . As young animals grow up in such a herd, they imprint on the animals they see nearby. Under wild conditions those are members of their own species, but captive young herd animals also see humans nearby, and they imprint upon humans as well" (p. 173).

But let's drop the mechanical term "imprint" and say they "love" them. Or at least let's return to *A General Theory of Love* and say that the young of each domesticated mammalian species require relationships to complete the formation of their brain structure and brain chemistry, that they suffer when these "open-loop" relationships are faulty, absent, or disturbed, and that they are more or less eager to experience relationship throughout their lives. Let's further say that these relationships can and even must be with humans, or the multitude of things that horses and humans have accomplished together would not have been possible. Young horses, intended for the most intimate and wide-ranging uses that humans can think of—for driving and riding and war and companionship—excel at forming relationships because the nature of the species demands it, as the nature of the human species demands it, or as the nature of the canine species demands it. But much of the horse's capacity for love, or "attachment" to humans, is unseen. In many cases, as with the man I met who had never thought of horses as having affections, the attachment behaviors of horses are ignored. In other cases, they are interpreted as carrot-and-stick behaviors, and it is true that horses like carrots and dislike beatings. But more than one horseman, at the racetrack and elsewhere, has noted that women have a special talent with horses and a special attraction to them. Perhaps this special talent is simply a talent for relating.

IF I HAD READ *A General Theory of Love* right after Biosymmetree, Jackie's dam, colicked and died, I might have been less sanguine than I was. I would have known that "many subsystems of the mammalian brain do not come pre-programmed; maturing animals need limbic regulation to give coherence to neural development. Without this external guidance, neural cacophony ensues: behavioral systems are constructed, but without proper harmony between the interdigitating parts. . . . The lack of an attuned mother is a nonevent for a reptile and a shattering injury to the complex and fragile brain of a mammal" (*A General Theory of Love,* p. 85). But a month must have been almost long enough for Jackie, because he has grown up to be easy for people to get along with and not unusually difficult to train. He has also been remarkably affectionate.

Like Wowie, the racehorse formerly known as Hornblower, Jackie started out his career as a racehorse, and at one point, both of the horses were living at a training farm south of River-

Jackie at two months, AJ at four and a half years.

side, California, out in the desert. The farm was hard to get to, and I didn't visit them much, but in late winter 2000, I managed to get there one morning to meet Eddie Gregson. Jackie was three and Wowie was two. They had been at the training center for two or three months. I arrived about fifteen minutes before Eddie did. The center was quiet—it was Sunday, late morning—and one of the managers told me where the horses were. I went to Wowie's stall first. He was eating his grain—he had galloped that morning, and at any rate he was a doer (racetrack talk for a glutton) of unceasing enthusiasm. I came up to his stall and spoke to him. He looked at me, stuck his nose toward me for a pat, and went back to his feed. I thought he recognized me, but my sudden appearance after several months didn't matter much to him. I crossed the courtyard to Jackie's stall. The stalls ranged around the courtyard were hidden behind shades to keep them cool in the desert sun, and as I stepped around the shade in front of Jackie's stall, I spoke his name. At the sound of my voice, he charged from the back of the stall, nearly banging open his Dutch door with his chest. His ears were pricked, his eyes were alert, his nostrils were open. I stepped up to the stall, and he greeted me with undreamed-of ardor: He snuffled my face, mouth, and nose. He ran his nose all over my hair, neck, and ears, whether to feel me or to smell me I have no idea. He could not get enough of me. He was climbing out of his stall. I petted him in long passionate strokes along the top of his neck, first one side, then the other. He melted under my hand, half closing his eyes for a bit, then resuming his inspection of me. He put his lips against mine for two or three minutes. What was he doing? I was kissing him, but was he kissing me? I have no idea. I was not making him do it by holding his head. It was very strange, but there was no mistaking the meaning of his actions—he was surprised and thrilled to see me.

Eddie arrived, and the grooms got the horses out. They went out to the exercise track and did their work, and they both did a good job. Eddie liked Wowie and asked me if I had nominated him for the Breeders' Cup. We agreed that he had an exceptionally large and smooth stride. Eddie was ten or twelve years older than I was and had thirty years' experience at the racetrack. I was deferential to the point of feeling that he could somehow anoint my colts with greatness just by looking at them. Jackie, I could see from a distance, had a beautiful trot, but he was only trotting. In his rehabilitation from an injury received the previous fall, he wasn't yet up to galloping. Eddie noted some good things about his conformation, but didn't pay much attention to him. I didn't say so to Eddie, but I noticed that, except for when he was on the track doing his job, the horse never stopped looking at me, always had his dark-brown head turned and his ears pricked in my direction. When we were finished, I followed Eddie to his car, still talking about racing, asking questions and trying to get a sense of what he thought of my horses. I went back after he drove away, and gave them each another pat and a carrot. But I was sad to leave Jackie. It was like visiting your child at boarding school and realizing that parting had to take place all over again. For Wowie parting from me was nothing, but it seemed as if for Jackie parting from me was something. When, a couple of months later, it became clear that Jackie simply could not hold up to race training, I brought him home with relief. Better, I thought, to have him nearby than to win a million dollars (yes, I did think that, but, then, I still don't know what it's like to win a million dollars, so I really can't compare).

What I now think is that stroking him all over when he was an orphaned foal was sufficiently like something he might have received from his dam that he came to be particularly attached to me. Maybe it was the stroking and brushing, but I also wonder if maybe it was only the degree of love I had for him. I was not his well-wisher and caretaker, as the manager of the ranch was, nor was I his friend and playmate, as his equine companions were; I was the one who adored him, for whom he was absolutely irreplaceable.

Even though lots of horsemen are uncomfortable with the idea of horses' having affections, or "loving" a human, horses in herds are very demonstrative of both affection and dislike toward one another—they clearly differentiate between individuals, they clearly have best friends, dear ones, more distant acquaintances, and enemies. They can also remember.

In that regard, Persey has a story, too. It is so unusual for a weaned horse to re-encounter his or her mother some years later that, when I told the story of Persey and Lucy to a lifelong New Zealand horseman, he told me that he had never heard of such a thing; but I saw it with my own eyes. After Persey was weaned from her neglectful and insecure dam, Lucy, at three months, the two horses didn't seem to have much of an awareness of one another. They lived on separate parts of the birth farm. When Persey was sixteen months old, I brought her to California rather than have her go through another cold Wisconsin winter in the closed-up barn where she was living.

When Persey was four, Lucy came to California, too. I assumed that the two were utter strangers, and that they would take some time to get used to one another when I turned them out together. But no. As soon as Persey laid eyes on Lucy, she was galvanized—ears rigidly forward, eyes wide, body at attention. She whinnied immediately. I opened the gate and put her inside the paddock; she rushed to Lucy's side and began rubbing her head against her. Lucy was more reserved, but displayed none of the suspicious behavior that horses normally display when they meet strangers. She neither squealed nor pawed. For the next few days, Persey shadowed Lucy, her head near Lucy's flank. She frequently rubbed the side of her head on Lucy's haunch or licked her on the flank or on the neck. Lucy allowed, and maybe even welcomed, this intimacy. As at the beginning, she was more reserved—accepting her daughter's attentions more than reciprocating them—but she, too, showed affection. If I took Persey out of the paddock, Lucy would call for her until I brought her back. When, a week or so later, I introduced them into a herd of about twenty horses that lived in a two-hundred-acre pasture, they were constant companions, and Persey habitually used her mother as protection from the other horses. They were rarely apart, but the division of labor seemed to be that Lucy would establish relationships with the other members of the herd, asserting and maintaining their status (which Lucy made sure was high—she acted like the queen from the moment she stepped through the pasture gate), and Persey would stay out of trouble. The following spring, Lucy began to show mysterious signs of the infection that would later cause her death. The main symptom was that she would seem to drop off to sleep with her head down, then stagger and return to consciousness. Persey always stood close to her, with her head down and turned in Lucy's direction, until Lucy woke up. They were entirely compatible, even eating out of the same feed trough or the same flake of hay. I never saw either one threaten the other.

When I talk to Alexis about horse love, she can hardly think of incidents of it. Mule love she remembers, from when she cared for Charlie O, back when the Oakland A's were winning the World Series. But horses at the racetrack live regimented lives, partly because so many of them are uncastrated males. Horse love is not much in evidence; in order to exhibit affection, horses have to be free to exhibit all sorts of feelings that might be inconvenient. At the racetrack, their behavior is highly regimented; for safety's sake, there is little variety, and interaction is discouraged. But if horses live in more open circumstances, then things that seem unusual are routine—horses come when they are called, for example.

I have had twenty-five horses or so over the years, and not all of them have related to me in the same way. Jackie, Mr. T., and one or two others have been attentive and interested—I would say that they show me affection that contrasts to the way they relate to other people. Mr. T., in fact, had the reputation of something of a crab around the barn, but he was always friendly and kind toward me. Once, I went to get him out of a large pasture, and as soon as he saw me, he whinnied and came to me at a full gallop. I stood still, on the principle that if he knew where I was he would be less likely to run me down by mistake. He slid to a halt right in front of me and put his head down for a carrot and a pat. Another time, I was petting him and he reached over and nipped me very gently on the chin. I was later told this was a horse's sort of kiss; when horses are grooming each other, they frequently nibble lightly and even carefully, opening their mouths just a bit, slowly, and laying their teeth on the other horse's neck and then scratching.

Some of my others are friendly toward me, and immediately notice my presence and come forward to see what I am doing, but they don't seem to express affection as opposed to general friendliness. Others gaze past me, sort of recognizing that I've appeared. A few ignore me completely. I have one mare whom I fed and petted and gave carrots to for six or eight months, three or four times a day. While she was living with me, she would allow me to pet her one time on the neck, then put her ears back and turn away. She never nickered or acted friendly. Now when I go see her or her foals, she maintains her distance—stretching her neck out to receive bits of carrot from as far away as possible. In the broodmare pasture, though, she is notable for the passion of her attachment to her chosen mare-friend. Her filly began being friendly only a year after weaning, but now quite enjoys petting.

One mare that I kept at my house became quite attached to me. She and her foal lived in my barn for six months, because the foal had been born prematurely and needed time for her stretched-out tendons to strengthen. She couldn't tolerate the rough-and-tumble play of other foals. Iona, the mare, enjoyed all kinds of attention. When the foal was old enough to be weaned (about seven months), I took the two of them to the nurse farm, and over the course of five to seven days, they were separated. When I went for a visit just after the weaning was completed, I was walking past the farm's biggest pasture, five acres in a long rectangle. The mares were at the far end of the pasture, grazing, and I called out, "Hi, Iona!" Her head popped up, and she whinnied loudly, then turned and galloped toward me, whinnying and whinnying. I stopped at the fence and she came straight to me, still whinnying. To this day, I think that she was attempting to express several things to me about the trauma of weaning (her first) and the stress of finding herself with strange mares in a strange place. I think that she saw me as the closest person to her and the likeliest one to help her. Her second and third foals have been among the friendliest and most eager for human attention.

The mirror of attachment is antipathy, and horses are good at that, too.

Not long ago, I went to a show and discovered that there was a horse on the grounds that I had once owned, named Fanny. I bought Fanny when she was almost three. Our relationship soured after about six months—she became balky to ride, and what Ray Berta called "selfish": Whenever I was in the saddle and required her to do anything at all, she would grit her teeth, pin her ears, and stop dead. If I pressured her, she would throw her head and neck upward and back and threaten to rear. Ray could get her to work, but only, he thought, because she provisionally accepted his domination. Around the barn, she was a nightmare. Once, a female groom went into the stall to put a blanket on her, and Fanny had pinned her against the wall with her very large hind end before the groom even realized what was happening. The horse was willing to do one thing, which was to be led to a large airfield, mounted, and galloped. She had a beautiful, floating gallop, and this pleasure persuaded me to keep trying with her. Eventually, though, Ray told me that I had fallen so low in Fanny's estimation that I could actually get hurt trying to reassert myself. I sent her to another trainer, who loved the way she jumped, and bought her. Even that trainer had some trouble with her determination to be the boss. The woman's strategy was to never act friendly toward the horse, and to allow no one to speak to her. Only when the mare approached the trainer submissively did the trainer treat her in a friendly way. Every time the trainer told me about her wonderful progress with Fanny's dressage training and jumping, I was thrilled that the horse no longer belonged to me. Subsequently, the trainer sold her to a fifteen-year-old girl, who took her to combined training events.

At the show, I could see her from a distance, standing in her stall. I went up to her and said, "Hey, Fanny. Remember me?" She hadn't seen me in about two years. Her instant reaction was to grit her teeth audibly in annoyance and to pin her ears. She looked away from me, but did not retreat or go into her stall.

The parents of her new owner came up to me and shook my hand and thanked me for getting Fanny off the racetrack and bringing her to California. They adored her. Their daughter adored her. She was a wonderful addition to their family. I probed a little. What was she like? "Oh, she's just Fanny, you know."

Was she manageable?

"Oh, very."

No problems?

"We just trust her completely with our only daughter."

When I saw her jump a course, I could understand this at least partially. She was a good jumper, fast and clean, but, more than that, a safe jumper. Her front legs seemed to disappear over a jump—she did have a certain sure-footed, athletic style that was about as safe as a horse could be. After that, I watched Fanny with the girl. Her demeanor was submissive and affectionate. A friend of the girl's was watching with me. I said, "What is Fanny like?"

"You know, she's a one-girl horse. She's awful with everyone else."

To the end of that horse show, every time I approached Fanny in her stall to attempt to achieve some sort of reconciliation, her reaction stayed the same—grinding teeth, pinned ears, annoyance. And this from a horse that I faithfully fed and cared for, a horse that I was never unkind to. Suffice it to say that Persey was at the same show and crossed paths with Fanny from time to time. Persey and Fanny had been stabled together for a period, and knew each other perfectly well. They did not seem to acknowledge each other's presence. Hali later said that Persey reported that Fanny had lorded it over her, crowing that she had left me and Persey had not, that she was a successful competition horse and Persey was not. Persey simply ignored her, or so she said. In fact, the world is full of horses who take a long time to find an owner to mesh with, after years of conflict and dissatisfaction on both sides, even when the unsuccessful owners are acting, as far as they know, with the best intentions.

A more dramatic tale of antipathy is the following. Two stallions, who lived on the same ranch, were separated for five years. When the stallion who had left returned at the end of that period, the stallion who had remained galloped across two fields and broke down two fences to attack his old enemy as soon as he stepped off the horse trailer.

The goal of horse training is to mitigate equine idiosyncrasy and to give every horse some fluency in the common language required to get along with people. There are always horses for sale and always buyers, and a trained horse is supposed to function reliably, to walk, trot, canter, jump, gallop across country, stand, cross-tie, be groomed and bathed, ride in a horse trailer, go to a few horse shows, and even foxhunt, or to do similar things as a Western-style horse. Horses who have not achieved some proficiency in the required areas by the age of six or eight are the exception rather than the norm. But there are horses who show affection, who share a bond with the owner, who do more than perform functions. They actively seek to please. Until you have owned a horse who seeks cooperation and behaves warmly toward you, you don't realize how many horses were just passing time in your company, half ignoring you or barely putting up with you.

Obviously, the source of affective behavior in horses is the mother/child bond, and there is no reason to assume that this bond is less strong in horses than it is in other species. One marker of this bond, according to Drs. Lewis, Amini, and Lannon, would be Persey's always evident "searching and calling" behavior. All horses engage in searching-and-calling behavior quite frequently, and most horsemen find it disruptive and annoying, and so most horses are prevented from forming strong attachments to one another—as soon as they show any signs of putting an attachment to another horse ahead of assigned tasks, the two horses are separated until they become apparently indifferent to one another. But in my experience, such draconian measures are unnecessary as well as unkind. My five horses live together in a pasture on top of a hillside on a ranch where the large riding arena is set into a bowl. They are good about going out of the pasture to work; if any one of them is being ridden in the lower arena, any other one who is being ridden down the hill greets the one in the arena as soon as he sees her, and the greeting is at once reciprocated, but there is no sense of desperation. The whinnies of horses not in the immediate family may or may not arouse a response. Many horses live in groups at our ranch, and it is common for horses left behind in the pastures to stand and watch them depart. When the horses return, they are always welcomed vocally. These horses generally greet their owners, too, as soon as they see them. In a situation where attachments are not discouraged, the horses' feelings for one another are evident all the time, but rarely inconvenient. Perhaps as with all routine attachments, family life wears thin, and the horses are happy to go off and do something, even if it means leaving the others behind for a while.

IF THERE IS any species of animal inextricably bound to human civilization, it is the horse. Horses engage in just about every human endeavor except literature and the arts. For most of history, they have been treated, in contrast to sheep, goats, cows, and pigs, rather as working partners than as agricultural commodities or companion animals. They have lived more like humans than like dogs, expected to be useful and to have productive working lives. Freud said in *Civilization and Its Discon-*

tents that human desire had to be deformed and channeled in order for civilization to emerge; this is even truer of the horse. However horses organize themselves, their families, and their herds in the wild, they may not do so in civilization. The signal example of the effect of civilization on the horse is castration. Stallions are widely presumed to be vicious by nature, and most amateur horsemen away from studfarms and the racetrack don't have much experience with stallions. Gunther Gabel-Williams, the great lion trainer, once said that an angry stallion is more dangerous and frightening than an angry lion or tiger. An experienced horsewoman I knew never approached any of her four stallions without a whip in one hand. Even Ray has told me that, though he expects a stallion to behave himself, everything a stallion does is more extreme than everything a gelding does. Most horses are gelded before they are a year old—just before they begin to exhibit sexual behavior.

Geldings are useful animals. They are trainable; they tolerate the presence of mares and other geldings without being over-stimulated; they live amicably in stables and herds. Nevertheless, and this is the point, geldings are far from lacking in affections or predilections. When allowed to, they are likely to form extremely close friendships with other geldings—one-to-one pairs who eat together, greet each other, stand nose to tail, flick flies for one another, call to each other when they are apart. If affection among horses were based solely on reproductive feelings—sexual feelings between stallions and mares, or maternal feelings between mares and foals—then geldings would have no feelings at all. What the strength and universality of their feelings shows is that relationships between horses are essential in and of themselves, whether there is a sociobiological yearning to pass on genetic material or not.

When we attribute certain feelings to horses—a prancing

horse is "proud," a nickering horse is "loving," a gamboling horse is "exuberant," a horse with his head hanging is "depressed," a horse with his head high and his ears pricked is "nervous" or "excited," a horse kicking is "angry" or "resentful"— we are not anthropomorphizing them, we are recognizing their mammal nature by using ours, and we are instinctively reiterating what Diamond points out in *Guns, Germs, and Steel*—horses mesh better with us than almost all other large mammals, including zebras, which have never been successfully domesticated. Furthermore, a horseman who fails to respond to the signals his horse gives him in an instinctive way—recognizing the emotions for what they are—won't get far with him. Not everyone's ability to receive and act on the signals the horse gives is equally good. Plenty of people infantilize their horses—pitying their fears and thereby reinforcing the fears rather than taking a confident lead and reassuring the horse that his fears are exaggerated—but plenty of others ignore their horses' emotions entirely, thereby promoting mechanical behavior in the horses and forgoing the satisfying extra dimension of companionship.

I suppose the remaining question, if I am saying that a horse can love his human, is, Can a horse show particular kindness to his human—in addition to manifesting attachment by looking for contact and affection, can he do something to benefit the human, can he knowingly give the human something?

I would have to say that I don't know the answer to this question. A friend of mine reports that when he and his sister were children a pony that they were riding without a saddle or bridle knowingly took them to the gate closest to their house and gently bumped them off in a patch of soft sand, as if he were babysitting them. Stories abound of ponies and horses seeming to take care of their child riders by raising their necks to push them back in the saddle when they are falling off. Eventing

trainer Denny Emerson has a picture on his Tamarack Hill Farm
Web site of a child leading one of his stallions. Adults sometimes need help, too—there is a famous video of an English
steeplechase in which the jockey becomes unseated but can't get
his foot out of the stirrup and is being dragged. The horse apparently makes some sort of move that launches the jockey back
into the saddle in time for the next fence. In the interview afterward, also shown on the video, the jockey testifies that it is his
opinion that the horse acted to remount him, something that he
had never seen or heard of before. On a more mundane level, I
often had the sense with my old horse Mr. T. that he was thinking of our safety when he declined to jump some fence, and also
when, in spite of my clumsiness and poor timing, he simply carried me along, jumping fence after fence. And, of course, he did
tell Hali that he felt my skills at jumping weren't good enough
for us to show, that it was dangerous for my welfare and his for
me to continue to try. I could tell a difference between Fanny,
who didn't like me and tried hard to buck me off or rear with
me, Persey, who when in the mood doesn't really care whether I
go off or not, and Jackie, who never rears and never bucks more
than a single time, and responds to a sharp "Hey!" by stopping
anything scary that he is doing. I could tell the difference
between a horse I owned who never really bonded with me,
whose fears were not amenable to any interference on my part,
and Mr. T., who always set aside his fear when I reassured him.
And the quality of "kindness" is common in horses. Some trainers see it as a good negative—when the trainer makes a mistake,
the horse refrains from taking advantage of it, or when the
horse feels himself at a disadvantage—cornered, for example—he
makes no attempt to use his power and speed against the trainer.
Others see it as a form of attachment—the horse wants to be with
his human, or humans in general. It is not submission but,

rather, generosity. Nevertheless, I think it remains a moot point whether kindness is a quality that a particular horse brings to a particular relationship, or whether it is a general quality of character that some horses (or many horses) possess.

AND DO HORSES' AFFECTIONS, or their capacity for affection, develop over the years? Recently, the twenty-year-old companion mare to my old mare Chipper suffered what appeared to be a lung aneurism. When the people at the farm found the two of them, the stricken mare was down and Chipper was nuzzling her head and neck, nickering in the throaty way that mares do to foals. When the humans were helping the other mare, Chipper went over to her hay and began to eat, but a few minutes later, the dying mare convulsed and went down. Chipper came running, whinnying and nickering, and began nuzzling and caressing her friend. The people stood aside, and Chipper tended to the other mare until she died. It is, of course, impossible to know how the mares themselves experienced this incident, but my friend who witnessed the incident, and who has seen hundreds of horses over the years, said to me, "You know, it's those old mares, the ones who've had lots of foals, that are really compassionate." And I believe her.

FIVE

By the Bay

BY THE END of March, I was of two minds about having a racehorse at Santa Anita.

Visiting the racehorse at Santa Anita was a vacation in itself.
Even though I didn't ever stroll through the Arboretum across
Baldwin Avenue from the track, and even though I never took
afternoon tea in the botanical garden at the Huntington Library,
and even though I hadn't shopped in the shopping mall that
abutted the parking lot, I appreciated that you could turn your
outing to the track into quite an elegant day of pleasures if you
so desired. Additionally, there are many statues and topiaried
shrubs and well-kept flowers and shady walks and quiet benches
at Santa Anita. It is a garden with horses in it and mountains
beyond the backstretch, rising against the blue of the sky.
That one's horse could get to such a place, and run, and even
get on the board by winning third under Chris McCarron, as
Wowie had done as a two-year-old, was one of life's bonuses. I
impressed myself with such a thing. And here was D. Wayne
Lukas, strolling along. And here was Bob Baffert. And wasn't

that Point Given out there? I was eager to retain this privilege, which was not quite like anything else I have ever done.

But the topiary and the shady walks cost money, and a racehorse has to win in order to support his training bill. To win, he has to run in races that suit him, and Santa Anita didn't offer races to suit my horse very often, turf races geared to grass horses of not-quite-world-class talents. American tracks in general, but southern-California tracks in particular, are very protective of their turf—literally. They keep horses off the grass course as much as possible, to prevent it from getting torn up by pounding hooves. In Europe, the turf is hundreds of years old, and horses work over it every day.* American tracks didn't use to offer turf races, but dirt runners and turf runners have different running styles, and with the proliferation of the intercontinental sales of racehorses, the American tracks have had to nurture grass courses. Since Wowie wasn't quite good enough to be a turf horse at Santa Anita, Alexis proposed that she send him to Bay Meadows, near San Francisco, where there is plenty of rain and the turf course is more frequently in use. Every three weeks, Bay Meadows ran a maiden turf race of a mile. Horses often go to other courses to race, then return to live at the home track. Many trainers maintain cooperative relationships with trainers at other tracks, and a few of the biggest ones have stables in several parts of the country. Even so, I couldn't help feeling that my child was being asked to leave Harvard and take a course at Boston University because perhaps that would suit him better. Of course, Boston University, like Bay Meadows, would have fine traditions and excellent facilities of its own, but fewer of the little flourishes that ask to be savored and are the privilege of a few.

*This is not to say that they work in the race courses themselves—they don't. They do work on grass, though.

The northern-California tracks, of course, have a long and famous history. When Charles Strub was just beginning to lure investors to Arcadia, the northern-California tracks were already going strong. In my imagination, though, there was something dark and hard-core about Bay Meadows and Golden Gate Fields, where I had visited once, in the winter, when the sunlight was wan and the weather was chilly. They made me think of Damon Runyon. They seemed a little forbidding, as if a nice girl like myself, a nonsmoker and an imbiber of Pinot Noir rather than whiskey, would be a little out of place, and even a little in danger up there. I didn't expect to get hurt, of course, but I did expect to be more nakedly in the proximity of sin. "He can come back," said Alexis. "I send horses up there and bring them back all the time."

On the evening Wowie was being shipped to Bay Meadows, Hali came over. I hadn't seen her in about ten days, and she didn't know the plans for the horse. After she had settled in and I judged that she was in the mood, I said, "So—how does Wowie feel right now?"

"Well, he doesn't know where he's going."

"Do you mean, like, what his fate is, or his larger purpose, or something like that?"

"I don't know. He just doesn't know where he's going. And he can't breathe very well. He's upset. He can't see. There's a lot of noise." She shrugged. "I don't know what he's getting at. Is there some construction at the racetrack?" Hali has never been to a racetrack. I said, "Well, actually, he's on a van heading to Bay Meadows up in San Francisco. He's probably confined in a stall about four feet by ten feet, and the windows are way up high. I'm not sure if he can see out a window."

She was unfazed by this confirmation of her abilities, and why should she be impressed? This happened to her all the time. She said, "Did anyone tell him where he was going or why?"

"I doubt it." This is a hard thing to remember with talking horses—that they like to know what's up. I said, "Tell him he's going to another racetrack to run in a race, because they don't have too many of his type of races down south."

"When is the race?"

"In a couple of days."

"All he wants is to have a look around. If he has a really good look around and sees everything that is going on, he can figure it out. And he wants a stall that has a view of the outside, so he can see as much as possible."

"I'll tell them."

The next day, Alexis and I had a little talk about whether the trainer she was staying with in San Mateo would be receptive to our unorthodox information-gathering system. She had no idea. On the one hand, Allen was a nice guy and a good trainer. On the other hand, he was a man. In my experience, horsemen tended to be more skeptical of the whole animal-communication idea. But, then again, he had spent years in the racing business. Most people in the racing business will give any harmless thing a try, if only for luck. I outlined Wowie's requirements. She promised to relay them.

The weather was cool up north; at Bay Meadows, right across 101 from San Francisco Bay, it was even cold. The grandstands seemed almost empty. There had been corporate flux at Bay Meadows, and much of the land was sold several years ago to build luxury condominiums, as yet mostly untenanted, that now looked down upon the crowded hustle and bustle of a rather old racetrack. The barns and the horses were moved into the infield, and so all sense of the pastoral—an attractive feature of even the most urban racetracks—had been lost.

At the barn, Wowie was standing in his bandages with his hind legs crossed meditatively. I asked whether The Instructions had been followed, and indeed they had: he was stalled where he could see the horses passing on the track, and he had been taken out and given a good look around twice the day before and once already that day. Alexis was careful and methodical preparing him for the race—even though the weather was cool, she had the groom hose him down, then she put a girth and pad over his back, and he was led, a groom on each side, toward the saddling enclosure. We followed. He was more than alert.

In the saddling enclosure, which at Bay Meadows is a large circular room underneath the grandstand, he was moderately misbehaved, but Alexis's precautions seemed to pay off—he got the saddle on and paraded out to the track without the sort of shenanigans that would draw the eye (and, I felt as his owner, the disapproval) of every bettor on the rail. He went to the post dry—an effect of the hosing, which prevented him from heating up and sweating, or "washing out," as racing people say. The gate was positioned right in front of the stands, crosswise on the green turf course. He disappeared into the third slot. The bell rang and the horses charged out, Wowie second by two lengths, then a length and a half. By the half-mile pole he was pulling ahead, and by the quarter-mile pole he was ahead by a length and a half. We were screaming—or, rather, my friend and Alexis were screaming. I was just staring in what I came to realize was disbelief as the horse ran out in front of the pack. And, alas, I was right. At the very last second, three horses came up in a line and nipped him at the wire—he ran fourth by half a length in a photo finish. I couldn't help feeling that my own sense of disbelief was the key factor in his defeat.

Opinions among the others were divided. The jockey thought maybe the blinkers Wowie was wearing had prevented him from seeing the charging line of horses. Alexis thought it was just bad racing luck. But it was an inspiring race, a real example of what the horse could do if conditions were right and we followed his instructions (calling him "Wowie" rather than "Hornblower," letting him explore) and he was feeling good. And it was cool. He preferred that. And he was near water, a Pisces in his element, more or less. After the race, when we followed him back to the barn, we got another glimpse into who he was as a racehorse—as the hot-walker paraded him around the ring, he was still prancing, his head up, his ears pricked, his attention directed out toward the track. He was still flowing with energy and ambition. In the meantime, one of his rivals appeared, a horse who had run up in the pack and finished second by a nose. Taramot was tired. He ambled around the walking ring with his head low and his tail drooping. Wowie looked like he had left his energy reserves entirely untouched. This was good, in that he still had them, but not good, in that he didn't care enough to tap them for the race.

When I spoke to him through Hali on the way home, he elected to stay in northern California, where the weather, now that it was early April, was cool and he could look around and esteem himself. Nor did he show any aftereffects of the race as the following week progressed. I was satisfied. In the generally accepted sense of the word, he was not a successful racehorse, having run eight times without winning, but he was enthusiastic and able to do it without physical stress or strain, which I considered to be a testament to my perspicacity as a breeder. After all, the great lament in all the horse publications was that the once sound and hardworking Thoroughbred horse had in the nineties and oughts become fragile—endangered by high finance and inbreeding and too much speed. Well, he was an outcross: cheap and sound, and he didn't have too much speed. So I patted myself on the back. Besides, there was a check I was going to get—six percent of the purse. That had been the original reason to take him to Bay Meadows, to make earning a return on my investment just a bit easier.

He ran again three weeks later. When I told people I was going to watch my horse run, I said, "I'm going up to Bay Meadows to watch my horse win."

I GOT THE IDEA to infect my guiltless and unsuspecting relatives with the racing bug. I called my sister in Palo Alto. As soon as we made our plan to go to the track, which was about twenty miles from her house, and to take the baby and the three-year-old, I began worrying. What if something happened? What if a horse broke down, got hurt, suffered right in front of the children? It had happened—in Wowie's fourth start as a two-year-old, his first with McCarron, just before the finish line. The horse that was passing Wowie on the outside simply fell down—his leg broken. From our angle on the rail, it had looked to Alexis and me as though the unlucky pair had been right on top of our lucky pair, and we were very shaken. But no, Wowie and McCarron were on the rail, and the injured horse was in the third or fourth lane out—McCarron and Wowie (who was wearing his blinkers) hadn't even seen them. Still, it was sobering to watch McCarron jump off our horse and run back to check on the fallen jock (McCarron was president of the jockeys' guild at the time), even more sobering, not to say tragic, to watch the horse ambulance pull up and the injured horse be carried off, certain to be euthanized before the start of the next race. Somehow, it was especially upsetting that the two horses had been close together, as if lightning had struck one but not the other. It was easy to reason that this "close call" aspect was only an illusion, but hard to really buy it. Chris McCarron saved the day, for us at any rate. After tending to the other jockey and making sure that the horse-ambulance people were doing their job, he came over to us, shook my hand, and said, "Your horse ran an excellent race." Then he gave us a blow-by-blow of everything he had done during the ninety seconds of the race and every way in which the horse had responded, from the opening of the gate to the finish line. It took him longer to tell it than it had taken to run. He was straightforward, analytical, and articulate. By the time he was done, I had taken from him not only the kind words he had to say about Wowie, but also his focus and his presence of mind. I saw that, with thousands of races and, at that point, almost seven thousand wins under his belt, he knew exactly what to expect and exactly what he was doing. Time that rushed by for us in a chaos of movement and hope and tragedy marched deliberately for him in a train of cause and effect. It was a lesson for me in the workings of a great athletic mind—the injured jockey and the injured horse came first, but once they were taken care of, he could clearly remember the job he had undertaken to do.

Nevertheless, the accident had rattled me and even Alexis, with all of her experience. What in the world would such a thing do to my sister and her three-year-old? I quailed, but I had issued the invitation and they were eager to go. I thought maybe, if I had to, I could just grab the three-year-old and hug him to my chest so that he wouldn't see anything, and then lie a lot afterward.

On the way to the racetrack, which was about half an hour from my sister's house, we listened to "Five Little Ducks," by Raffi, seven times. The subject of the song was the decimation of a duck family—"Five little ducks went out one day, over the hills and far away. Mother duck said 'Quack, quack, quack,

quack. Only four little ducks came back.' " And so on, until they were all gone. It was the only song Will would listen to. Will was curious about where we were going and eager to get there, not like my own children, who seem to fall into a coma at the words "horse race." Once we got there, Will was eager to know how everything worked and what everything meant. He seemed to understand my explanations perfectly. In horse-breeding parlance, judging by her two sons, my sister and her husband are a "nick," which means their two bloodlines mesh to produce offspring of better quality than either of the parents (which is not to denigrate the high quality of these particular parents, of course).

We met Alexis and Allen at the horse's stall and made our way toward the grandstand. My sister and Will were gawking. She said, "I had no idea this was even here. I mean, I drive past here all the time, and it's so big, but I never even realized."

I held Will firmly in my arms and watched Wowie make a serious ruckus in the saddling paddock under the grandstand. He was rearing and kicking out, leaping from his stall, dragging the groom around. His eyes were rolling. The concerted efforts of three or four men finally resulted in a horse with a saddle on heading for the track, but he was sweaty and hot, and even though, as a group, my sister, nephew, and I chanted, "Wowie, you're the man! Wowie, you're the man!," I felt rather glum.

My sister followed me to the betting windows, where she put ten dollars across the board on the horse. I coached her: "Say, 'Number-three horse in the fifth race, ten dollars across the board.' " She took her ticket, still marveling. She said, "Do they do this all the time?"

"Spring and fall here, summer at the fairs, winter at Golden Gate Fields, near Berkeley."

"It's a whole world." But not a very populous one, I thought, glancing around at the almost empty betting hall. It was a regular weekday. There were maybe a hundred fans in the grandstand.

I picked up my nephew while my sister was placing her bet, and carried him up to the glassed-in Turf Club. I stood him in front of me on the windowsill. The gate was in front of us, and the horses approached it. I wondered what he could see—if the swaths of green and the tote board and the video screen made any sense to him. The horses suddenly looked faraway and small, and then, of course, they disappeared. I said, "Watch those doors! The doors with numbers above them!" He stared obediently, and then the bell rang. The gates opened. Once again, our maiden stormed out in second place, about a length behind the leader, with another horse right behind him. The three of them had it all between them. At the half-mile pole and the three-quarter pole, Wowie was still second. Only at the last moment did he drop back to third by a length. It was exciting. It was a duel. Will watched every distant second with his hands on the window and his eyes wide. When it was over, I hugged him and gave him to my sister, a little dizzy at the thought that, though the horse hadn't won exactly, during the month of April he had come up with enough purse money to pay his training bill. My sister was fingering her betting slip thoughtfully. She said, "Now I go back to the window and turn this in, right?"

"That's how much you get, on the board there. Three dollars on a two-dollar bet means you get fifteen dollars back, plus your ten." She had that look—the look of someone who had never realized that this investment opportunity was available to her. She called her husband to relay her success—she had lost only 16 percent on the thirty dollars she had bet to win, place, and show. I could see her thinking, If only I'd done a little more research.

I staggered off to find Allen and hear what the jockey had to say. A moment later, I glanced around to see if my sister and Will were behind me, and I saw the three-year-old lying on the floor in the classic tantrum attitude. She wrestled him into her arms. We were surrounded by men, old men. I could see she was embarrassed. I murmured, "What's the tantrum about?"

"Oh. He's having a tantrum because the horse didn't win." Ah, yes. A tantrum every bettor in the room could identify with.

Allen was disappointed by the finish, but I wasn't. For one thing, there had been no accidents. But, more important, he had been fifth. He had been fourth. Now he had been third. I could see a pattern shaping up. And again after the race he was still on his toes, still ready to go around again. As Alexis and I agreed in our customary postmortem, it is a big effort to leave the security of the pack and run out ahead of them, a big mental effort, maybe the most counter-instinctive thing a racehorse has to learn. Other breeds of horses achieve status by biting, striking, rearing, threatening, kicking. He who pushes another horse around is the one who is the boss. But Thoroughbreds, through an inherited drive to run as well as a trained-in desire to go faster than a rival, must claim a human aspiration as their own. Wowie still had to decide whether he was a horse or a racehorse. I said, "So—all we know is that he has to learn it step by step. But if he does learn it step by step, maybe it will be a lesson more perfectly learned. And, anyway, it's like everything else, you don't know what success feels like until you have some. He'll learn." Alexis and Allen nodded—yes, they did. I wondered if Charlie Whittingham, a trainer famous for saying, "Owners are like mushrooms. Keep them in the dark and covered with plenty of shit," had nodded, too, while his parade of owners expounded their theories.

In the meantime, two races and two checks had given me a

fondness for Bay Meadows. Yes, it was run-down, in comparison
with Santa Anita at least, and, yes, there was a dark, damp, cool
northern-California ambience about the place. The sun, when it
shone, seemed to shine only on the front entrance to the grandstand, never on the track itself. The barns in the middle of the
infield gave it something of a hockey-arena feel. But the dirt
track had excellent, resilient footing, and the turf course had a
name, the Johnny Longden Turf Course, which gave it history
and sweep—Johnny Longden was not only a famous trainer and
a great jockey who rode Count Fleet and Whirlaway, he was also
twice lucky. As a five-year-old child, set to board the *Titanic*
for immigration to America, he had run away from his family,
who were waiting to embark, to be found only after the gang-
plank had been pulled up. And trainer Dave Hofmans told me
another story: Longden had once been standing behind a restive
yearling. When he looked down at his catalogue, the yearling let
fly with both hind feet and kicked the hat off his head. I liked
the idea that they'd named the turf course after such a lucky
man. It was a brilliant green swath all spring. And Wowie indicated that he enjoyed the place—the cool sea air especially. And
there was money to be made. Nothing to dislike about that.

THAT WEEKEND, I went to L.A. for a literary festival. When I
was finished with my panel (Boswell, Blake, Dickens, Amis),
Alexis called and said that there was a surprise for me at
the track—my two-year-old filly had turned up unexpectedly,
shipped from the training farm some two weeks before she was
due. I called the Iranian limousine-driver provided by the book
publisher to make sure that I got where I was going on time, and
told him we were going to Santa Anita. And when we got there,
I in my silk suit, in the backseat of my brand-new Mercedes

limo, with my respectful and dignified driver at the wheel, the gate guard waved us through without even asking for my owner's license. For a day, I was not just a gal with a cheap horse at the track, who carefully showed her owner's license on every occasion for fear of being mistaken as an intruder, but maybe the wife of some mogul, perhaps my own blond *Horse Heaven* character, Rosalind Maybrick, purring up to the gate, seeking access to my stable of million-dollar racehorses. Santa Anita again. Back in the big time of sunlight and gardens full of bird-of-paradise, hanging flower baskets in the shedrows and National Register of Historic Places Art Deco carvings on the grandstand. Tiles instead of concrete.

Here was my eight-thousand-dollar filly, as black as a Thoroughbred can be, not a white hair on her body, shining in the

Waterwheel as an unkempt foal. We never did catch her that day.

sunlight, her head up, her tail up, dignified, self-assured, and sexy. In accordance with Wowie's instructions, this filly was without a name. He had deemed the name I gave her in the spring of 2001, "Fiscal Panic," unworthy, and we had yet to come up with another that satisfied Alexis, me, Hali, and Wowie. Or, rather, the one we liked, "Mae West," the Jockey Club considered a trademark, therefore not usable. I wanted to try "Mai Ouest," but I wasn't sure how that would look on the cover of *The Bloodhorse.*

The black filly was my tenth-born. After Jackie, the foals had proliferated a little more quickly than I had expected them to. I had not designed her breeding, though; rather, I had asked a friend to find me a commercially bred mare so that I could get a foal who would turn into a yearling who could go to a sale and be sold for a profit. Except that, when the time came to send her to the sale, I could not bring myself to let her go, so I kept her and sent her to the training farm along with the uncommercially bred foals whose matings I had designed myself.

Alexis had seen the filly before—we had met at the training farm and watched her gallop there. She was little, hot, and bright, always tossing her heavy forelock over her fiery eye and looking right at you as if daring you. She had told us she was ready to come to the racetrack—when Hali asked her how she liked life at the training farm, she said that it was fine, but she wanted to run in front of more people than those in the tiny viewing stand. When we asked her whether she was intimidated by running with bigger horses, she indicated that, though she didn't want to be "hipped" (her word for bumped, possibly), she thought she could easily avoid this by getting out in front and staying there. She was like certain students I had had in writing classes—too responsive for their own good, too ready to throw all their energy into any new thing.

When Alexis brought her out of her stall and stood her up in front of the shedrow, she was a riveting sight. She had been here less than twenty-four hours, but she already gazed around with complete self-confidence and focus. And a few days later, when I called to see how she was settling in, Alexis said, "You know what she does? She narrows her eyes when she looks at something."

We started referring to Wowie and the filly only as "He" and "She," as if they were such powers in our lives that they didn't need to be identified. But I couldn't come up with a name. Her sire's name, "Grindstone," was singularly unpromising, especially for a female ("Pumice"? "Sandy"?), and her mother's name, "Our Wild Rose," led only to clichés. The best possible Grindstone name for a filly was already taken, "Emery Board." Everything else was too geological.

I continued on my book tour, and Wowie ran again while I was in New York, where once again it was impossible to find a simulcast.

By now it was May, bright and sunny in New York, and I was sitting in the library of the Princeton Club, waiting to give a talk about Charles Dickens. On the cell phone, Allen was less communicative than Alexis, but when I looked at the chart later, I could see why. The race was an exciting one. Wowie broke fourth but pulled ahead immediately, until he was in second. He continued in second place from the three-quarter pole until the homestretch, where he pulled ahead of the number-one horse. They actually dueled down the stretch, with Wowie in front much of the way, only to lose in the end by three-quarters of a length. It was, from one point of view, a perfect race—he had hooked on to another horse, and the other horse had tested him. He had not won, but he had not given up, either; rather, he had tested the other horse, too. There were no surprises, as in the race where the three horses had come to him at the last second. Both horses knew what they were doing–battling to win a race–and both horses had worked hard enough and long enough at it for the experience to sink in. I said to Alexis the next day, "I bet he learned that it's better to win than not to win, because he could see the win before he ended up losing it." I was happy. In the two April races, he had won over four thousand dollars, more than enough to pay for his oats. In the one May race, he won thirty-six hundred dollars, again more than enough to support himself.

Disney movies promote the fantasy of a horse who is like a dog, only better–prettier and more useful, but just as devoted and companionable–and it is tempting to compare horses to dogs, until it becomes clear that horses lose by the comparison, and so does the owner's reputation for sanity. If one could have a dog, which costs a few hundred dollars to buy, twenty dollars a month to feed, and a few hundred dollars a year for veterinary care, why would one pour thousands down the horse hole just for some devoted companionship? It is only when you compare horses to your children that their advantages can be truly appreciated. A child, for example, starts out at eight or nine pounds and requires seventeen or eighteen years to mature to, say, 150 pounds. A foal starts out at about a hundred pounds, and weighs a thousand pounds two and a half years later, on a much simpler and cheaper diet. A child doesn't become useful for even minor chores around the house until he or she is at least seven or eight. A horse is ridable at three and well trained at five or six. Doctor bills and vet bills run about the same; bills for education and training are similar, too, in amount, but last far longer with the child than the horse. Though it costs as much to keep a racehorse at Santa Anita as it does to keep a child at Harvard, the payoff can come within months, and accrues directly to the owner, who would never expect to be repaid by the child for expenses incurred. Compared with dogs, yes, horses are an expensive headache, but compared with children, they can be the source of much unalloyed pleasure. If they live in a group of three or four, they don't even have to be entertained–they entertain one another. And, in the worst case, a case of complete incompatibility, they can be sold or given away to someone they like better than they like you. These are the thoughts I began to have when Wowie started to produce an income.

SIX

Ambition

CHEERFUL'S MOTHER IS named Chipper, and she is a daughter of The Axe, a son of Mahmoud. It is hard to communicate to someone who does not breed Thoroughbreds how Jurassic such a pedigree is. A Thoroughbred generation is not quite comparable to a human generation, but let's say it is about five years—long enough for the winners of the Kentucky Derby and the Epsom Derby to breed their first set of mares, and for those mares to produce foals. Mahmoud was born in England in 1933, seventy years or fourteen generations ago. A three-year-old like Cheerful is roughly akin to a twenty-year-old great-grandson of someone who was born in the time of Oliver Cromwell (of course, the monkey wrench in this analogy is that, whereas women are able to breed for about one human generation, mares are able to breed for about five horse generations).

I saw Chipper for sale on the Internet, and I bought her sight unseen, as a sort of "Seed Savers Exchange" acquisition—even though she was old and even though she hadn't produced many winners, I thought I would like to have some offspring of her bloodlines. I also bought her because of a sign. I was sitting with my friend Jim Squires in the dining room at Keeneland, talking about whether I should buy the mare, and I saw Penny Chenery across the room, the owner of Secretariat, and it seemed blasphemous not to take the mare. Chipper was then shipped to Jim and bred to an Irish horse in Kentucky named Corwyn Bay. After that, she came to me and the ranch in California where my mares and foals live.

Chipper not only had Jurassic breeding (no Northern Dancer, no Nasrullah or Nearco, the only connection to Native Dancer through that horse's older sister), she had a Jurassic look. Bright chestnut, with a big blaze, four white stockings, and a white patch on her belly, she had the outline of a Thoroughbred (low-set neck, high withers, longish back, sloping croup), but the feet of a draft horse and the musculature of a quarter horse. She looked every day of her age—twenty-three—not because she was in bad physical condition, but because she was built like old-fashioned horses, coarse, wide, and strong, with a long slim head, long ears, and a broad forehead. Cheerful was her eighteenth foal.

Mares don't go through menopause; some breed into their late twenties, and even produce good racehorses, but Chipper seemed very old to me, and I saw signs of senility in her. When I went to give her carrots, she seemed barely to recognize what a carrot was, and not to recognize me at all. All ideas seemed to take a long time to dawn on her, including, in the end, the idea of giving birth. The usual gestation period for a horse is 340 days. Chipper was still standing at 372 days. She had gone to a breeding farm to be bred to another stallion right after the birth, so I didn't see her at the end, but when I went to visit Chipper and her foal, what I saw rather startled me.

Cheerful as a foal. Something of an ugly duckling.

Cheerful (whom I named before he was born just because I liked the idea of a "Chipper" giving birth to a "Cheerful") was also bright chestnut and loudly marked with four white legs and a white blaze. His legs were so long that even at ten days old he could hardly get around and had to be helped by the groom. Chipper, though, was wide awake. It was as if the new foal had rejuvenated her. She was as directive and alert as any of my other mares, and perhaps less disappointed in the foal than I was.

When they returned from the breeding farm, Cheerful seemed more normal, but it was clear that he was going to be built just like Chipper, a strange jumble of parts, not a Thoroughbred–draft-horse/quarter-horse melding, but a construction. He was sweet as pie, though, and, more important, every day Chipper lived in the real world of bossy motherhood, and she seemed to enjoy it. Over the summer, Cheerful's chestnut coat fell out, and he turned out to be a gray, like his sire. At my wish, he stayed with her for almost eight months, because she had not gotten in foal after the birth, and I strongly suspected she would not get in foal again. Since he was nice, I wanted her to enjoy him as long as possible.

Not long before they were weaned, my vet happened to be giving the foal a vaccination. He glanced up for some reason, and the angle from which he saw the foal's left eye showed him something we had not seen before, a cataract. By the time we had had the foal examined by a veterinary ophthalmologist, it was clear that he had a congenital cataract in the left eye and that the right eye was defective, too, though still perfectly sighted. I called Eddie Gregson, who said, "Well, I would train a racehorse that was blind on the right, but not on the left, because the rail is on the left, and the horse has to be able to see the rail." I wondered if I should send the horse to France, where they run clockwise. It is true that blind horses have had racing careers—Real Connection, a filly whose dam kicked her in the head as a foal, was blind on the right. She ran more than a hundred times. In her first race, she came out of the gate, stopped dead, and looked around, then ran like hell after the others and actually got on the board. Subsequently, she won over a million dollars. But that was the right eye. As usual, I came up with some crackpot theories to account for the cataract. The vet explained to me that congenital wasn't the same as genetic—the problem with the eye could have been a developmental accident in the womb rather than an inherited trait in the DNA. Still, Cheerful was a sweet foal. Strangely put together, humbly bred, blind in one eye.

Off and on we gathered evidence that he might have some

usefulness. Andre, who cared for the foals, reported that there was no outward sign of impairment. When the band of colts ran at top speed through the supports of the rain shed or among the trees, Cheerful ran with them, never having an accident and giving no sign that he was cocking his head or turning it to see where he was going. New spaces didn't intimidate or challenge him. He explored them at a gallop just like other young horses. Though the ophthalmologist reiterated several times that he didn't have any sight in that eye, we knew he had something. The ophthalmologist was not sparing of hope, however. The right eye, though defective, could remain sighted, and if it did so until he was four, the age when horses are physically mature, it would probably be fine for the rest of his life. And the lens of the left eye would gradually reabsorb into the horse's body, allowing light to strike the rods and cones directly at the back of the eye, giving him some distance vision.

Dressage, I thought, was his destined discipline. Dressage takes place in a rectangular dressage court and is not about getting anywhere; a horse doesn't have to be perfectly sighted to do it. In some sense, a horse doesn't have to see at all to do dressage, since he is supposed to be 100 percent responsive to the instructions of the rider and not to think for himself in any way.

Cheerful resided pleasantly at the ranch for another year, and then the trainers there began to worry that he was getting big and strong and therefore dangerous, so I picked him up and brought him to Ray. I was wringing my hands, envisioning a horse so unpredictable that he would never be useful, would get more and more dangerous, and would have to be euthanized before the age of two, but as we began Cheerful's training by leading him around his new home and allowing him to investigate with nose, mouth, and sight everything that made him nervous, Ray reassured me that he was no different in degree of skittishness from any other eighteen-month-old colt.

We discovered about two weeks later that he was different in one way, though. Ray had been working him in the round pen, and I had been sitting in a tree nearby, watching. After about fifteen minutes of the horse's trotting and cantering calmly in both directions, backing, yielding, and a few other things, Ray asked him to step away from the rail, crossing his front legs to do so. The horse looked at him for a moment. Ray reiterated his request. Instead of trying anything, Cheerful gave a low groan and lay down, first on his chest, and then out on his side. He closed his eyes. Ray stood there, looking down at him. I said, "What's that all about?"

"I don't know."

"Is he sick?"

"No."

"Are you going to try to get him up?"

"No."

"Are we just going to watch him?"

"Yeah."

So we watched him. He lay there, breathing gently. His eyes continued closed, but he didn't seem to be asleep. After a few minutes, Ray sat down on his shoulder and began stroking his neck, and pretty soon I did, too. We stroked him all over, and at one point, he opened his eyes, then raised himself onto his chest. We sat astride him, not entirely weighing on him, but partly supporting ourselves. We petted him all over, ears to tail. His coat was fine and silky. We relaxed like this for maybe fifteen or twenty minutes, and when we were done, the lesson was over. I felt that he had let us get intimate with him, and that the lesson was for something unorthodox, something not the same as learning to go forward and obey, but more about trust.

Cheerful with Ray, deciding he would rather lie down than figure it out. Kiss Me looks on with interest.

His lessons progressed in every way. He was naturally affectionate and submissive.

I first noticed Cheerful's ambition on a rainy winter day when we had him in the covered arena, where some small jumps were set up for the student riders. Ray had yet to ride the horse—he trained him with a halter and a twelve-foot rope or a lariat. The horse had progressed to working at some distance from Ray, with the loop of the lariat around his neck. Ray asked him to step over a pole on the ground and then a low jump. Cheerful did it beautifully, snapping his toes into the air so as not to touch the wood. I said, "Too bad about the eye. He might make a good jumper."

A week or so later, we were back in the covered arena. This

time, a couple of jumps, about two feet high, were set at an angle to one another. Because it was raining and training space was at a premium, Ray had decided to work Jackie and Cheerful together. They started by galloping around the covered arena, learning to move together. The idea was that the older, more experienced horse's movements would signal the younger horse what to do. It was fun to watch their exuberant playfulness come under Ray's control as they grew more and more attentive to him. They galloped. I was a little worried that they would bump into the jump standards, but Jackie avoided them gracefully. He always knew where they were and where he was, no matter at what speed he was traveling.

Cheerful, it soon became clear, also knew where the jumps and the standards were, whether he was approaching them from the right or the left. I was just in the midst of exclaiming about this when he veered off his path and jumped over a jump. I started to laugh with the pleasure of it. He had done a voluntary, unnecessary, serendipitous, and joyful thing, a thing that many horses (including Jackie) would not have done. Then he came around and did it again, and what's more, after coming over the first jump, he turned and went over the second one, even though it was not in his path. We laughed and laughed.

When the first of May rolled around, and Cheerful had been in training for six months, I brought another filly down from the ranch who was his same age, Kiss Me. Ray liked her immediately. Though she had had far less handling than Cheerful, she took to working with great enthusiasm, and Ray was riding her within a week. Cheerful worshiped her. They lived together in a large pasture, and they immediately began living as a united pair, their bodies always parallel and close together, eating out of the same bin, not sparring, the way male horses do, but going steady. She was the boss. Though he was affectionate, she always came to me first and got the first carrot. She always put her nose into the feed first. Ray worked them together almost every day. When the filly didn't understand or like something he asked her to do, she bucked like a rodeo horse but quickly settled down. Cheerful never bucked or reared. When he didn't understand something, he gave up, lay down, and closed his eyes. They were both gray, and people asked me whether they were related. But they were about as unrelated as two Thoroughbreds could be.

I still envisioned Cheerful as a dressage horse. For one thing, he was built for it, with haunches of jaw-dropping proportions, a well-set, naturally arching neck, and a good overstep. One day, when the ranch personnel had to do something in their pasture, I turned Kiss Me and Cheerful into another pasture, nearer the large herd of horses, a situation that required Cheerful to show off everything he had. He had a lot. Ears pricked, tail up, he did several beautiful extended trots across the paddock, moving with fire and and speed over the uneven ground. His gaits were square, with lots of suspension.

In the fall of his four-year-old year, Jackie started going to a trainer whose method was to rig her lariat (the same sort used on calves in calf-roping contests at rodeos) around the horse's head and nose, teach him some simple voice commands, and then put him over obstacles as a way of teaching him to jump without compromising his form with a rider (me). The principle is a good one. The horse learns how to use his body and balance himself on his own. If he gets into a fence wrong, he learns how to extricate himself. He gains confidence as he goes over lots of different types of obstacles, and the trainer on the ground can control him with voice commands that will later serve the rider. The most famous exponent of this sort of training in California was a man named Gene Lewis, who jumped his horses on the rope from the back of another horse, over every sort of fence. He was a great one for taking the trophy out from under the noses of the fancy and expensive horses and trainers. My new trainer, Karen, had been a student of his.

Except that, one day, Jackie was suffering from hives, an allergic reaction to what we later figured out was oats, and so there was nothing for Karen to do, and so, just for the fun of it, we got Cheerful out and taught him his voice commands, which he learned within minutes, and then we set up some poles on the ground and a jump, and so, just for the fun of it, Cheerful went over everything in perfect form, and Karen and I ended up staring at each other, our eyebrows up to our hairlines. I said, "He doesn't seem to be cocking his head."

She said, "There's no sign in either direction that he can't see what he's doing."

"Or that he's hesitant."

"He goes fine to the left, fine to the right."

"I was planning on making him a dressage horse. Look at those haunches. You know he could sit down and passage and piaffe and all."

She said, "There are plenty of one-eyed jumpers."

"Who rides them?" Not me, I thought.

Ambition is, of course, a psychological characteristic that individuals possess, but it implies the larger world—a place in which the individual can realize his or her ambitions. Of Diamond's "big five" large domesticated animals (cow, sheep, goat, horse, and pig), only the horse has been regularly given any other activities besides eating, being slaughtered, being milked, growing hair for shearing, and reproducing. The basic requirements that horses fulfill that make them domesticatable (sociable with one another, easily herdable, ready to adopt a human leader) hardly begin to describe what the horse has been willing to do for us over the millennia. The other four big animals, according to Diamond, helped create the hegemony of Western European civilization passively—that is, they provided their keepers with concentrated calories and immunities from animal-borne diseases that enabled them to prevail in the clash of civilizations. But horses have been active participants—carrying burdens and riders, waging war and offering sport, pulling carts and carriages, working livestock. It is impossible to imagine the spread of European civilization around the world, or even the constant conflict of Europeans among themselves, without the horse. And Europeans (let's say Indo-Europeans, since the horse was first named and tamed in the Caucasus) have repaid their debt by elevating the horse to an object of love and luxury still unparalleled in the animal kingdom—what other being on earth (Nobel Prize winners included) earns five hundred thousand dollars for a single shot of semen? If the big five are the only large mammals who could be domesticated, then the horse is the only one of the big five who could shape civilization, make history, the only one who was given a multitude of tasks and the opportunity to achieve glory. An ambitious horse is a horse that makes something of the opportunities that are offered to him, even when those opportunities are man-made rather than natural. Ambition is not agreeability or willingness. It is a seeking out rather than a receptivity.

Ambitious horses, like horses with other distinct qualities, show themselves by contrast to their peers. When, in morning training at the racetrack, two fillies go out to breeze, one shows her ambition not only by going fast but also by going straight, not only by galloping out strongly—after three-eighths of a mile in thirty-five and two-fifths seconds, she effortlessly covers the next furlong in a manner that shows she is relaxed and enjoying herself—but also by not being distracted by the other sights and sounds on the track. Her companion might try to duck out through the opening and head back to the barn, but the ambitious filly doesn't even notice the opening. The other filly might have to be taught that first you trot and canter clockwise, then you turn around and take off, but the ambitious filly knows this through either observation or desire. Each time the horse has something the trainer thinks he or she must learn, the horse is there to meet her, the unknown lesson already half learned. This is not submission.

When I was teaching fiction-writing in college, I noticed this characteristic in my most talented students. They repaid one's critique with an abundance of understanding, producing a response to a suggestion that went beyond the original intention of the suggestion—I could imagine how their stories could be improved, but their ability to improve them was beyond my imagination. This was distinct from raw inventiveness. There were plenty of students who had the energy to try anything to fix a story, but few who, untrained, had the intuition to try the right thing. Ambition produces mental quickness, but also willingness. When Edison maintained that genius was 98 percent perspiration, he wasn't just talking about mindless drilling. I think the example of Wayne Gretzky, the hockey player, is a good gloss on Edison's prescription. Gretzky was famous for practicing his shots over and over again. He didn't practice them because he had to, he practiced them because they were interesting to him—each variation on the same shot told him something about the puck, the hockey stick, his hands, arms, body, and mind that was interesting to him and that he learned from. An ambitious horse is not likely to have the freedom to practice, so she makes the most of her opportunities. Other horses, even horses right next to her, are distracted by fears or aches or the wish to get back to the barn or to have a companion or the deer trotting down the hill, but the ambitious horse is distracted by nothing.

The more interesting question is why a horse would be ambitious in the first place. A horse like Jackie, who is studdish by nature, has certain ambitions that are readily accounted for with ideas of herd status. His favorite equestrian activity is dressage, which is based on the movements of stallions displaying themselves in front of mares. When I ask him to arch his neck and proceed in a big, fancy trot, the movements I am asking for constitute licensed showing off for him—they tap into his already present feelings of pride. The evidence for this is that when members of his mare-band are present his performance is brighter and more energetic. His feelings about galloping and jumping are quite different. Most Thoroughbreds enjoy the free and vigorous movement that is bred into them, but Jackie is easily intimidated by too much of a jumping challenge. A thought that he can't get over that whatever-it-is intrudes into his mind as he approaches it; he's a good and talented jumper, but he's not an ambitious one.

Racing is more or less natural for a Thoroughbred, and so a racehorse's ambition is a marked example of something that is inside the realm of normal Thoroughbred behavior. Alexis's only job, as far as I can see, is to keep the ambitious filly sound and safe, give her enough opportunity to do what she wants to do so that she can learn from it and not feel frustrated by inactivity and restraint, but not so much opportunity that she will hurt herself or burn herself out. When I say that I hope my dark filly will realize her potential, I am not speaking only of my investment or of my reputation as a breeder (and I didn't design this mating anyway, or even choose the mare, so I am the passive beneficiary of her breeding), I am also speaking of her ambitions for herself; even though she can't articulate them or probably even imagine them, it seems clear that she feels them.

One of the great photographs of equine ambition is the picture of Secretariat winning the Belmont Stakes by thirty-one lengths. The legendary horse is thundering across the finish line, his nostrils flaring, his ears back, his chest as wide as the front end of a car. His jockey's head is turned as he catches a glimpse of the clock that records the horse's 2:24 time in the deep Belmont sand. Thirty-one lengths is some six seconds, or half a furlong. The split times of the Belmont that year showed that Secretariat just kept getting faster as the race progressed. No normal horse behavior accounts for his speed, not rivalry with other horses, not pressure from the rider, not evolution or biomechanics or any generalization about horses or mammals or the need to reproduce one's DNA in future generations. The horse could do it and he did it. He wanted to do it. His engagement with racing was like Wayne Gretzky's engagement with hockey—not inherited. Secretariat's groom maintained for the rest of his life that after the horse's racing career was over he was never so happy again. He went back to being a horse, disappeared from the racing culture that allowed him to exercise his genius.

THE RECORD JUMP by a horse carrying a rider is pictured in the *Guinness Book of World Records,* Alberto Larraguibel Morales on Huaso, jumping an 8′ 1¼″ wall in 1949. The horse high-jumping record and the human record are about the same, but the horse is required to lift his own body (ten times the weight of a human body) and that of the rider. Horses in certain types of jumping classes routinely jump over seven feet. Why? No horse can be forced to jump a solid wall that stands two feet above his own height. Horses that do so are an unusual sort, but a friend of mine from Australia has another friend who specializes in finding down-and-out horses in knackers' yards and teaching them to high-jump. He offers no insights into their psychology, beyond opining that such horses are more common than you think.

Cheerful's progress in jumping on the rope was enlightening and at times inspiring. For ten months, he jumped every week or two, to the right and to the left, usually about eight or ten fences. Sometimes they were set up singly, with a trot pole placed about eight feet in front of the fence. Other times they were set up in a grid, two or three fences in a row that he had to bounce through. We kept them low—between two feet six and three feet three, in deference to his age (two and three), not wanting to strain his legs and feet before he was mature. But it seemed as though he couldn't get enough. He was always ready to heed the signal and go down the line, popping over whatever was put in front of him. From the beginning, I was delighted at the sight of the one-eyed horse doing so well and enjoying himself so much, but soon enough Karen began setting him greater challenges, and then I was impressed. I think the first time was about three months into his training, when she set up a triple combination—he had to jump three fences in a row, with no intermediate strides, had to jump, land, jump, land, jump, land—a feat of strength, willingness, and coordination. He did it so perfectly on the first try that we were afraid to try again, for fear he would make a mistake and then we would have to keep at it until he did it right again, but he did it just as well the second time as the first. Karen said, "I know lots of experienced horses who couldn't have done that on the first or second try."

This is not to say that Cheerful showed a global sense of

ambition. By normal standards, Cheerful was a pretty ordinary horse, though he had an impish quality—when turned out with another gelding besides Jackie, his boss, he would be playful. One game they enjoyed that I had never seen before was a tongue-grabbing game. First one horse and then the other would stick his tongue out and clamp down on it. The other horse would then try to grab the tongue. Toward Jackie, his pasture-mate and rival for the three mares who lived with him, he was submissive and alert, as well trained to show respect as any buck private or Mafia lackey. For example, if I came to the gate with carrots, Jackie would not allow Cheerful to approach the gate. I had to enter the pasture and wave the more dominant horses away in order to give Cheerful treats. All of the mares besides Kiss Me, his old friend, showed contempt for him.

Karen moved away, and her place was taken by another protégée of Gene Lewis's named Trudy. Trudy had a different demeanor and a different set of requirements. Whereas Karen wanted the horses to go down to the jumps calmly, Trudy wanted them to go down to the jumps deliberately, looking to her for every signal and every command. She was exceptionally meticulous in what she demanded of the horses, and at first they were confused. Cheerful's response was to slow way down. If she wanted him to walk toward the fence, well, he was happy to walk right over it. Slower? How about a nice halt? I said to her, "Minimum effort is the name of the game with him." But, really, I meant that he fulfilled instructions like a student who wanted to learn. She shook the rope at him, a move designed to energize him a bit, and one not very common for her. In the next lesson, though, and in subsequent lessons, he had gotten the picture. He stepped toward the jump, ears pricked, body alert but contained. He glanced at her. She indicated he could take a trot step. He did so. Now he was focused on the jump, brought his hind end underneath himself, and rolled into the air. His motion was so slow and powerful that he seemed to hang above the fence. He landed. Trudy stood up straight and was about to praise him and draw him toward her when he noticed another jump, a gray wall constructed out of plywood painted to look like stones, about three feet or so high. He jumped it. Trudy turned to me in her serious way and said, "You're going to have to watch out for that with him."

"What?"

"That you're standing in front of a fence and he decides to jump it."

"You didn't ask him to jump that one?"

"Nope."

Trudy was especially leery of kissing to him—a command that in her system said to the horse, "Look for a jump and jump it." It was a useful command for a show horse, who might come around a turn in a jumping class and not quite know what he was supposed to do. Should the rider make a kissing noise, he would know to sit back on his haunches and look around, which would render him just that much more ready for the rider to steer him to the next jump. But Cheerful was so interested in jumping that a kiss just invited him to look for jumps on his own.

Toward the end of Cheerful's ten months of training on the rope, Trudy set him a series of tests. One windy day, she brought large squares of canvas in yellow and black and laid them over a fence. They were likely to do anything, including blow upward into the horse's face as he was approaching. Cheerful hardly cocked his ears. She set him odd-looking or deceptive-looking jumps. One in particular was four poles set on two standards, the two parallel top poles about three feet three inches off the ground and three feet apart, two other poles about nine inches below those, and nothing close to the ground or on the ground.

This jump would have been hard to gauge for the horse—normally, a horse likes to know where the ground is in order to judge his takeoff. Cheerful acted like he'd been jumping that sort of thing for years. The horse continued to have the ability to judge, the first time he saw any fence, what might be the best way to get over it. The only mistake he made was sometimes ticking his back toes on the second pole of a wide fence, but soon enough he learned to lift his haunches in the last nanosecond so that his toes would clear. His arc over the fence continued to be something of an optical illusion. The other horses who were jumping on the rope went up and came down. Cheerful seemed to have airtime, to be going so slowly over the fence that my heart reacted by thumping because I was sure he was just going to drop straight down at the apex of his arc. Trudy was unfazed. "Well, look at his haunches," she said. "He's got such power."

After the second testing session—a lesson where Trudy jumped Cheerful for maybe ten minutes over four or five new fences that were increasingly challenging—she said, "Put him away. The hardest thing is to hold back, and remember that he just turned three a couple of months ago."

It was true that our glee in his ability, our pure enjoyment of his enjoyment of his talents, sometimes smote me with dismay—had we done too much? A horse isn't necessarily the best judge of what his body can take, especially a young and enthusiastic horse.

Nevertheless, Cheerful came to jumping in a state of relaxation. He was not afraid of what he was being asked to do, and so stress hormones, like cortisol, were not coursing through his body, contributing to the breakdown of joints and soft tissues. Lots of great racehorses, especially well-known ones like Kelso, John Henry, Citation, and Seabiscuit, ran dozens of times and remained sound (soundness and injury are not the same, but unsoundness does predispose a horse to injury by unbalancing him). An unusual case of equine endurance is provided by the 1873 mare Moorhen, who, starting as a three-year-old, ran seventy-seven times both in flat races and in steeplechases, and in the course of her seven-year racing career had twenty-six wins and several foals—while pregnant and after foaling, she would continue to race.

Does it matter that, when Hali asked Cheerful what he wanted to do in life, he said that he wanted to "jump over the sun"?

If we make the case for ambition in the horse, then we are entering into the realm of a certain branch of intelligence theory, as described by Howard Gardner in his introduction to the tenth-anniversary edition of *Frames of Mind: The Theory of Multiple Intelligences,* "contextualization," which propounds that, "rather than assuming that one would possess a certain 'intelligence' independent of the culture in which one happens to live, many scientists now see intelligence as an interaction between, on the one hand, certain proclivities and potentials, and on the other, the opportunities and restraints that characterize a particular cultural setting" (p. xiii). In other words, a creature, horse or human, is stimulated by the opportunities in his or her environment to display capacities that other environments might not call for. In the varied civilizations that humans have developed, both humans and horses "volunteer" for particular activities that bear little or no relation to biological urges to survive, reproduce, achieve status in the herd, or stabilize relationships. Some horses, like some humans, are more prone to do this than others are.

Many horses are not ambitious at all, but what the ambitious ones show, I think, is that horses are truly domesticated creatures, that they are not in fact victims of civilization, but participants in it. Breeding for certain characteristics has enhanced both their ability and their willingness to do what people prize, but there is something extra beyond that, something that is a gift rather than standard equipment.

SEVEN

Betting Interest

As of June 6, when Wowie raced again, my nine-year-old son, AJ, still had more than a week left of school. I had gone on the record (in *Horse Heaven*) as being opposed to taking children out of class so that they could go to the racetrack. Nevertheless, on the morning of the race, I called the school and said that AJ would be leaving early for a family trip, but that he would be back the following day. AJ himself was told that we were going to visit our cousins in Palo Alto. Happy to be out of school, he didn't investigate any further until we were about halfway there. He said, "Are we going straight to Will and Griff's house?" My brother and his family lived in Menlo Park.

"No, they're still at school."

"So what are we going to do?"

"Well, we're going to pick up Francie and her Will"—both my brother and my sister had made the same mistake, naming their oldest sons after the one quality that would give the parents the most trouble—"and then we're going to the racetrack."

"The racetrack!" He was dismayed.

"Yes, the horse is running in a race today. It'll be fun."

"Can't you just leave me at Kristie's until they get home?" AJ was quite fond of my sister-in-law.

"No."

He sighed a big sigh.

I decided right then that the whole history of racing must mean something, and the whole history of racing had been, not about fabulous races and great equine personalities, but about two simpler things—who won and who backed the winner. When, in the seventeenth and eighteenth centuries, English landowners and horse breeders came to realize that they couldn't afford their sport if they were to just pass around a few plates as trophies, they understood that what they really needed, like all capitalists, was an infusion of funds from outside, and so racing, bookmaking, and crowds of working-class men converged to become the sport as we know it. I said to AJ, "You know, if the horse wins, and I think he's going to, I'll buy you something. What do you want?"

"A game for my GameCube."

"What about if he's second?"

"A game for my GameBoy."

"What about if he's third?"

"A toy of some kind."

"That's what we'll do, then."

It worked like a charm. But more than that, I thought, it had a pleasing aesthetic and philosophical appropriateness—the beloved horse would demonstrate to the beloved child that an equine was good for something, that he was useful and allied to the boy's interests. And wasn't it true that you had to appeal to a child in a language that he understood? One of the great things about winning a horse race, thanks to the bettors, is that it is most emphatically not abstract. In addition to the pleasure, in addition to the vindication, in addition to the win photo, there is prize money—more prize money for first place in one small race at a second-echelon track than there is in any literary prize in America. Thank you, betting public.*

When I stopped to pick up my sister, it was only the darling Will who was going to accompany us. I was remaining calm. I didn't have the usual misgivings, what Penny Chenery, the owner of Secretariat, has called "the emotional fatigue." I felt something sharper and more invigorating than hope.

Once, when I was researching *Horse Heaven,* I was walking from the barn area at Saratoga to the main entrance of the grandstand. I glanced behind me and saw a horse who was graying out in what looked like polka dots. I watched him cross the road and follow the other horses toward the track in preparation for the next race. I didn't bet on him, but I knew with absolute certainty that he was going to win the race. When he did win, I decided that I had just liked him because he was gray, or oddly colored, or something, but that moment of conviction stuck in my mind. Almost a year later, I happened to be at Turf Paradise, near Phoenix. It was a lazy day at Turf Paradise, a day in the middle of the week when there were almost as many horses and horsemen at the track as fans. I had been there for four races and was about to go to my car when I caught sight of a horse in the paddock, a chestnut filly. This time the feeling was stronger than at Saratoga, as strong and distinct as the ringing of a bell. I went back to the rail and watched the horses leave the paddock and enter the track. The chestnut filly ran easily in about the

*Purses in races in the United States run from a few thousand dollars to five million (in the Breeders' Cup Classic). The winner traditionally gets 60 percent (with 10 percent of that going to the trainer and 10 percent going to the jockey). Second place earns 20 percent, third place 12 percent, fourth place 6 percent, and fifth place 2 percent. Jockeys earn a small, flat fee for riding in a race, but a percentage of the purse only if they win, no doubt to make winning more appealing.

fourth position most of the way around. In the homestretch, she put on some speed and won by a length at the end. I knew she would. I knew she would possibly before she knew she would.

This was how I felt about Wowie's race. I was happy that he was quiet in the paddock and allowed himself to be saddled and led out without a problem. I was happy that we could call out, "Wowie, you're the man! Wowie, you're the man!" just to show our support. I was happy that we had relayed Hali's instructions to Allen and to the jockey—at the crisis point of the race, the jockey was supposed to say exactly these words, "Wowie, win for Jane." I was especially happy when we looked at the numerology involved—on the sixth day of the sixth month, Wowie started from the third hole, and in addition to that, we had a three-year-old and a nine-year-old with us, and three was my sister's lucky number. The silks were blue, the same color as the saddle cloth, and the sky was blue, and the dappled gray of the horse's coat made him look like he had been cast for a movie. I was happy about all of these things, but I wasn't surprised. Allen said, "I'm so glad you came. Not very many of my owners do that anymore." We went to the glassed-in trainers' boxes in the grandstand, and I explained to AJ the concept of odds.

When the horse-owning class chose to cut the betting class in on the action, they did so in a systematic way—out of all the monies bet, they took out a certain percentage (called, of course, the "takeout"), which in the United States is about 17 percent. The rest they divvied up among the bettors in proportion to how they happened to favor particular horses. If almost everyone backs one horse, then he is the favorite, and there isn't much more in the pool than what is bet on him, and so after the takeout the bettors don't get much more as a return than their original bet. The odds on the long shots rise as the proportion of the bet pool wagered upon them diminishes. As with the stock market, handicappers are often right–the favorite wins about 30 percent of the time. What interested AJ was that, even though Wowie was the favorite, his odds were still two to one. That meant that, when I put five dollars down on the horse to win for AJ, he would receive fifteen dollars back–twice his bet, plus the value of the original bet. Since I was bankrolling him, of course, he had even less to lose than five dollars. AJ, who has to do homework, read books, practice the piano, and maintain a positive attitude throughout these activities in order to earn money, thought that he had finally found the something-for-nothing route, and, to keep him quiet, I let him think so.

There were twelve horses in the race. Several of them had been running in this maiden turf race all spring, and now formed something of a club–Governor Moonbeam, Aly Aly O, and Hopso had graduated, but Wowie, Taramot, Swift Hero, and some of the others had seen one another before–in fact, Taramot and Swift Hero had finished second and third the day Wowie was surprised at the wire and finished fourth. In the next two races, though, Wowie, third and second, had beaten both of the others. It was probably with these former races in mind that the handicappers made him the favorite. To myself, I remarked that it all began when everyone around the barn started calling him Wowie rather than Hornblower.

Up in the turf club, we stood by the window and watched the doors of the third hole. As they opened, Wowie seemed to rise up and charge forth, leaping to the front as if he couldn't get there fast enough. But the younger horse, Ship Ahoy, broke even better, and went out ahead. For a while, Wowie was at his side, and then he dropped back. By the half, which they did in a quick (for Wowie, anyway) forty-six and three-fifths, Wowie had gained all the ground he'd lost and was only a head behind.

Seconds later, he pulled in front and just kept going, striding, running, without apparent effort. As he entered the home-stretch from the turn, he left the other horses behind and galloped for the finish line, which he crossed alone by three lengths, never seeming to let up, even though no horses were threatening him.

We were yelling and jumping up and down, shouting, "He won! He won!," and AJ turned and looked me in the face, puckered up, and gave me a big smacker right on the lips, the perfect expression of family solidarity and betting success. We stood there until Allen said, "Want to go down to the winner's circle?" That's when I thought I was going to faint. I guess I was more surprised than I realized.

I staggered around the winner's circle for a bit. All I remembered afterward was a short man coming up to me and telling me that Allen had done a patient and dedicated job teaching Wowie to remain calm in the paddock, and Wowie himself, still alive with adrenaline, his head up, his ears pricked. We stood in a bunch away from him, two moms and two kids who seemed to have wandered into a beautiful day at the races, all of us squinting into the sunshine while the horse turned his head the other way, toward the track. Let me say now what I said then to everyone I knew who had the least interest in either racing or me—the horse ran a beautiful race, dappled gray on the green turf, steady and smooth and expert. He was fit and a little fast, and he cared enough to keep going even after he had left the pack behind. Two weeks later, the tape arrived of the race and I memorized it, especially those last hundred yards, Wowie alone, heading for the finish line, his body rhythmically stretching and contracting as his four legs reached and folded, reached and folded. Racing tapes are silent, so he seems eerily ethereal and eternal, too.

Of course, there was the congested drive down Highway 101,

to be followed by the equally congested evening of Thursday homework, but I don't believe either AJ or I noticed the tedium of the usual routine. I had that endless perfect gallop in my mind, and he had a copy of "Tony Hawk's Pro Skater 2" in his possession.

MY OLD VET, a longtime racing man, told me that my horse's breaking his maiden was "like losing your best friend." There would be no tidelike return of that maiden mile on the grass at Bay Meadows, offering up small variations on the theme of the same ten or twelve grass horses trying over and over again to get there first. Now there were races against winners, many of them very experienced, and many variables of distance and class for Alexis to take into account as she tried to build on Wowie's educational spring campaign. But my fantasies knew no bounds. I assumed a rather dictatorial tone—not toward Alexis, but toward fate itself. "So," I said, "a mile and a sixteenth is good. Just a little longer. I mean, that finish showed he was strong at the end. He could have gone another furlong. Time for him to stretch out a little. Put him in whatever you can find." Inwardly, I continued, Well, a couple more lower-level races, then we'll move ever upward in September, and that would be plenty of time to have him ready for the Breeders' Cup Turf (a mile and a half). I got a speaking invitation for the last weekend in October, but I turned it down. And, of course, a win in the Breeders' Cup Turf would set him up perfectly for the San Juan Capistrano in the spring, and then the Arc the following fall, that would be the fall of 2003, then the Breeders' Cup again, then the San Juan Capistrano again, and by that time he would be carrying a lot of weight because he had won so much and was such a great racehorse, and so he might be remembered, like Forego, as a great weight-carrier,* but, gee, after winning those races he would go on as an Olympic Three-Day Event horse, where he would have to carry not 140 pounds, but 175, which is what international eventing horses must carry, and jump big jumps in the process, not to mention turning in an exquisite and even legendary dressage test, especially for such a famous ex-racehorse, and the commentators for the Olympic coverage would replay his Breeders' Cup footage and marvel again and again on the versatility of a good sound Thoroughbred, even one of modest breeding, but, then, no Thoroughbred is of modest breeding. I fantasized for five long weeks, almost until the meet was over at Hollywood Park, at the end of July. I passed the time staring at the video of his win. So silent and heavenly.

But we couldn't get into a starter allowance—a race written for recent maidens, to break them in a little more easily to the tougher company of winners—only a claiming race on the turf with a purse of thirty thousand, but I discovered Southwest Airlines. No more the humble car journey to southern California: two and a half hours to Atascadero, then two more across the windswept badlands to Highway 5, then up and down the Grapevine into L.A., wondering noirishly for the last two hours about the meaninglessness of life, only to watch the race and turn around and try to get back to the Monterey Peninsula before midnight. Now there were the helpful reservations agents and the accommodating system of one-way fares and the smiles of the gate agents in their T-shirts and shorts. I signed up for air

---

*One of the things that racing secretaries do, other than setting up racing schedules, is to impose the weights that horses must carry in a race. Often, these are standard "weight-for-age" imposts—all the three-year-old fillies carry 117 pounds, for example—but in certain races, the racing secretary attempts to even the chances of all the horses in the field by giving the more successful horses higher weights to carry. Theoretically, a pound equals a length, so, if one horse carried 140 pounds and another horse in his race carried 123 pounds, then he was giving that horse seventeeen lengths.

miles, expecting to accumulate plenty of free tickets as my splendid horse piled win upon win.

There were twelve horses in the race, up to the ages of eight and nine. The three four-year-olds were the youngest. Horses that run on the grass often last quite a long time—they have less opportunity to race because there are fewer turf races on a typical card, the turf is natural and forgiving, they are bred for distance rather than speed, they frequently have more bone compared with body weight, and they also have a characteristically smooth action that is easier on the horses' tendons and ligaments. A stayer stays around. At any rate, Alexis warned me. She said, "He's racing against veterans now—veteran horses, I mean. They're tough and experienced." Just as Wowie had dominated the three-year-old next to him in the gate in his winning race, he would now be dominated by the twelve-horse herd of eight-year-olds, seven-year-olds, six- and five-year-olds. They would feel his youth and he would feel their maturity. But, of course, over against that there was the great boon of Southwest Airlines.

He was pretty and affectionate in the barn, he was wild in the saddling stall, he settled for the jockey, he lingered in the gate, but once he was out, he made a game effort to get into the fray. In the middle of the pack on the first turn, he tried to go around and move ahead in the backstretch, gaining about three positions. The other horses closed him out in the end. And the time was fast—just over 1:10 at six furlongs. He beat the other four-year-olds.

I pointed out to Alexis that the four-year-olds all carried the same weight as older, stronger horses. They didn't get the sort of weight allowance that Wowie had been giving the three-year-olds all spring. The jockey, Goncarlino Almeida, said, "He needs to break in front and go for a longer distance. The others can push him a bit." We nodded. Independently, Hali later said,

"He says it was so long between races that he didn't really realize what he was doing until the race was already started. And he wonders why the finish line came up so fast." So we all, even the horse, agreed that this race was meaningless, a drop score, not significant in the larger ascent to permanent success. The fact was, I felt so good about the whole Southwest thing that it didn't even bother me that Wowie dwelled a bit in the gate and then forgot, somehow, to catch the others as they ran for the finish line. Failure was startling, really. So startling that I hardly noticed it at all.

THE DARK FILLY had been with Alexis for two months now and was still without a name. The only one that Alexis liked was "Waterwheel," but Hali maintained that this had something of a ditzy vibration, and certainly the filly manifested "ditzy"—she would not allow herself to be bridled. "She isn't nutty about it," said Alexis. "She just puts her nose way up where you can't reach it, and she holds it there. It's not like she isn't looking at you the whole time, trying to see what she's going to get out of it. So I give in. I offer her a bit of something to eat, and she eats it, and puts her nose up again, but as soon as she knows, as *soon* as she knows she has us over a barrel, she takes the bit."

Then she got sick, and had to receive medicine. "Oh, she was wild," said Alexis, affectionately. "She's smart. She has us perfectly trained now. We do everything her way."

I said, "Hali says 'Waterwheel' has a ditzy vibration."

"I like it, though."

"Try 'Bump and Grind.' "

Alexis was silent.

" 'Bump and Grind' has a really strong vibration."

"Well, I'll write it on the blackboard and see if anyone responds."

I remembered when I named my older daughter Phoebe and my mother called me on the phone, objecting on the ground that it was too uncommon. "Try something else," she said. "How about 'Charlotte'? How about, say, how about 'Ciara'?"

We kept referring to the filly as Waterwheel, and pretty soon "Bump and Grind" disappeared from the blackboard. But there was this mishap and that mishap. She got a bump on her leg and a scratch on her head, and after her first breeze (thirty-five and two-fifths for her first three-eighths of a mile, nice and fast), she got a little bit of gas colic. "She's too much," said Alexis. "She's got to have it this way and got to have it this other way, but as soon as you head to the track, she's all business. Nothing scares her. She'll investigate anything. She's so interested! I love her."

I said, "It's like she's more than she can handle. Her eyes are bigger than her stomach."

"Exactly."

Waterwheel's foalhood had not been untroubled, either. She was bred in Kentucky and came to me out of the November Keeneland sale of 1999, when I decided, on the advice of Eddie Gregson, to buy a mare in foal just for breeding racehorses. The mare, Our Wild Rose, was a daughter of Once Wild, who had set an Aqueduct track record for six furlongs of 1:08.6; though he wasn't a famous sire, the mare was good-looking and good-moving and young—only four. Grindstone was a winner of the Kentucky Derby and a son of Unbridled. The foal's bloodlines were outside my usual habit—neither antique nor distance lines. The mare was small. In fact, she was just what Eddie recommended, a horse I could keep as a business proposition, not as a member of the family. He said, "Now, don't fall in love with it.

When the foal is born, don't pet it or even name it. You're going to sell it as a yearling. Don't get attached. Think of this mare as your factory."

The foal was active but tiny. Foals born later outgrew her right away, and the mare manager quickly discovered that, for whatever reason, the mare wasn't producing much milk. For a while, it was touch and go whether the foal would have to be weaned and bottle-fed, which would have been difficult, since she was suspicious and hard to get near (though the mare was friendly enough). Finally, Andre managed to get enough food into the mare so that her quantity of milk went up, and the foal began to grow, but she was never big. She was always, however, in front. When the mares took off, Rose led them. When the mares and foals took off, the tiny filly, about as big as a black dot, led them all.

True to my pledge, I didn't make up to her or befriend her, and neither did anyone else. This posed a problem when it came time to take her registration pictures, since she wasn't used to being handled. We could not get a halter on her, or even touch her, so we followed her around the pasture, waving off the friendlier fillies, and every time she stood still, we snapped the picture. The Jockey Club requires four views—each side, head-on, and tail-on. We managed exactly four shots of the filly standing perfectly, by herself in the field, as if she had been trained like a show dog to take a position. In between, we got twenty shots of her running, rearing, bucking, playing, and in general demonstrating her real opinion of us.

By the time she was ready for the yearling sale, she had been halter-broken and taught some manners, and she had already shown her particular ability to focus. One Saturday, some six weeks before her departure, the ranch where the filly lived put on a picnic-demonstration of horsemanship techniques. We in the audience stood about the round pen, talking, shuffling our feet, leaning against the railing. It is possible that the filly had never seen so many people at once. But she paid no attention to us after the first few moments in the round pen. She circled the periphery for a minute, perhaps, then gave her attention to the trainer, who was soliciting it from the back of another horse, with the flag. She understood full well that the man and the horse had more to do with her than the spectators did, and she learned very quickly to approach them, to allow him to touch her, both with the flag and with his fingers, and then, after about ten minutes, to allow him to put his finger on the halter she was wearing and lead her along next to his horse.

I watched her. There was an intent quality to her readiness to learn. She was bright and full of energy, which she directed toward the trainer and no one else. And she was beautiful, so dark, shiny, and compact, but not small or petite-seeming. I, who had vowed not to name her or pet her or grow attached to her, couldn't take my eyes off her. I, who could not afford another racehorse and had already paid money to put her in a yearling sale, pulled her out of the sale. I, who had vowed not to send another horse to the track until Wowie, then running as a two-year-old, was paying everyone's way, began beating the bushes for training money.

I tried to put the touch on my brother, who had sold his company and was, I was sure, looking for a questionable investment. I took him and my sister-in-law and Will and Griff to the farm. I extolled the filly's virtues. I said how much fun it was to go to the racetrack and what a wonderful place it was for children. My brother had been a hedge trader on the Mercantile Exchange, so I appealed to his gambling instincts (though hedge traders aren't really gamblers, more like insurance companies). I had never really tried to sell anything to anyone in my family

before, and it didn't work. I understood from my sister in a subsequent conversation that it might have worked if my sister-in-
law hadn't doubled my brother's potential outlay by suggesting
that if he bought a racehorse she would like to buy a bedroom
suite. That was a deal breaker.

In the end, Hollywood came through when a British film-
making company renewed an option it had purchased on a
novel of mine. "British?" I said to my agent. "Ask them if they
would like to invest in a racehorse on the side. Brits love racing."
There was no reply to this offer. But there was enough for training, and that was enough for me.

EIGHT

IQ

IN THE BEGINNING, there was Mr. T. Mr. T. was born some-where sometime in the late seventies. I was born at Los Angeles County Hospital on September 26, 1949. Our lives converged in northern Wisconsin on July 20, 1993. As with most horses, Mr. T.'s history was a closed book. All I got was what I saw—a tall enough white Thoroughbred maybe thirteen years old, but maybe older. He was kindly, it seemed, and with good gaits, as well as some jumping ability, but woefully underweight and covered with bites. When my friend George went to look at him, he almost turned him down on first sight, but after he rode him, he changed his mind. The horse had an air, and George had an instinct. My first reaction was similar—surely I deserved a better horse than this plug. But he was easy and comfortable to ride. He felt safe. He made me feel like a good rider already, not just some middle-aged woman trying to remember lessons learned twenty-five and thirty years before.

I don't know what presuppositions Mr. T. brought to our relationship, but mine were fairly basic. When I grew up riding,

Mr. T. in Wisconsin, 1993. Taken about a week after I bought him, still showing the effects of considerable neglect. His normal weight would be about three hundred pounds more than this.

I had been told over and over again that horses were mechanical, Cartesian, behaviorist beasts, who noticed only the person who was carrying the feed bucket or the carrot. Right there in my copy of the *World Book Encyclopedia,* the picture of the horse on the intelligence scale was low down—tenth, below the pig as well as the dog. And I had read the manual of the U.S. Cavalry, a standard reference for both my teachers and my fellow students. It stated on the second page, "The horse's intelligence is too rudimentary for him to understand or calmly accept the out-of-door phenomena which affect him." Another expert, Harry D. Chamberlin, wrote in his chapter on breaking, "The prominent characteristics of the equine mind are: 1. an almost infallible memory; 2. little intelligence (although this varies greatly in individuals); 3. small reasoning power; 4. the trait of mimicking other horses; 5. resentment of unjust punishment; 6. appreciation of rewards when merited; 7. attentiveness" (*Training Hunters, Jumpers, and Hacks,* p. 130). The experts at my barn were in full agreement with this assessment of the horse's intelligence. I hated the idea, but resigned myself to it and contented myself with worshiping my equines as if they were animate idols, unappreciative and unable to reciprocate, but available as objects for observation and no small degree of longing. They were much like teenaged boys in this: the pleasure for me was in having the crush; it was not possible that the crush would be returned. I loved my horses as far as I knew, though—I cared for them, groomed them, rode them, went out wandering upon them. I expected them to ignore me, and so they did. My most consistent experience of being with my horses was of moving along in a fog of happy solitude, adjacent to the horse but not communicating with it, trying to ride it by performing various prescribed operations upon it that usually worked. It was bliss enough. At first that was my view of Mr. T., too. But I was an adult now, and, besides, behaviorism was dead. When Mr. T. appeared to have affections and intelligence, I believed what I saw.

About six months after I got him, I deciphered Mr. T.'s tattoo and sent the numbers off to the Jockey Club. The information they sent back opened a whole new world in my mind. The bad news was that he was a year older than I had thought, but even so, the skinny white horse was a world traveler—born in Germany, trained and raced in France. (At Longchamp! How sophisticated was that! Winner of stakes races!) In the United States, he had run in California, Louisiana, Florida, Maryland, and Saratoga, ending up at Sportsman's Park outside Chicago, which was where he had left the racetrack after his nine-year-old season and got within range of Wisconsin. He had been places and seen things I didn't know. Except for the fact that he could tell no tales, his life seemed to me as interesting as that of any new boyfriend—full of adventures and excitement among exotic people. He had won $150,000, nothing to sneeze at. I learned how to read his past performances, and saw that in his first six starts in the United States, at Del Mar, Hollywood Park, and Santa Anita (as high-class then as now), he had run second three times, third once, and first once. His claiming price in one race was $150,000, the equivalent of valuing a horse of today at twice the sum. Only about 1 percent of Thoroughbreds win stakes races. Even fewer win stakes races, race for seven years, and remain sound and well disposed. His value rose in my eyes by leaps and bounds.

Most important, though, he was a good and agreeable horse. He might have gotten bad-tempered, or at least overenergetic, as he returned to normal weight, but he remained amenable and willing. He carried me to horse shows and combined training events, over jumps, through lessons, through experiences of pleasure and delight that I hadn't had in at least thirty years, and maybe had never had as fully.

The first example of his intelligence had three parts. In January 1994, we went to Texas for four months and took the horse with us. When we returned to the barn where I kept him when we wintered in Iowa, I turned him out in the outdoor arena, and at once he spied a grassy field across what appeared to be a low fence. What he didn't see was an electric wire set about a foot and a half above the visible part of the fence. He galloped across the arena, jumped the fence, and snapped the wire. I could tell it stung him, because he started. He was nonetheless happy to get to that grass. That was May 15. At the end of July, we were in Wisconsin again, and our barn was giving a small horse show. It was decided that another rider and I would jump a course as a pair, and that we would take down the electric fence and set up a jump going out of, and then back into, the arena. Mr. T. would neither go near nor jump this jump until I dismounted and led him up to it and let him investigate it to his own satisfaction. He looked at and sniffed the jump, and he looked at and sniffed the standards to either side of the jump and the electric fencing still intact to either side of the jump. Once he had ascertained that no wire crossed the jump, he was happy to jump it as many times as I wished. Three weeks later, I took him to a combined training event west of Chicago. On cross-country, which he normally liked and ran boldly, he was fine until we approached a chicken coop set in a fence line. He started backing up ten strides out, and would not be hurried or forced. When he got to the coop, he stuck his nose over the fence, then turned around of his own accord, took two strides, and jumped it. It was only upon reflection that I realized that electric fencing ran away from this coop to either side, and that he had noticed this and decided to check things out for himself.

He had other habits that I considered evidence of intelligence. For one thing, if given the choice of going back to the barn or wandering about the trails, he would wander about the trails, eager to see new things. If something startled him, he would jump back but then move toward it, with his nose out to investigate. Once he had investigated it, whether it was a scrap of paper, a combining machine, or anything else, he ceased being afraid of it or shying at it. He was curious, and he believed the evidence of his senses.

After we moved to California in 1996, incidents of his intelligence proliferated. One morning, bored with the work we had been doing, I said to him as I mounted, "You can do whatever you want today." I put the buckle of the reins down on his neck, and he marched briskly out of the stable courtyard. I fought back the temptation to interfere with his intentions, and over the next hour I became convinced that what he had been wanting to do for months was to explore the grounds of the stable and hotel where I kept him. At one point, we found ourselves in the parking lot of the hotel kitchen, where the garbage Dumpster sat. With no interference from me, he sniffed and inspected the closed garbage Dumpster for ten minutes—every corner and edge and wheel, first the front, then the back. It is second nature to a horseman not to let the horse get himself into a tight spot, for fear he will be startled and hurt himself (and for this reason I am not recommending people do the same experiment with their horses that I tried with Mr. T.), but I staved off that instinct, too. I let the horse go wherever he wanted and look at whatever he wanted. He walked boldly along, never trotting, never spooking, checking out cars and horse trailers and buildings and vegetation (but not stopping to graze). After I moved him, a few months later, to my own house, I realized that his curiosity was constant. He had a steady yearning to escape the confines of our three acres, and he knew where the gate was. Once, when the gate was standing open and I had him tied to the hitching rail, he pulled back, broke his halter, and ran straight for the gate. I had to run after him with the gate-closer in my outstretched hand, clicking it furiously. He almost made it—only the rattle of the metal gate beginning to close startled him into pausing before exiting. I later got comfortable enough to let him graze at large on the property (something not allowed the other horses), but I always made sure that the gate-opening hose was rolled out of the way. There was the chance he would step on it accidentally. I also felt there was the chance he would step on it intentionally.

Back in Iowa, my trainer had told me of an incident in which she was watering flowers by the house and out of the corner of her eye saw the two horses next to the barn step back from the electric fence, then charge it, and break it, only to gallop past her down the driveway. She swore that Mr. T. was nipping the other horse on the flanks to keep him going. They came to the end of the driveway and turned left down the country road while she ran for her car. As she came to the end of the driveway, they disappeared over a rise. When she got to the rise in her car, here they came back—they had not been able to bring themselves to cross a scary wooden bridge over the creek at the bottom of the hill. They passed her at the gallop, and she backed around to chase them the other way. But when they came to the intersection of two country roads, they found another spectacle—a hundred hogs in their pens, squealing and banging their feeders. The horses quailed and turned back. When they met her again, this time by the farmhouse, they put their heads down and followed her back to the barn. She always thought that if it hadn't been September, with the corn across the road a seven-foot-high wall, they would have headed that way. She also always thought that Mr. T. had instigated the whole thing.

Given the opportunity, he would open his stall door and let himself out—the evidence that he had done so was that he neither opened the door all the way nor closed it behind himself. He could readily manipulate a dog-leash snap or a spring snap. Once, when he was staying at another barn for a few days, he unbuckled a halter being used to tie closed the gate of corral, and let himself in with the mare in there. He was fond of mares.

In the fall of 1998, I went out in the morning to feed the two horses, and Mr. T. was recumbent in the paddock. This had happened once before—I knew he was having a bout of colic. But he didn't rise on my approach, and one look at the paddock told me that he had been up and down, rolling around, all night long. I went into the paddock and tried to rouse him, but he only groaned and stayed down. This was panic-inducing, especially since AJ, then six, was inside the house alone, waiting for his breakfast. I called the vet and some friends, a horsey couple, who rushed over to watch the horse while I dressed the boy. Mr. T. didn't even seem to notice their arrival. The three of us then urged the horse to get up, but he resisted, and only stretched out on his side and groaned. I said to my friends, "Do you think he's a goner?"

They nodded regretfully.

The schoolbus came and went, taking my son to first grade. Some ten minutes later, I saw the vet's truck at the big gate, and ran to open it. The vet's truck rolled down the driveway and came to a halt outside the paddock. Before the vet even opened his door, the horse had rolled up onto his breastbone and levered himself to his feet. He met the vet at the paddock gate with his head up and his ears pricked. The vet gave him a shot of Banamine, a strong painkiller, right there. The strangest thing of all (and we were all standing there, staring) was that this was not the horse's regular vet. He had seen him only three or four times in three years. In fact, it turned out that the colic was painful but not serious. Mr. T. was not shocking—his gums were still pink and his hydration level was still good. With the shot and a dose of mineral oil, he was back to normal in twenty-four hours, but I was always amazed that he not only knew who had arrived, but also anticipated that his pain would be relieved. And he was not a horse who liked vets—at his first annual checkup and vaccination appointment after I purchased him in 1993, he had bitten me on the sleeve of my jacket every time the vet injected him.

The horse was just plain smart.

I've had other horses do smart things. Once, when Persey was two, she got chased in her paddock by my newly acquired and not very obedient year-old Great Dane. A friend of mine and I came running, and shouted to the dog to stop, which he did—he stood still and looked at us. The horse was behind him. He didn't see her walk up to him. She bent her knees against his shoulder and side, and rolled him over. This was not normal horse behavior—as far as either my friend or I knew, horses do not express dominance or submission by rolling each other over. But it worked with the dog: the filly established that she was the boss; he skulked out of the paddock and never chased her again.

Trainer David Hofmans told me that when the woman who trained the horse who played the title character in the movie *The Black Stallion* had her horse at Hollywood Park during filming, she trained him within a couple of days to follow the command "Find Dave!" The Arab stallion would leave his barn at one end of the Hollywood Park backside, and seek out Hofmans at the other end, undeterred by fillies, chaos, distracting sights and sounds. And the trainer Pat Parelli once trained a large Friesian horse to lie down so that his wheelchair-bound owner could ease herself from her chair onto his back, at which point the horse would get up and carry her around.

Janet Burleson, who trains miniature horses to guide the blind, reported to *Time* magazine that her minis quickly learn to distinguish between red and green lights, and are reliably house-broken. Another owner of minis had a mini who liked to come into the house and lie on the couch, but would always bang the door to get out if he needed to relieve himself. Other horses have been trained to urinate in designated areas or even in buckets ("Make pee-pee" is the command one woman uses), and to perform all sorts of tricks.

A woman I know once witnessed a horse and a chicken cooperate for over a month. The chicken had quite a few chicks, which all liked to roost during the day on one side of the stall and nest at night in the feed trough on the other side of the stall. My friend was out waiting for the vet to come to another horse, and she saw her mare go over to the roost and extend her head toward the chicks. Two chicks walked up onto the horse's poll and clung there while she ferried them across the stall. At the feed trough, she lowered her head and the chicks disembarked. Then she went back for a couple more, until all the chicks were delivered, at which point the hen flew across the stall to the nest.

A man I know saw his mare transfer knowledge she gained from one situation to another—he taught her to work cows when she was seven, although her original job was three-day eventing and dressage. She went to a cattle-working clinic every couple of weeks, and after the second or third one, she got the picture—she could put her ears back and grit her teeth and lunge slightly toward the cow, and the cow would move off. In my observation, this is not normal horse behavior, but something the mare learned to do. Pretty soon, she started using this technique in her pasture, against her lifelong boss, an older mare. Within a few days she had raised her status, and in the last seven years she has remained on top of an ever-increasing group of mares.

I mention all of these incidents because ideas of horse intelligence still owe a lot to the U.S. Cavalry and other traditional experts. But the huge variety of disciplines and activities that horses around the world perform with their humans is not only evidence of their generosity and willingness, it is also evidence of the quickness of their intelligence and its adaptability. In the course of his twenty-year lifetime, the variety of things, large and small, that the average Thoroughbred must learn almost defies listing. He must adapt continually to the conflicting demands that successive groups of humans place upon him, because, inevitably, every horseman treats every horse somewhat differently from every other horseman. Most horses pass from one human to another—some horsemen and -women are patient and forgiving, others are rigorous and demanding, others are cruel, others are ignorant. In the course of what you might call his institutionalization (most horses live in stalls, supplied with food and controlled exercise, like prisoners in a medium-security facility), the horse has to learn how to, at the minimum, walk, trot, canter, gallop, go on trails, and maybe jump, to be handled by strangers and children, to be shod by the farrier and treated by the vet, with sense and good manners. Talented Thoroughbreds must learn how to win races, and if they can't do that, they must learn how to negotiate courses and jump over strange obstacles without touching them, or do complicated, dancelike movements, or control cattle, or accommodate severely handicapped children and adults in hippotherapy establishments. Many horses learn all of these things in the course of a single lifetime. Besides this, they learn to understand and fit into the successive social systems of other horses they meet along the way. A horse's life is rather like twenty years in foster care, in and out of prison, while at the same time changing schools over and over and discovering that, not only do the other students already have their social groups, but also what you learned at the old school hasn't much application at the new one. We do not require as much of any other species, including humans. That horses frequently excel, that they exceed the expectations of their owners and trainers in such circumstances, is as much a testament to their intelligence and adaptability as to their relationship skills or their natural generosity or their inborn natures as a member of the "big five." That they sometimes manifest the same symptoms as Romanian orphans—distress, strange behaviors, anger, fear—is less surprising than that they usually don't. No one expects a child, or even a dog, to develop its intellectual capacities living in a box twenty-three hours every day and then doing controlled exercises for the remaining one. Mammal minds develop through social interaction and stimulation. A horse that seems stupid might just have not gotten the chance to learn.

Human-intelligence theory has blossomed only in the last generation, as the study of the brain has yielded insights into the relationships of brain structure and chemistry to brain function and psychology. No doubt it is far too early to extrapolate to horses, but I am going to, anyway. It is one thing to recognize anecdotally that people, or horses, are smart. The average person recognizes smarts all the time. But it is quite another to understand intelligence—how it works and what it is for. I think the best preliminary theory is described in Howard Gardner's *Frames of Mind: The Theory of Multiple Intelligences.* Gardner posits seven types of human intelligence, each of which is located in a specific area of the brain. The evidence that intelligence is not a global or general capacity that can be measured by one yardstick is furnished by records of injuries or other deficits suffered by humans, who lose certain capacities but not others, or who are born with certain out-of-proportion capacities that contrast to strong inborn deficits. Much of the work of Oliver Sacks, in such books as *The Man Who Mistook His Wife for a Hat,* covers the same material in an anecdotal way. Other evidence for different types and locations of human intelligence is cultural and anthropological—different groups of humans in a variety of ecological niches have developed different forms of "genius" that apply only to their worlds and not to all human worlds.

The seven types of human intelligence, according to Gardner, are: verbal intelligence, musical intelligence, spatial intelligence, logical intelligence, kinesthetic (body) intelligence, and two forms of psychological intelligence, the one that deals with the self and the one that deals with others. Gardner's theory has served to equalize the status of the seven forms of intelligence. Wayne Gretzky, for example, is no longer considered a dumb athlete, but the possessor of an extreme degree of kinesthetic intelligence, akin to Bach's or Mozart's degree of musical intelligence, or T. S. Eliot's degree of verbal intelligence. One feature of geniuses in all of these areas of intelligence is that they seek out the experiences that inform and shape their preferred intelligence. We know from anecdotes about Bach's childhood, for example, that he was so curious about music that he was willing to defy strict prohibitions in order to copy out and practice new pieces.

No one has categorized types of horse intelligence, but clearly verbal intelligence is not one of them, at least in the sense that a horse would be able to produce symbolic speech, though horses understand their names and respond to them, and seem, in some sense, to understand the idea of naming (yes, I realize I wrote a whole section about talking to the horses that contradicts these assertions, but I am not counting on the reader, especially the scientific reader, to accept that section). Equally clearly, kinesthetic intelligence is one of a horse's essential capacities. The horse is inherently more athletic than the human. When the horse and the human are required to learn their roles in a particular athletic task, such as running races or performing dressage, the horse needs fewer repetitions in the course of his training than the human does. But other examples of kinesthetic intelligence abound. My horses live in a pasture where there are quite a few ground squirrels. I used to fear that one of them would step in a hole and break a leg, but no horses in these pastures have ever done so, and I ceased worrying about it when I saw my mare Persey trotting along. She put a hind foot in a hole. She pulled it right out and kept trotting without missing a beat. Kinesthetic intelligence told her that there was nothing under her foot. When the racehorse Alysheba went to his knees in the homestretch of the 1987 Kentucky Derby, then lifted himself up to run on and win, it was his kinesthetic intelligence that had the understanding about running and racing to allow him to do that. He knew that the task was not only to keep his balance but also to win, and he did. On a simple level, I once witnessed Jackie try jumping a bank jump in the arena at our barn. He stood next to it, sniffed and inspected it, jumped onto it from a trot, turned around, and jumped off it at a trot. Then he started galloping around and around the arena, and every time, he flew off the bank jump with his ears pricked, his knees bent, and his chest out. He was having a good time, but he had investigated the problem and tried it out first before going at it full-bore.

Psychological intelligence of one type is another of the horse's outstanding abilities, as is illustrated by the famous case of Clever Hans, a horse who was supposedly able to count and add in the early part of the twentieth century. Clever Hans was exposed as a fraud—he was not actually adding or counting, even though his owner seemed to think that he was. What he was doing was keeping a sharp eye on his owner and on the other people around him as he neared the end of the sum he was supposed to be doing. When their body language changed, he stopped pawing and got his reward. He was far more astute about the small movements and signals the humans were making than they themselves were, even though he did not actually possess a humanlike form of logical intelligence.

Spatial intelligence is an especially interesting idea as applied to horses. Horses operate in more dimensions than humans (this idea is explored in greater detail below, in Chapter 12), so their sense of the space around them must be more complex than that of humans. They have more to deal with, but they also have more sensory input to learn from. It is well known that a horse approaching a large jump cannot see it in the last couple of strides as he approaches it, because the set of a horse's eyes creates a blind spot directly in front of his nose. Courses of jumps set without tall standards to either side of the fence often disconcert even experienced jumpers, indicating that the horse uses the standards to either side of the jump to tell him where the jump actually is, a form of triangulation that helps the horse decide when to launch himself into the air. But horses learn quickly—the jumpers that can't jump without standards for the first few times do so readily and consistently after a couple of tries. Gardner's theory connects spatial intelligence with sight— the primary use of spatial intelligence is to perceive forms and shapes. Horses are notoriously quick at recognizing other horses; they are rarely mistaken about identities. Conversely, horses can be quite disconcerted when other beings look equine but don't behave in a familiar fashion. When Persey was a four-year-old, she saw her first Tennessee Walker produce his special gait. She was terrified. Her visual experience of the novel way of moving overrode her other sensory experiences of the animal's horseness. Quite often, horses react very anxiously to mules, ponies, and mini-horses if they have never seen them before.

But horses are spatially handicapped as well. Gardner shows that being able to predict how a shape will change as it moves in space is an indicator of spatial intelligence. Every horse trainer knows that objects change identities for horses, depending on the direction of the horse's approach. An object seen with the left eye is not the same to a horse as the object seen with the right eye—each side of the horse requires habituation. A jump must be approached from both directions in order for the horse to learn to jump it. The horse doesn't necessarily learn from jumping it north to south that it can be jumped south to north. Needless to say, some horses have a greater ability to generalize than others. Horse A might spook at the same object in the same spot day after day, year after year. Horse B might look at it twice and never worry about it again. In fact, horsemen often use this difference as a rough-and-ready measure of general intelligence.

IN THE YEARS I lived with Mr. T., we worked out a way to be together that was congenial to us both. I recognized and accommodated his evident desire for ritual—wherever he was on the property, when I came out of the house and went to the barn, he wanted to greet me formally, over the door of his stall, so he would ignore me until he had positioned himself, and then he would look at me and nicker. I gave him the chance to do a little exploring, and he never panicked or got into trouble. I fed him on time and supplied him with equine companionship. He was a good riding horse, who was willing to try everything I asked, including galloping around at the end of a line in a large circle around my trainer, with me standing in my stirrups, which had been shortened to their top hole (an exercise my trainer came up with to improve my balance), including jumping and making tight turns and ambling down the street and crossing roads and bridges and encountering dogs and children and bicycles and other strange sights. He was willing to perform the occasional intelligence test: A couple of times, I set small pieces of carrot in a precarious row on the top of his stall door. His job was to pick them up one at a time with his lips without knocking them to the floor. He could usually manage five out of six. If something aroused his suspicions, he was always willing to stop and have a look at it, and accept it after a minute or two.

By contrast, his fellow resident Yukie never got used to their living situation, just over the fence from a busy road. The headlights of the cars on the road every night still startled him after two years. If he saw a plastic bag under a bush next to the arena, he could not approach it or get used to it. If another horse wasn't with him at all times, he was ill at ease. New things remained forever new. Certain old things, like trailers, remained forever suspect. Perhaps most important, he never believed me. I could not reassure him by habituating him to the bag or systematically reintroducing him to the trailer, because he didn't ever come to have a real relationship with me—his psychological intelligence was lacking. As a well-trained horse, he was ridable in many structured situations, but around the barn his body language showed that he was more attentive to Mr. T. than to me. What I had to teach him or show him, he never learned. I would say that Mr. T. and Yukie contrasted in intelligence—one could learn and the other could not.

Gardner makes it clear that the seven human intelligences rarely act alone. For most people, one or the other might predominate slightly, but human survival, for individuals and for the whole species, is predicated on all of the intelligences' being developed to some degree. The case could be made, too, that some activities rely upon the integration of several intelligences—novel-writing clearly makes use of verbal intelligence (for the style), psychological intelligence (for the characters), logical intelligence (for the plot), spatial intelligence (for the symbolic and metaphorical content as well as the setting), and even musical intelligence (for pacing and rhythm). Novel-writing is an activity that often begins late in life, after the novelist has learned a little about lots of things, whereas musical composition and mathematical theorizing can begin quite early. Perhaps it can be said that horses, too, learn to integrate their intelligences.

Mr. T. in Iowa, 1995. A saint in a box.

I came to see that a clever horse is one who can open gates and pick up small pieces of carrot that he can't see. An intelligent horse is a horse who learns his set tasks quickly and also accepts their importance, even if they are not "natural" horse activities. And a wise horse, one who has integrated his psychological intelligence with his others, is one who recognizes opportunities for learning (which are really opportunities for adapting to the life he leads) and who actively seeks to make his life easier by figuring things out and by attending to the most knowledgeable being in his world, which might be a horse or might be a person. I know a vet who was able to rescue a horse from a trailer accident in which his legs were jammed through the sides of the trailer, because the horse, without sedation, let his owner quiet him and keep him still. He allowed his attachment to and trust in the owner override his potential panic.

Do horses have consciousness—that is, a psychological intelligence of the self that complements the psychological intelligence directed toward the group? Those who say they do are few and far between. In fact, there are experts on human intelligence, like Daniel Dennett, who maintain that humans don't have consciousness, either—that human consciousness is a false by-product of the workings of the brain. Nevertheless, let's say that humans do have consciousness, and that consciousness is the sense of a consistently felt self experiencing the world. Perhaps I can say, "I am running, I am jumping," but perhaps a horse can only say, "Am running, am jumping," or even, "Running, jumping." Theorists of consciousness in humans admit that they can't prove their theories, either for or against, because to do so would be to devise an experiment that replicates the same world that the subject of the experiment experiences. Thus also with the inner life of the horse or the dog; I can infer it, but I can't prove it, just as I can infer the inner life of my friend, but can't prove it exists. I do think, though, that there are a few hints that horses have an "I."

For those who accept that humans develop an actual sense of self, the stages through which this development progresses are fairly well defined. In the second year of life, experiments have shown, the human child begins to distinguish himself from those around him. Gardner writes, "The child is starting to react to his own name, to refer to himself by name, to have definite programs and plans that he seeks to carry out, to feel efficacious when he is successful, to experience distress when he violates certain standards others have set for him or that he has set for himself" (p. 246). With the possible exception of referring to themselves by name, horses give evidence of each of these perceptions. They quickly learn to respond to their names, even when they are given several names over the course of a lifetime. They clearly have plans (how else would one account for the chick-transporting episodes mentioned above?). And they clearly express satisfaction after achieving a task. Anyone who sets horses tasks—that is, trains them systematically—will notice that when they fail to do what is required (say, step backward in response to gentle pressure with the leadrope, or step over by crossing one hind leg in front of another) their body language may remain stiff or get more agitated, but when they do perform the required action, they lower their noses and chew or lick their lips even before the trainer has a chance to praise them. They also prick their ears and look alertly toward the trainer, either for praise or in readiness for the next command. After a race or after successfully jumping a new jump, the horse's body language can express pride or exuberance—swelled chest, high head, bucking or kicking up. As for violating self-imposed standards, I saw a beautiful example of this with Mr. T. himself. One time, I took him down to a jump, and we jumped so awkwardly that he broke the pole of the jump. The fence was low, and the pole was fairly rotten; the horse was unhurt. Most horses go right back to jumping, and usually jump better after hitting a pole or making a mistake, but Mr. T. seemed to become convinced that he could not jump at all, even trot over a pole on the ground. The more we asked him, the more agitated he became. The usual riderly recourse to a little bit of force (with a whip) undid him completely. He began to tremble and refuse to look at the even smallest jumps. It was as if, we said at the time, he felt that he had committed a terrible transgression, and he wanted to put it out of his mind completely. A week later, when we tried again, he was back to normal.

Horses do not learn to use complex symbols, as far as we know, even though they readily learn to respond to word commands, such as "trot" or "whoa," but they do learn to respond to groups of signals—particular applications of the leg and the hand and the weight of the rider's body results in particular movements by the horse. Some of the movements are very complex, especially for high-level dressage horses and circus horses. The horse's mind is interpreting the signals and producing the movement—surely this is a rudimentary understanding of symbols, and not the rider's subtle touches coercing the horse's huge body into various postures.

Gardner maintains that the personal intelligences are linked, and that there are two ways of looking at them. One set of theorists emphasizes the growth of autonomy—the child becomes a symbol-using individual who develops a stronger and stronger sense of self as he grows up to be a fully formed ego, essentially separate from the group. Another set, who tend to study non-Western cultures, emphasizes the growth of the child as a functioning member of his group, who gradually learns to take up his role and position among other members of the group. His self is made of his understanding of his role rather than his experience of separation. Both forms of growth happen in all children, but every culture promotes one or the other. Gardner writes, "Stated most strongly, without a community to provide the relevant categories, individuals (like feral children) would never discover that they are 'persons'" (p. 248). Obviously, horses living in a herd learn something about themselves. I don't think it is too outlandish to assert that they discover they are "persons" (not humans, of course, but there is no word implying consciousness that is used for horses)—that they have status or they don't, that they have jobs, that they differ from one another, and that they expect other horses to act in a certain way; at the very least, the high-status horses expect the low-status horses to give way, and the low-status horses expect the high-status horses to push them around, but also to stand between them and frightening experiences. There is a famous and strange story that I think is evidence that horses have a sense of self. A horse at a southern-California racetrack had been winning good races—low-level stakes—but his trainer fired his groom for some sort of misbehavior. The disgruntled groom got to the horse one night and shaved his mane and clipped off his tail. Although he wasn't actually injured, the horse showed every evidence of depression and even humiliation—low head, low energy, lackluster facial expression—for many weeks thereafter. And he never won another race. I think the easiest interpretation of this story is that the horse's sense of himself was damaged by his altered appearance.

If horses have a sense of themselves, then one of our jobs with them is to be alert to how their sense of themselves is evolving as they learn new things. Like people, horses can learn to fail if they are asked too often to perform a task for which they are unsuited. Or they can learn simply to not succeed. A woman I knew had a mare who ran at Bay Meadows for several years. She never won, though she ran thirty times and was second twenty-three times. She earned plenty of money, but her owner eventually retired her, remarking to me that the mare's window for learning to win had closed. She had been confirmed too many times in her view of herself as "not a winner."

The fact is that, although it may seem sentimental or unscientific to attribute consciousness to horses, if we do not, then we give up one of the principal tools in our training kit—the dimension of imagination that permits us to try ideas that might work when conventional methods have failed.

NINE

By the Sea

IN THE SUMMER, racehorses in New York move to the famous spa town of Saratoga, where, supposedly, the air is cooler, or at least cleaner, than in the city. In southern California, racing moves to Del Mar, a town right on the beach about twenty minutes north of San Diego. At both Saratoga and Del Mar, there is a strong sense of white-suit-and-panama-hat leisure. The track at Saratoga is festooned with red-and-white-striped awnings that keep off the sun but also look like summer. The saddling enclosure and the walking ring are out in green grass, under large trees. There are windows into the room where the racing silks are kept, and they hang by color in festive rows. Del Mar is newer, but the sea air and the vacation rentals and the families on the beach are just as luxurious and soothing. At both tracks, purses are high and many classic races are run. Famous trainers and famous three-year-old horses are trying to make good on the promise they showed in the Triple Crown races; famous trainers and fast two-year-olds are demonstrating whether they have the potential to run in next year's Kentucky Derby.

And Wowie had a problem. After the spring meet is over at Bay Meadows, racing in northern California adjourns to the fair circuit. For two months, races are run all over the state, in a manner that used to be fairly common in other parts of the United States. The purses are small, compared with those at the big tracks, and the tracks are small, too—narrow, short, and with tight turns. There is no turf track,* since grass requires steady nurture over decades or centuries. Wowie had to take the summer off, go to the fairs, or go to Del Mar. To take the summer off meant to lose both his fitness and his edge. To go to the fairs meant greater risks without much potential compensation. To go to Del Mar meant storming the castle once again—the castle of expensively bred horses who were fast and bold, horses he had not had much luck against in the winter, or in his July start at Hollywood Park. Going to Del Mar meant challenging the numbers.

I thought I was perfectly confident, even undaunted.

Three days before Wowie was to run for the first time in his life, in my life, at Del Mar, I took my *New Yorker* out of the mailbox and had a revelation. Malcolm Gladwell was writing about face recognition, and happened to mention that Sylvan Tompkins, a face-recognition pioneer, had spent his fortunate youth at the racetrack, handicapping horses for a betting syndicate. I've always said that handicapping isn't rocket science, it's harder, and the fact that geniuses like Sylvan Tompkins can often be found re-creating themselves with a *Racing Form* is proof of this. Tompkins' betting system, as reported by Gladwell (who, I felt, didn't accord it the importance it deserved), had to do with herd status—a horse confident in his status relative to the horses around him would run and win. That confidence

---

*At U.S. tracks, the turf track is usually built inside the main dirt track, and so is shorter. Only at Belmont Park, where the main track is a mile and a half long, is one of the two turf tracks equal in size to the average dirt track.

could come from various sources—age, size, an inborn sense of dominance, a sense of dominance produced by previous wins. It was especially important, according to Tompkins' theory, who was on either side of a runner in the gate—that is, who the horse would immediately measure himself against while waiting for the start. I am not exaggerating when I say that, upon reading these paragraphs in Gladwell's article, I began to flush hot and cold. And then the phone rang, and it was Hali, and she said, "Wowie has been talking to me all day about the race Saturday, and he wants to know who is next to him in the gate, and who is in the third position."

"That hasn't been decided yet. They don't enter until tomorrow. But listen to this." I told her about the article.

The race was a mile and three-eighths, a long race by any standards, and a quarter-mile longer than he had ever run. But we were following his instructions—after his last race, he had said, "Why did it end so soon?" Alexis was a little worried about running him such a distance, but I said, "The horse gets a vote, too. Let's do it his way one time."

Once Alexis entered, two days before the race, we agreed that as soon as the *Form* came out Alexis would do as Hali said the horse wanted—she would tell him all there was to know about the other horses in the race.

There were only seven of them. He was in the second hole. The horse in the third hole was a horse up from Turf Paradise— no threat. The horse in the number one post position had no speed, either. She went down the list. She was sitting on the trunk outside his stall, and, evidently, he was listening to her. At least, she said, he was looking at her. The speed horse, the big horse, was out away from Wowie, in the sixth spot. One of the other horses was used to running long distances—he had run in Europe, several times at a mile and a half. After we read him the

Form, I was sanguine, even though he had gotten the second-longest odds, and the house handicappers were dismissive.

Friday night, he said, "No blinkers." I relayed this to Alexis. Though she had to put something on him, because she had entered with blinkers, she gave him the "cheaters," blinkers with only a narrow rim that hardly blocked his vision at all.

I retained my sunny, hopeful outlook all the way to San Jose, all the way from San Jose to San Diego. Then, on the bus to the rental-car area, I became fixedly annoyed at a young family—pretty blond wife and heavyset, prosperous husband, who had dared to produce four blond children. Why was I so crabby? I wondered between catty thoughts. And then, at the Budget Rent A Car agency, when they handed me the keys to my tiny white Hyundai Accent, I went into full-fledged Status Anxiety. *How* could I drive to Del Mar Race Track in a Hyundai Accent? *Why* had I named my racing stable "Laughingstock Racing"? (Did people realize that was a pun, that my horses were *happy?*) *Who* did I think I was? But of course now it would be even more shameful to trade in the Hyundai Accent for an SUV.

I was carrying the silks. The old silks had been lost, and I had ordered a new set. I called this set the lucky set. The old set, the unlucky set, had disappeared somewhere at Bay Meadows, and the set he had won in had been a borrowed set that looked something like my design. The new set, the *lucky* set, were in my hands. We were late. We ran, ran, ran to the jocks' room to turn in the silks. Nothing was smooth. Second position, second race, eighth month, third day. A chaos of signs. But the clearest sign was the sign I kept giving myself—that I was just lucky to be here, my horse was cheaper than my rental car, and I really didn't mean this whole horse racing thing.

I will say that this has been a strange facet of my horse-breeding and racing career—that I am hugely intimidated by the big money and the big names. When Wowie was a two-year-old, having his first few starts, I used to wake up in a panic with a strong "How dare I?" sensation. I mean, I am generally self-confident. I've taught freshman composition! There's no tougher audience than that! At the racetrack, by contrast to reluctant college freshmen, people are friendly and welcoming. The racing secretary no doubt thanks his higher power every day that the less expensive horses and their hopeful owners show up to eke out the fields. And a long shot can win. Long shots win every day. Nevertheless, driving around in my Hyundai Accent, hustling my silks to the jocks' room, reflecting on the slurs against my horse in the *Form*, I was not preparing myself mentally for a thrilling win.

Alexis was not rolling smoothly downhill toward a win, either. Upon arrival at the barn in the morning, she had discovered not one but two of a horseman's greatest nightmares. Both involved fillies. The first was that one of the fillies, a two-year-old named Ever Rafter, had been sleeping with her head pointed toward the door of her stall, and in the course of her nap, it seemed, had slipped her head and neck so far under the wire-mesh gate bolted there that when she woke up she was pinned, her shoulder against the bottom of the inward-opening gate. Even beyond the tendency of horses to panic when they are trapped, there is also the fact that horses' bodies are so big that when they lie on their sides for too long the lower side begins to deteriorate from the weight. And three stalls down from Ever Rafter was Bird in Spring, also a two-year-old filly, who was standing in the middle of her stall absolutely unable to move her right foreleg in any direction. The skin and flesh on the point of her shoulder were puckered, her shoulder and foreleg swollen, hot, and painful.

One thing about horses is that they want what they want when they want it. If they are standing in their stalls early in the morning, waiting for the feed, you cannot tell them that this morning it is going to take a little longer while rescues and diagnoses are going forward. They whinny and bang their feed tubs, get agitated and excited, seem to be hounding you, threatening colic and worse. This is not to say that they are unaware of the crises their companions are in—they are aware, either by means of the regular senses or of other senses. Just the day before, at the ranch, in front of lots of horses and several people, a mare in season had backed up to Jackie, who was standing innocently in his pasture, and kicked her hind leg through the gate. When she pulled it back, it did not come through, but twined itself around a bar of the gate, so that she was stuck, and stuck good. Everyone nearby was equally astonished. The horses immediately pricked their ears and started whinnying to her; possibly they were communicating encouragement, but more likely they were just saying, "What in the world are you doing?" The people were struck dumb, at least for as long as it took to think the thought, How are we going to get her out of this?, and to watch her get her own leg out, awkwardly, painfully, but with only a scrape, not a fracture.

By the time I got to Alexis's barn before the race, the trapped filly had been freed, had not panicked or injured herself, and seemed fine. The swollen filly had received the vet, who had given her lots of antibiotics and taken her blood. Alexis was back to her normal composed demeanor, her good-humored, measured responses that disguised how rattled she really was. While I delivered the silks, she prepared Wowie for his race, using every trick, including hosing and girthing him in the barn, to quiet him so that he would save his energy for those long, long two minutes on the turf course. Then the groom walked him over to the front side, and after that around the beautiful Del Mar walking oval, which is grassy and green and embellished with flowers. I walked along parallel to him, telling him what a good guy he was, and he stared at me for many strides.

The jockey complimented me on the silks.

I met Caroline, the twenty-year-old Irish rider who exercised both Wowie and Waterwheel in the mornings. Alexis said, "Oh, Caroline knows the Baby Jesus, don't you, Caroline?"

Caroline nodded.

At the betting windows, I pulled out forty dollars and bet it on Wowie to win—an essential vote of confidence.

He broke perfectly, just as the jockey, Goncarlino Almeida, had predicted he ought to—went straight from the second hole to the lead, and started galloping in his steady, smooth way. Since the race was a mile and three-eighths, the gate was in the

The paddock at Del Mar.

middle of the backstretch. When they passed us the first time, my blue-and-yellow silks were a length in front. I didn't have to look at the clock to know that the race was slow—forty-eight and three-fifths, nearly two seconds slower than the race he had won. But he stayed in front, and the seven horses looked graceful in the sunlight, the grass of the turf course all around them like the backdrop in a movie. At a mile, far away from me on the backstretch, just before the third turn, the horses galloping behind him began to eat him up, first the five horse, who had won a good deal of money, and then the six horse, the favorite (so much the favorite that he had gone off at odds of less than two to one), a sharp horse by Affirmed, the last winner of the Triple Crown. Wowie didn't let them go ahead without a fight, but it was a short fight, and over before they were well into the turn. By the time he passed us again, crossing the finish line, he was sixth, beating only the obscure horse and obscure jockey from Arizona. The race lasted two minutes and thirteen seconds, which seemed like forever, seemed like a race in France, where they run endlessly on long stretches of turf, their hooves almost silent, in the shadow of great stone piles of buildings constructed by peasants in the distant past.

Alexis spoke first. She said, "A mile and an eighth," meaning maybe that would be his optimum distance. We ran down to find Almeida for the postmortem. He is tall (for a jockey) and lean, with a bright smile and an intelligent manner. He looks as if he might have been a cavalry officer in another lifetime. He shook my hand and shrugged. No analysis needed. Simultaneously, we all said, "He really tried." And, yes, he had, he had tried to give Goncarlino what he asked for, especially at the crisis point, when the horses were overtaking him. But he didn't have any more to give. Still in the grips of my Status Anxiety, I thought, Well, that's the difference between an Affirmed (twenty-five-thousand-dollar stud fee) and a Grand Flotilla (two-thousand-dollar stud fee)—thirteen lengths, or two and a half seconds. The winner had run the last three-eighths in under thirty-five and a half seconds. Wowie had run the last three-eighths in about thirty-eight seconds. The slow pace he set allowed the others to save themselves, but it had used him up. And, though I didn't say it aloud, the winner was an Aries.

Back at the barn, everything was peaceful. The filly who had gotten trapped under the gate that morning was dozing on her feet. Wowie and his hot-walker were strolling around the walking area, pausing every so often so that the horse could take a drink. Waterwheel was grubbing for stray bits of grain in the shavings under her feed bucket. "You know," said Alexis, gesturing toward Waterwheel, "I was out here the other day, sitting over here by the office, eating an apple. She heard me take a bite and started nickering at me. So I got up and went over and pushed a piece through the fencing, and she gobbled it right down. Most of them at least sniff it." She laughed. She said, "I love her." She opened the door of the pen and went in. The filly immediately offered her head, and Alexis started stroking and rubbing it vigorously. Waterwheel stretched out her neck. I could see that the affection was mutual. Alexis said, "Oh, you just know everything, don't you? You are the smart one!" She laughed. We were being very grown-up about the race, I thought. And the horses, all the horses in the barn, were all right.

In her dim stall (the barns at Del Mar are built of adobe), Bird in Spring was moving her right leg stiffly, but much more easily than she had in the morning. Her shoulder, chest, and forearm were still painful and swollen, however. She presented her head, and I stroked her lightly between the eyes. As Alexis was pointing out where the mysterious swelling had been, my cell phone rang. It was Hali. She said, "I have something to tell you."

"What?"

"Well, you know, he got through to me last night, but I didn't call you. I remembered when you had that bad news for Alexis about the horse who was going to get a fracture, and you didn't tell her ahead of time, so I didn't think I should tell you."

"What was it?" I felt a little alarmed.

"After she read him the *Racing Form* yesterday, he knew he couldn't win the race."

"Why?"

"Because he was intimidated. It was too much information. He felt that he didn't know how to do it. And today, when they came up and overtook him, it surprised him. He said he didn't know he was going to have to find a fifth gear."

"That makes sense."

"He says that his learning process is such that he only learns one thing at a time. The older horses know more than he does. He was intimidated."

Oh, I thought. Status Anxiety. I hope he didn't see me drive up in that Hyundai Accent.

Later, when Alexis and I drove back to the grandstand, I as usual expounded my theories to her. Status Anxiety; Owner-Horse Reflexivity; something just plain off about the whole day. She nodded and smiled. "Well, he's a plodder. He'll find a race."

I agreed. "Yes, he's a perfect plodder."

"It's not like he's a rototiller," she said. "You look at some of them and you just wonder how they get around the track."

Another theory occurred to me. "There's the stride-versus-strength theory, you know. Some horses have a long, smooth stride. That's in the joints. But they don't have much muscle power to go with it. Other horses have a lot of muscle, but the muscles restrict the freedom of the joints. They're very strong, but they have to produce more strides to get around the track. The power gives them speed, but the number of strides they have to produce wears them down. There's something, in the end, to be said for a pure plodder like Wowie. A nice trade-off between strength and stride length."

"He's sound," she agreed.

"And he's earnest. He wants to learn, even if he only learns one thing at a time."

"He's got some speed. He's not without speed."

"His sire peaked seven and eight."

"I don't think we'll have to wait that long."

We headed for the grandstand again. I said, "You know, even if this is all bullshit, it is a way to give him a story that allows the passage of time and makes us more patient."

She smiled.

Sunday was Waterwheel's day. At nine, when we showed up at the track to watch her morning work, she was tacked up and ready to breeze. Caroline was there with Samantha. Whereas Caroline was slight, blond, and a bit shy, an Irish girl from four generations of racing people around Tipperary, Samantha was muscular and frank, an English girl who seemed to do the asking of questions, not the answering. She got on Ever Rafter, the filly who'd been trapped the morning before but was now fine. Caroline got on Waterwheel. While they walked to the track one way, we drove there another way. We looked for them as soon as we got to the box, and they were hard to spot. In another section of the grandstand, the track was hosting breakfast. Nicely dressed couples were sitting at linen-clothed tables, drinking coffee, while the announcer identified horses and stables doing their morning works. Godolphin horses and riders—owned by the Sheikh of Dubai—were scattered about, easily identifiable in their azure shirts and saddlecloths. Our two fillies were more modestly tricked out, two brown fillies and two girls in anonymous clothing. Waterwheel, in particular, had no identifying marks, just dark, dark, dark. They came toward the finish line from the wrong direction, trotting, then turned and began trotting, then cantering, around the oval. They were to work three-eighths on the straight—from the quarter pole to the seven-eighths pole—and across the finish line right in front of us. They cantered easily down the backstretch, disappeared behind the video display, reappeared. Waterwheel began moving away from the other filly, and at the quarter pole, Caroline let her have it her way. She shot forward.

Much of a horse's individuality is in how its body moves. No rider has ever ridden two horses who felt the same. Every horse's level of energy combines with the size and nature of its stride, the degree of spring or smoothness, the sense of the horse's bulk between your legs, and the amount of horse in front of you and behind you. All of this is modified by the horse's own intentions: Is he with you or not? Focused or not? Happy or not? Mr. T. was smooth as silk but a little lazy—he felt best in a new place, energized into big strides by novelty. Jackie's strides are suave and powerful. Persey goes as if she has a diesel engine, always straight forward, which is nice over jumps but harder in dressage, when you want the horse to lift itself and show off a bit. I had never ridden Wowie, but I could see why the riders enjoyed him, because his gallop was long and even and pure, each stride just like the one before. Waterwheel, though not very large and still inexperienced, galloped in yet another way. She was long-strided for her size, but also quick; she was fast, effortless, and dedicated. She didn't require Caroline to ask her for anything—she simply offered it. You could almost see the energy she had, her laminar flow. "Perfect," said Alexis. She had worked the three-eighths in thirty-six and two-fifths seconds without even trying.

"Oh, she's a pocket rocket," said Samantha when she got back to the barn. "My filly wanted to do this and that. At the opening on the far side she wanted to duck out, but that filly of yours, she just looks ahead and goes. We couldn't keep up with her, and Caroline was right not to hold her back."

"I love her," said Alexis, again.

I said, "Look, Alexis. You have to lead Wowie past her pen every day and say, 'Here's your reward. Do a good job so you can keep your *huevos* and she's yours!'"

Alexis laughed.

LATER THAT AFTERNOON, for the feature race, the San Diego Handicap, Trudy McCaffrey, who has many good and famous horses, sat down with us. She is a trim, brisk woman with dark-red hair and a down-to-earth manner. Alexis asked how her earlier races had gone.

"Oh!" she said. "I had such hopes for that filly, but the bridle broke as they got in the gate, and, you know, she's so particular. They had to use one of their spares that they keep at the gate, but she didn't like the bit, and then, during the race, the saddle slipped forward, so you can imagine!" She shook her head. I recognized from her manner that this was a story for her, but not a melodrama, as Wowie's career was a melodrama for me.

"Didn't you have one in that maiden race, too?"

"He was fine. He ran pretty well."

She looked at her *Form*, and then out toward the gate. One of her good stakes horses, Bosque Redondo, was approaching the gate with the others.

The race was full of horses and trainers that everyone has

heard of—Bobby Frankel was running Euchre; Bob Baffert was running the famous Congaree, who was a son of the famous Arazi. There was an air of expectedness about the race that goes with well-known horses and plentiful sportscaster commentary. Alexis and I watched it with the disinterest that comes from respect for others combined with low aspirations for oneself. The high-status horses left the gate. Congaree, big shining chestnut, galloped to the front with what looked like supreme self-confidence and speed—he ran the first quarter in just over twenty-two seconds, a sprintlike time. The first half was just over forty-six, a little slower, but still a stakes-horse sort of time. Way behind the field was the pitiful Grey Memo, an almost white, rather awkward-looking five-year-old by an obscure Chilean sire, who sometimes ran a big race, but hadn't figured in the pre-race commentary. He was being ridden by Eddie Delahoussaye, but, then, even great jockeys have bad days. We watched the bays and chestnuts battle it out. At six furlongs they were still fast—1:10 and change—but then here came Grey Memo, so strangely white on the dark track, running like a rototiller yet mowing down the fancy horses. The time at a mile wasn't much faster than Wowie's winning time had been at Bay Meadows, and the time at the wire was practically slow—a good deal slower than the big race for fillies had been the day before.

I don't know why watching this was so invigorating, even when Trudy McCaffrey's horse was, disappointingly, eased in the stretch. Perhaps it was that the winner had looked so hopelessly outclassed, and yet had turned out to know better than all of us who was who and what was what. Trudy went down to see what had happened to her horse, and Alexis and I watched the pictures being taken in the winner's circle, full of the kind of pleased benevolence you feel when something good happens that doesn't benefit you in any way.

A little while later, another trim, matter-of-fact woman stopped to say hi. "Oh, Juanita," said Alexis. To me, she said, "This is Eddie Delahoussaye's wife, Juanita."

She was holding a package. She exclaimed, "I'm just glad it isn't those candy dishes anymore." She pulled out the end flap of the box and held up a square metal object with "Del Mar" and some other letters engraved on the front. She said, "What's this? I guess it's a clock of some kind."

She was talking about the trophy Delahoussaye had received for winning the race. This was an aspect of winning that I hadn't thought about—the accumulation of meaningless knickknacks around the home, maybe more like years of Christmas presents from virtual strangers than a gallery of triumph. Jockeys like Delahoussaye, McCarron, and Lafitte Pincay had thousands of wins, many of them stakes wins. Did that mean they had thousands of clocks and candy dishes stashed in storage units somewhere?

It was, indeed, a clock, battery-operated, oval-shaped, about four inches by five inches by two inches. We all looked at it. I don't know what the others thought, but I thought it was deflating, reducing the effort of the gray horse and the canny jockey to a piece of idle corporate giving. Looking at the clock made me think about racing in another way, not just as a castle I was storming with my pretty horse.

The paradox of horse racing is that a huge infrastructure of money, corporations, and governments is essential to maintain the venues and facilitate the flow of revenue, and the operations of these organizations always contextualize racing as just another entertainment opportunity, or investment strategy, or business, and then the horses come out of the gate and run around the track, and beauty and unpredictability seize the imagination. Yes, horse racing is largely about gambling and money, just like the stock market or capitalism in general, but, unlike the stock market, racing is repeatedly redeemed by the horses themselves. Twenty years ago, the powers that be in racing decided to pitch their appeal to the habitual gambler, whose bets sustained track revenue, but in doing so, they narrowed their possible audience. The worst effect was a natural demographic one—as traditional gambling racetrackers age, like farmers, they are not being replaced by younger men, who these days are fans of other sports.

Most of the time when you go to the track, the people you see look seedy—for one thing, they smoke cigarettes and cigars with the open regularity that you used to see in the 1950s. The racetrack might be the only place in the world where a twenty-first-century child will see someone light up a stogie. Racetracks overtly serve juicy carved sandwiches trimmed off upright joints of meat that actually look like the legs of cows, and the meat is delicious, but it is as if the customers have never heard of cholesterol. A natural audience for a horsey activity, girls and women, who have not been appealed to, tend to feel out of place at the racetrack. I like the track, though, because the grandstand of a racetrack, the parking lot of a racetrack, the betting hall of a racetrack, the walking ring and paddock of a racetrack are friendly and safe places. Racing fans are exceptionally nonviolent, because they have to keep reading the *Racing Form* and getting their bets together for the next race, and also because they are inured to disappointment. Fans never riot at the racetrack the way they do after football games and soccer matches. They sigh and tear up their tickets once again and get back to work.

SUNDAY NIGHT, Alexis took us to a party, where she promised to introduce us to the real horsemen. From my point of view, there were two disadvantages to this. One was that it was likely to exacerbate my Status Anxiety, since I would now have to worry about whether I was not a real horseman as well as whether I had a cheap and talentless horse. The other was that, in groups of real horsemen who are all standing around hoisting glasses of wine, I am about a head and a half taller than the conversation, not all that convenient for eavesdropping, which forms the main part of my plan to turn myself into a real horseman. Nevertheless, observing the wildlife in its natural setting is a must, so I put on my party clothes and off we went. It became evident almost upon arrival that my cover was blown, since the hostess knew that I wrote books, and therefore was in the business of observation and betrayal, but I eavesdropped as best I could, anyway. Right when I had decided to leave and also that I would never go to a party again, the Baby Jesus appeared. The coming of the Baby Jesus had been much foretold, and he fully lived up to his billing—he was about five feet tall and slight, with creamy white skin and long reddish-blond curls, a full mustache, and a neatly trimmed beard. He spoke in a lilting Tipperary accent. Caroline was standing with her very handsome fiancé, Bhupat, who worked for Bob Baffert. Both Caroline and Bhupat were heirs to generations of horse racing families, hers in Ireland and his in India, now toiling on the shores of the Pacific for one horse trainer from Arizona and another from Greece by way of San Francisco. Football offers nothing so inclusive. Anyway, it didn't take much to get the Baby Jesus started. The scene was southern California, the occasion Christmas, and the circumstance that the Baby Jesus, then known as Patrick, was so drunk that he couldn't walk, and so some friends of his laid him in a convenient manger, in a crèche outside a private residence, after first removing the doll and tossing it on the lawn. Too drunk to move, Patrick lay there curled up, dreading that the owners of the home would come out and find him; but instead, Gary Stevens and some other racing people came along and noted the striking resemblance between Patrick and the Saviour, and nick-named him. Patrick became universally known as "the Baby Jesus" by the next morning. He turned to me now and said, "And, you know, I didn't mind, except that my parents were coming to visit, and my mother is tremendously devout, and I thought she'd be upset, but then I just told her, once something gets around at the racetrack, well, that's that—you've got to accept it."

He took me aside. He said, "You must know, I've been dreaming of that horse of yours, Hornblower. He's a good horse and he wins, but in the dream, I keep calling him Valhol." He grinned. The joke was that Valhol was a 1999 Kentucky Derby prospect whose name and career, along with those of his trainer and his owner, were forever tainted when his jockey was con-victed of using an electrical device called a buzzer to goad him at the end of the Arkansas Derby (a video camera picked it up being dropped from the horse's neck after the race, and it was found on the track by an official). I didn't quite know what to make of this dream, but I thought it was a compliment that he kept dreaming of my horse.

The next day, Alexis promised that Wowie would run again at Del Mar.

TEN

Personality

AT ONE POINT or another, possibly while applying for a job, many Americans have taken some version of the Myers-Briggs personality test or the Keirsey Temperament Sorter. These systems analyze human personality by posing four pairs of opposites. The four sets of opposites yield sixty-four types. They attempt not to assess or even address issues of development or pathology, but, rather, to sort human populations in understandable terms into a manageable number of types, then to predict what sorts of qualities each type would have and how these qualities might express themselves in the various roles that humans are asked to play. David Keirsey points out, in his book *Please Understand Me II,* that attempts to define and differentiate human temperaments have a long history, and that the categories Myers, Briggs, and Keirsey himself have come up with are comparable to the categories Plato, Aristotle, Galen, Shakespeare, and others came up with in their day. Above all, the Myers-Briggs categories are *useful.* Rather than address the idea of the individual and how he needs to fix himself, they address the world of human endeavor, and ask how each type gets along and makes his or her way. The system is based on the test-taker's knowledge of him- or herself. The analytical tool these categories produce has sufficient complexity to be informative, but is simple enough for laymen to understand, and after answering seventy questions, a subject might be surprised to discover where he or she fits. The Myers-Briggs sets of opposed pairs are:

introverted/extroverted   judging/perceiving
intuitive/sensory   thinking/feeling

I, for example, turn out to be an "extroverted, intuitive, feeling perceiver." However my brain chemistry works, however my limbic system was formed, I find myself occupying a certain human niche and feeling suited to it. The system itself makes no judgments about which of these qualities are desirable, it only attempts to describe them singly and together and to assess how many people fall into each. It is not about the psychology of the individual but, rather, types of human personalities and how they contrast with one another.

Horses may be simpler than humans, but they have pairs of characteristics that readily express themselves in herds of horses as well as in relation to humans, pairs of characteristics that add up to personalities and can be used to analyze how they, too, might get along and make their way. I think the most obvious of these are:

dominant/submissive   curious/afraid
energetic/phlegmatic   friendly/aloof

Every horseman recognizes all of these traits every day, in large part because, when a horse has to do a job, he expresses one or the other of these traits in his approach to the job. First and foremost, a horse's behavior with his pasture-mates partakes of these categories. For example, when I brought my horse Essie (born in 1999, the eighth of my foals) from the ranch where she was born to live with Jackie, Kiss Me (number five), Persey, and Cheerful, she showed herself right away to be submissive (she yielded to the other horses at the feed tub), friendly (she greets me and the other horses every time she sees us after even a short separation), curious (on her first afternoon in the pasture, I saw her walking across the hillside far away from the other horses, her head up and her ears pricked, apparently checking out the accommodations), and, in comparison with other Thoroughbreds, a bit phlegmatic. By contrast, Jackie is dominant (he is the boss of the herd), curious (he is always inspecting whatever tools or equipment humans are using in his vicinity), energetic (loves to gallop full-out, and is very hard to tire), and friendly (his ears prick at the sound of my voice, and he nickers and whinnies regularly to all his associates). This combination is sometimes frightening, because it can lead to unmanageability, but it is also rewarding and interesting. Persey's personality is submissive, afraid, energetic, aloof. The submissiveness and the fear gain power from the energy when she spooks and bolts, and the aloofness means that she is less susceptible to influence coming from any attachment to her rider. Fanny would fit into the categories of dominant, curious, phlegmatic, and aloof—in other words, she doesn't want to expend energy except on things that interest her, and she can't be made to do so. Having attached herself to her ambitious fifteen-year-old rider, as I described earlier, she can feel like the boss and also spend her time galloping cross-country and jumping, activities she likes that frightened me when I owned her.

As with the Myers-Briggs scale, a horse could manifest each

quality more or less decidedly. The result, to an observer, would be greater or lesser vividness of personality. Everything horses do inspires Myers-Briggs sort of questions. I can imagine a few of the horse questions that could be posed at the track: "The first time you walked through the gate, did you find it interesting or frightening?" or "When you work with a partner, do you want to outrun him, or would you rather stay with him?" or "After you work a sharp six furlongs, do you want to do it again, or go back to the barn and take a nap?"

For an aspiring jumper, questions might go like this: "The first time your rider showed you a water jump, did you want to jump over it, or run away from it?" or "When you and your rider disagree about how fast to approach a jump, do you take hold of the bit, pin your ears, and go as fast as you please, or do you do whatever she wants, even if you know she's wrong?"

Horses pastured with a group might answer such questions as "When you first entered the group, did you approach the group, or did you stand off and get them to approach you one by one?" This is what Persey's mother, Lucy, did after the two were reunited and introduced into a herd. The result was that she was allied with the herd boss by the next afternoon. Or perhaps the horse might remember, "The last time you lived in a large herd, were you strongly attached to one other horse, or pretty much on your own?" When I first bought Mr. T., he was covered with bites and very thin, signs that he was aloof, submissive, and energetic—in other words, that he couldn't find an ally in the herd, and therefore didn't get enough feed to keep his weight up.

Horses in stalls have personalities, too. An energetic horse might develop bad habits such as chewing wood or stall-walking because of inactivity. A friendly horse might whinny and make a fuss every time another horse came near. A curious horse might do what Mr. T. did—fiddle with locks and latches, or sit on the automatic waterer and tear it off the wall. A dominant horse might do what Fanny did when she pinned the woman who was coming to blanket her against the wall with her haunches, or what Jackie did every time he came out of his stall—overreact to the activities of horses who didn't have anything to do with him and start rearing or bucking or whinnying from the stimulation. Myers-Briggs theory is not about transforming introverts into extroverts and feelers into thinkers (though self-knowledge can be a powerful motivator). Many of the psychologists who use it do so to help people choose careers, or for hiring and promotion in companies. It is about understanding what jobs are easier for some personality types than for others, and guiding individuals toward an "Arbeit" that might suit them. It is about heading off potential difficulties of fit before too much has been invested, by either the individual or the company, in unsuitable employment. Horses, too, have jobs and "co-workers," their owners and riders. As with humans, many horses are required to perform their jobs whether or not they suit.

It is a truism of racing that great horses have big personalities. Sometimes what the trainers are referring to is legendary meanness—the unparalleled sire, St. Simon, was given a cat as a companion animal. He killed it instantly. The owner of Claiborne Farm, Bull Hancock, is said to have had to scare off the stallion Nasrullah with a broom when the horse was twenty-seven years old. Eddie and Alexis's biggest money-winner, Super Diamond, tried to bite every passerby. John Henry was so impossible to train at first that his owner gelded him, put him out to pasture, and passed him off to a sucker who turned out to be the luckiest man in the history of racing, since the horse ran until he was nine and won $6.5 million. Sir Tristram, the greatest sire to stand in New Zealand, had to be caught with a length of rope that always hung from his halter, then led between two poles. He wore the same halter his whole adult life, because no one could get close enough to take it off. Perhaps what these horses were expressing was extreme dominance and extreme aloofness that got only more extreme with years of breeding, successful intimidation of humans, and isolation (stallions at breeding farms rarely if ever live with a companion). One farm, Three Chimneys, where Seattle Slew was a stud for many years, recognized this problem and alleviated it by having all the stallions, including the great Slew, ridden every day, just so that they would regularly experience submission.

But curiosity and energy can express themselves, too. The two-time winner of the Breeders' Cup, Tiznow, likes to run after sticks and fetch them back, like a dog. Citation had so much energy that he regularly worked a mile—one horse went with him at the beginning and another went with him at the end. Fusaichi Pegasus, who won the Kentucky Derby in 2000, was reported by his exercise rider to be not only opinionated, but extraordinarily curious. What appeared to observers to be balking was really the horse's taking an interest in his surroundings. The personality of the horse bulks large in the mind of the racehorse trainer. Even though running fast and far might come naturally to almost every Thoroughbred, entering the gate or training energetically, or allowing himself to be rated and controlled by the jockey, or going out ahead of the pack, or taking dirt in the face, or battling back for the win, or eating with good appetite even after a stressful experience like a race, might not. The trainer frequently finds himself or herself threading the horse's personality very carefully through the obstacle course of the racing world, and great trainers are those who can do so with horse after horse, year after year. Sylvan Tompkins' theory about the horses' sense of their status relative to the other horses in the race would fit in here, but on a smaller scale—a horse standing in the gate in a fifteen-thousand-dollar claiming race at Turf Paradise might not consider himself a Secretariat, but he might have plenty of confidence relative to the two on either side of him.

It is not true, however, that all strongly marked personalities belong to great horses. Big personalities belong to horses who are allowed to develop them and who have owners and trainers who can recognize them. Riding horses' personalities are in evidence all the time.

Let's say a horse, Scout, who belongs to a friend of mine, has never met a person she respects. Her owner can't do a thing with her, and neither can any trainer. She is pushy and mean, and her resistance is growing—tasks she used to be willing to engage in, she now refuses to perform. Most dangerously, she will not go forward when the rider asks her to. She is a big, broad, strong mare, five years old. No creature she has ever known since my friend got her as a foal has been able to dominate her. When she is brought to our ranch and put in with the mare herd, she dominates them as effortlessly as everyone else she has ever met. When my trainer Ray begins with her, the first thing he asks her to do is turn her head, and it may take a whole morning for him to get her to turn her head in both directions without resistance. Is she the most dangerous?

Another horse, Zeus, is remarkably aloof. He can barely tolerate the presence of people, and can't tolerate at all the presence or activities of other horses. When his owner is riding him in a large arena, and other horses pass him, he rears up and tries to get away. Since he is a big, energetic horse, he is dangerous. Once again, trainers he has known can't figure out what to do with him, and the owner is afraid of him. Is he the most dangerous? What is the ethical thing to do? Surely it is not to sell him, and if the owner can't handle him and he might cause injury to another horse or human, it might be to put him down. Instead, he comes to Ray, who works first on submission, not because the horse is focused upon domination, like Scout, but because he wants to redirect the horse's attention away from the stimulation of the other horses and to establish a connection between himself and the horse, making the horse attentive, above all, to the rider's wishes, a first step toward making him comfortable with other horses and humans.

As for Jackie, full of energy, temporary fixes like tiring him out by working him hard only give him more energy in the long term, because they make him ever more fit. His head is up all the time. His ears are pricked, looking for something. I can feel his energy come up and stay up, in contrast to other horses, who perk up but then quiet down. Is he the most dangerous? Since I know him, I suspect that his testosterone and adrenaline levels were unregulated when he was a foal because he was orphaned, but at this point the cause is irrelevant. My job is to intervene when his head goes up and his ears snap forward, or even before they do, when the first small charge of energy passes from his body to mine. I have to prevent the stare that precedes the buck and use his energy for my purposes.

Maybe Persey the Fearful, who sees monsters everywhere, is the most dangerous. Some days, she can't go anywhere alone without encountering terror after terror. A panicky horse knows nothing besides fear. One time, Ray was riding a young horse up a trail. There was a wall on the left and a steep drop to the right. The horse spooked at something that landed between her ears, and went right over the cliff. Ray had to throw himself off to the left as the filly went to the right (fortunately, she landed on a ledge some twelve feet below the trail, and was able to scramble back up the declivity). A dominant horse, an aloof horse, or an energetic horse can at least pay some attention to his own safety, but a panicking horse might not.

None of these, of course, are ideal amateur horses. The best amateur horse, I think, would be somewhat phlegmatic, somewhat submissive, neither afraid nor curious, and very friendly. An amateur horse's job is to be safe and willing, and each personality trait should promote safety and willingness. A phlegmatic horse might subside into less energy, but the rider could learn to use a crop. A submissive horse may try getting pushy, but would be easily intimidated. A friendly horse always rewards the owner's treats and affection, and the owner can easily establish a warm connection even after a bad ride. A horse that is neither too curious nor too afraid gets into less trouble and therefore sees the vet less often. I am describing horses that can occur in all breeds, but are more likely to be quarter horses, Morgans, and other horses descended from horses that once did daily work around the place, like drawing the carriage or working cows. I was lucky to find such a horse in a Thoroughbred, Mr. T. But few horses fit the ideal amateur-horse profile. Breeders of all kinds, all over the world, are breeding horses for athletic ability and looks rather than temperament. Thoroughbred breeders breed for racing ability. Warmblood* breeders breed for beautiful gaits and jumping ability. Quarter-horse breeders breed for speed, looks, and show-ring talents. Most trainers and prospective owners look primarily for the potential to win, because that's where the money and status are, and hope, in the end, to fit the horse somehow to the rider, by either changing the horse or improving the rider. And big money is passing back and forth. I know a fourteen-year-old girl who wept, a couple of years ago, at the idea that her parents would buy her "only" a $40,000 show hunter. The ones she liked cost $125,000. And the

---

*A "warmblood" is a cross between a draft horse, such as a Percheron, and a Thoroughbred. The balance between the draft blood and the Thoroughbred blood varies from breed to breed. Bred for equestrian sports, they excel at dressage and jumping.

prices have gone up since then. Eyebrows don't lift too much when a $275,000 amateur jumper from Europe bucks his rider off five times in a month. The burden and opportunity for trainers mushroom as horses get more athletic and more expensive.

People fit into the horse categories, another example of what we share with horses that has allowed us to domesticate and use them in so many ways. If I were to characterize myself using these categories, I would say that I am more submissive than dominant, more friendly than aloof, more phlegmatic than energetic, and more afraid than curious in my relationships to horses. I like a horse who is energetic because I don't want to push him, and a horse who is friendly because I want to feel my affections are reciprocated. I like a horse who is curious because he gives me self-confidence, and I like a horse who is dominant enough to have self-confidence, but not so dominant as to interpret every interaction we have as a test of who is boss. If we don't get along, who changes, he or I? It is the trainer who mediates this negotiation. I would like to be more energetic, more curious, more dominant, but people change more slowly than horses.

Experienced trainers have their personality profiles, of course. Ray is curious, dominant, aloof, and energetic. The aloofness means that he maintains his objectivity toward the horse; the curiosity means that he gives no thought to fear—he is always thinking about the next step rather than what might happen. The dominance is something the horse picks up on instantly, and gives him an advantage from the beginning. The energy means that he keeps going until the horse learns what he needs to learn. In his case, energy gives him patience. It helps that Ray is also athletic and experienced. He has superb timing—a kinesthetic trait, no doubt. At any rate, he can mold just about any horse to his requirements. But a former trainer I had who was also fearless, dominant, experienced, energetic, athletic, and aloof, but not so curious (that is, not so alert to the idiosyncrasies of the horses), could ride one of my horses, who was always openly challenging the rider, very well, but was too strong for another, and when he rode *him*, the horse seemed to fall apart. Another trainer I know, also on the dominant and energetic side, can ride almost anything, though he met his match in a half-Connemara who was able to scare him by bolting down woodland paths and knocking him against large overhanging limbs. A woman trainer I know, not so dominant and energetic, but extremely curious, has imagined and thought her way around many training difficulties that stump others. She has a knack for subverting the horse's failures of cooperation with subtle, jujitsu-type methods. All human personalities mesh better with some horse personalities than with others.

In the 1980s, there was a famously difficult mare named Touch of Class. She was a talented open jumper, and many riders tried her, but she had the habit of cantering "disunited"—that is, her legs did not move in the standard sequence.* All of the riders she had before Joe Fargis made her change to a proper canter, because it is a piece of standard equestrian protocol that the horse's canter be correct at all times. Joe Fargis let her canter how she pleased, and she went over the jumps for him. After she had experienced his allowing her to decide (ceding dominance, you might say) for a while, she got to be a calmer, happier horse. And she stopped changing her lead behind while galloping

---

*If a horse is cantering around a circle in the orthodox manner, the outside hind steps forward first, lifting the horse; then the inside hind and the outside fore go forward together, supporting the propulsion; then the inside fore goes farther forward than the outside fore, and receives the force of the leap just before the outside hind steps again and sends the horse on again. The horse is called "disunited" if the legs that go forward simultaneously are the outside hind and the outside fore rather than the conventional diagonal pair.

down to the fence. She won the gold medal in the 1984 Olympics. Fargis was able to cede dominance to her because he was curious enough to see how she wanted to do things, and then she was able to back down, too.

A friend of mine told me about an experienced cowboy she knew who had a two-year-old filly who one day made it clear that she did not want to have a bit in her mouth. First she put her nose up in the air; then, when he tried again to put the bit in her mouth, she stuck her nose under his arm. When he tried a third time, she knelt down on one knee and pressed her nose against the ground. Rather than attempting to dominate the filly, the trainer went into the tack room and found a hackamore, which is a bridle that has no bit. He was smart enough to realize that not only was the horse enterprising and intelligent, she was trying to communicate something. For her future work with cows, he wanted to develop her ability to dominate them, so he rewarded the resolution with which she had communicated her preferences.

If we project our four horses into the future a few years, we can see how each one might blossom according to his or her inborn personality traits. Jackie is now an event horse. His natural energy and curiosity, combined with fitness and a learned ability to relax, enable him to gallop over cross-country courses with efficiency, ease, and enjoyment. (That's my fantasy, anyway.) Zeus works calmly in the arena at the stable where he is boarded and lives amicably among other horses, whom, because of his natural dominance, he bosses around. He has a job, directing the activities of more submissive horses, and his owner, to whom he is more friendly, likes him better and has been able to develop his athletic talents so that he can go to shows. Scout has become an exceptional trail-and-pack horse, reliable and strong, able to get out and about because she is no longer bossy and dangerous. She no longer has to stand around the paddock feeling bored. She is still the leader, but she is cooperative, and, above all, her life is more regulated and interesting. Persey is a useful animal, going on the trail some days, having dressage lessons other days, having jumping lessons, too, from time to time. She takes her rider in small shows and has a satisfying relationship with both that rider and the other horses she lives with. She is no longer fearful about every new experience.

Of course, much in the way of bad luck could intervene between the two halves of these pictures, but all of these horses, because of their personality quirks, are in danger of being mishandled or even abused. Horses who don't fit in, who are bad at their jobs, who offend their owners and trainers, get sold or passed on in some other way. They are then at the mercy of their new owners, who may like them less and have even less invested in them. Zeus and Scout are like most of the horses Ray gets—their redemption depends upon what their riders are able to learn. Both horses have succeeded in frightening their riders, and their riders have sent them to Ray as a last resort. But the riders also have a task—to overcome their fears (and maybe some of their own personality defaults) and to learn the techniques and the attitudes that Ray uses to manage the horses. A "trained" horse is a dynamic being. He has to be kept up to snuff. The uncooperative part of him is a territory that expands and contracts, especially if the uncooperative part comes from fear or the desire to dominate. When Zeus and Scout go back to their owners, it will be well if the owners have become relatively adept at what Ray does, more perceptive than before, with more courage and better timing.

But back to racing, where a seventy-five-hundred-dollar horse can easily find himself outrunning a hundred-thousand-dollar horse. Well, maybe not easily, but often enough. I would like to project Wowie a few years into the future, too. His personality (he's a Pisces, after all) hasn't seemed all that suited to racing. He is on the fearful side, though full of energy. He was less than dominant, and friendly rather than aloof, but none of these qualities has been pronounced. He's a beauty, but he doesn't have a big personality (or his personality seems big only to himself, as we talk to him through Hali). Is he learning, through both luck and practice, to focus his abundant energy on winning, to overcome his fears through days and weeks and months of only confidence-building experiences? Will more months as a stallion give him a greater desire to dominate? Will the way racing is set up continue to work for him, by affording him good systematic training and excellent riders and jockeys as well as appropriate levels of competition, or will it come to work against him, by making it impossible to maintain him at the level where these good things are routine? The sociology of racing is rigorously class-based. If a horse can't make it in the upper classes, he slips down the slope toward the lower classes—forty-thousand-dollar maiden claiming races at Santa Anita this year, five-thousand-dollar races for nonwinners, five years old and up, at Canterbury Downs, outside St. Paul, Minnesota, two years from now. It is not his body, in terms of speed, or even soundness that necessarily makes the difference. Horses of all types, in all races, at every kind of track run twenty-three-second quarters and forty-seven-second halves. It is his personality that makes the difference—how he fits into the populations of racehorses and of their human connections. As much as Alexis and I see him as a unique and valuable personality, learning how to win literally by leaps and bounds—fifth to fourth to third to second— to everyone else in the racing world, he's just a set of numbers.

ELEVEN

Reality

A FEW DAYS BEFORE Wowie was to run again at Del Mar, Alexis called me and said, "I put him out in the pen next to her. He's out there now. Right away they started putting their noses up over the tops of the pens, trying to touch."

"Trying to kiss," I said.

"Trying to kiss. Then he started making stallion noises. I've never heard him do that before. He was arching his neck and everything."

Imagining Wowie arching his neck and going "huhn-hunh" in a deep voice was rather like imagining my son, AJ, shaving. I said, "That sounds very romantic."

She laughed. "Now she's gone across to the other side of the pen, but she keeps looking over her shoulder at him. Turning away, then turning back."

"Very coquettish. So she didn't squeal as if he'd impugned her virtue?"

"Oh, no. And I don't think she's in season, either. She isn't showing any signs."

I instantly got into the courtship spirit. "You should work them together. I wish you would."

"She's so much quicker than he is. It might discourage him."

"But she has such a sexy ass. It might inspire him!"

Though Alexis wouldn't commit herself, she did say, "Oh, I like working the two-year-olds with the older horses. It does steady them. I'll say that."

I didn't pursue it, but I did think about it. Equine romance. The beautiful gray stallion, so lovely and so elegant, but lacking in—what? Well, speed, of course, but something more, some divine spark. And the tough little know-it-all filly, lacking only experience, but still female. Wasn't she turning to look over her shoulder? Wasn't she interested?

Standard mare/stallion behavior, produced countless times all spring, all over the world, proceeds according to biology. Where the mare is in her ovulation cycle dictates how she feels about the stallion. All breeding establishments have breeding stallions and teasers. The teasers are male horses—sometimes ponies or geldings, sometimes lesser stallions—whose job it is to approach the mare and find out if she's interested. The stallion proposes, but the mare disposes. If the mare is at a fertile moment in her cycle, she will welcome the teaser, and then the help will take the teaser away and bring on the breeding stallion. If the mare is not ready, she will squeal, pin her ears, and maybe even attempt to strike at or whip around and kick the teaser. The breeding stallion is too valuable for such antics.

When old Chipper, the dam of Cheerful, went to Gainesway Farm in Kentucky to be bred at age twenty-three, after seventeen foals and in a state of what I would consider at least moderate physical breakdown, she put on such a display of something— behavior? pheromones? experience?—that the teaser, a pony, nearly came over the top of his stall door to get to her, and Corwyn Bay, who had seen quite a few mares by that time in the season, was no less interested. The grooms at the farm started calling her "Mae West." She was an inspiration to crones everywhere. Horses are not sexually dimorphic, like humans—that is, mares have very few overt sexual characteristics and do not look especially different from male horses—but they do have relatively large haunches, and Chipper's are very big, especially for a Thoroughbred mare. Who's to say that some combination of size and sway wasn't especially sexy to the stallions?

At any rate, standard horseman's wisdom is that the stallion is always ready and the mare is ready when her biological clock dictates a yes. Nevertheless, I have noticed that some geldings and stallions get fewer squeals and threats than others, no matter what point of the cycle the mare is in. Jackie happens to be very appealing to mares. They almost always return his nosings and greetings without protest. His own three mares accept his attention all the time, whether they are cycling or not. Surely they must notice that he never fails to greet them with his member hanging down. Cheerful, on the other hand, is careful all the time not to make any overtures that might give offense. The other thing I've noticed is that geldings (because I don't have much to do with stallions) who are beautiful to humans, like Jackie, are also the ones who get away with more familiarity toward mares. It is as if there is some trans-species standard of beauty that holds for mares and people alike.

And so it was no surprise that Waterwheel would be taken by Wowie's looks and manners. And I suppose that it was no surprise that I should be instantly matchmaking—fantasizing the two of them as a nice dual-career couple who would share the ups and downs of making it, only later to retire to some verdant spot to make babies and live off the interest of their earnings.

Except that conventional Thoroughbred breeding arrangements would have her living with the mares and seeing him once a year for about ten minutes, during which she would be booted and caped and twitched and not allowed to actually *relate* to him, while in the meantime he would live alone, or, if amenable, with a companion goat, and he would service many other mares with whom he had not even the memory of a kiss or a look or a few congenial works around the track.

Yes, I am *anthropomorphizing* shamelessly. At the same time, Jackie, Cheerful, Kiss Me, Essie, and Persey show certain things about horses' social and family arrangements that critique conventional arrangements and persuade me that the best living arrangement for horses, even Thoroughbreds, who some horsemen consider too delicate and/or crazy and/or hard to keep to live out, is the small, stable, mixed herd in a pasture of two or three acres.

The first point to make is that horses like to stand right next to their preferred companions. They swish flies off one another, touch one another, press into one another. Horses communicate their feelings in part by pushing one another. They also give and gain reassurance by proximity. Many horses aren't allowed to get close to other horses, but only to touch noses through the bars or look at one another. No wonder they get crazy.

Horses are curious and like to wander. At the ranch where Jackie and the others live in a small pasture, a large herd of twenty horses have two hundred acres to roam about in. In the mornings, they come down to the feeding areas under the trees, and they eat there; then they wander around to the front of the hill and watch the day's events taking place in the valley below; then they eat again in the late afternoon; and when the hay is gone, they wander over the hill and spend the night out of sight. Jackie and his group have less territory, but they have made a similar routine. They watch things from one corner, they watch things from another corner, they gallop around, they eat and drink. Besides exercising their muscles as they hike up and down the hills, they also exercise their minds—they see deer and other wild animals come and go, they feel the weather and react to it, they play as a group and individually. Sometimes, all of them gallop around together, kicking up their heels. Other times, Jackie and Cheerful spar in a typically male way, mounting one another, rising up on their hind legs, picking up objects and tossing them, trying to grab one another.

As noted earlier, they *like* to form hierarchies. Jackie is the boss. Kiss Me is the first female. Persey is the second female. Cheerful is the underling, and Essie is the bottom female. When I set out three feeding stations, Jackie eats by himself or with Kiss Me; Persey eats with Cheerful; and Essie, the youngest, though only by a few weeks, eats by herself or with Cheerful, depending on his mood and her cycle. All the other horses are more or less aware of Jackie's wishes, though Cheerful is the only one habitually on the alert, reacting to Jackie's signals instantly. Essie is more aware of the other mares, knowing that her status with Jackie can rise if she is in season and they aren't. Kiss Me doesn't pay much attention even to Jackie, because she is entirely self-assured. The point of these intricacies is that they exist, and they are interesting to the horses because they are naturally equine. Horses deprived of the time and opportunity to form hierarchies will form them with their humans, and the human might find herself in a surprisingly subordinate position. When a horse has horse society to occupy his mind, human society is of less significance, because he or she knows who he or she is and doesn't have to find out from the human every day.

In addition, outdoor horses use their bodies in freer, more various ways than they would living in stalls and training once a day. They learn the nature of their terrain, which may be rough, and how to manage it. They do not greet the outdoors with surprise, fear, or irrational exuberance. They are used to lots of things, and fewer things faze them. In a mixed herd, the males don't long for females and the females don't long for males. Day in, day out, they are relaxed and give off a sense of wellbeing. When I am concocting dates between Wowie and Waterwheel, I am wishing for the same thing for them, but with the added attraction of that potential foal, that perfect melding of his soundness and consistency with her speed and ambition, of his elegance with her muscle. Kentucky Derby, anyone?

Several years ago, the anthropologist Elizabeth Marshall Thomas wrote a couple of books about dogs and cats, *The Hidden Life of Dogs* and *The Tribe of the Tiger.* She asked the question, What do dogs and cats want? Her conclusions were that dogs want companionship of their own kind, including mates and offspring, a somewhat secret place to congregate, and something to do (using the neighborhood as territory, for example). Cats, she decided, want unchallenged possession of a territory, but, barring that, they prefer having something stimulating to do (like performing in a circus) to living in the wild without a territory or living in a confined space. With that precedent, then, we can ask what horses want.

Like dogs, they want other horses, too. They want to live in relationship to them, in close proximity with them, to be part of a group. As with cats, being the boss of the herd has advantages and perks (Thomas found that feline possessors of territory had more highly oxygenated blood, better health, better coats and skin than cats without territory), but horses in groups, even underdogs, like Cheerful and Essie, colic less, stay sounder and healthier. The danger comes not when horses live in groups, but when the population of the group constantly shifts, so that the horses have to re-establish their status over and over.

But there is something else, too. Like dogs and cats, and even more so than the other "big five" domesticated mammals, horses have crossed the boundary, genetically, between wild and domesticated. Even feral horses who have been living apart from men for several hundred years in the American West are not truly wild, like zebras. With some readiness, they hook on, learn to cooperate, take up jobs, and become affectionate and trustworthy companions. They *want* something that can be found among people even when they have never experienced it. It doesn't have to be his own idea to move a cow in order for a formerly feral horse to enjoy it and to become eager to do it. It doesn't have to be his idea to run in a race in order for the horse to become eager to do so. Horses, like circus cats, want mental stimulation and physical movement.

BY THE TIME Wowie raced again, it was September. The Del Mar meet was almost over. I had overcome my Status Anxiety, but there weren't as many horsemen around to trigger it, either. The Pacific Classic, the Del Mar Debutante, the other big races were history. Some of the barns were empty, and the backside was quiet. Alexis was about to send her son up to Pasadena to go back to school, and to ship the horses back to Santa Anita. Where Wowie would ship was pretty clear, but he had one last chance to enlist for Santa Anita rather than Bay Meadows. She badgered the racing secretary about writing the race we wanted— a starter allowance on the grass, a mile and a sixteenth. "Wait till he wins again," she told me. "Then you'll have a real problem, because he'll have to run against winners all the time."

I had done a very bad thing the morning of the race. I had gone to the dentist, had an X-ray, and discovered that one of my molars was doomed. The rest of the day was fine—I ran into a friend, I easily made my plane, I enjoyed my book. I was in a good mood, but I wasn't in a soon-to-be-struck-by-lightning mood. I was not in the mood to defy the bettors, who had him ten to one, the fifth favorite.

Alexis said, "Look at him. He's ready. He tried to bite me a few minutes ago."

Wowie's easygoing, playful demeanor, which I had enjoyed on my previous visit to Del Mar, was gone. The horse had his ears permanently pinned back, and the look on his face was testy. I went over to Waterwheel, who under Alexis's care had now become a first-class sensualist. Caress my head? Stroke my neck? Fondle my back and run your hands down my flanks? Let me get closer to you, honey. Her ebony coat had developed a brilliant polish and was soft as the breast of a bird. I couldn't take my hands off her, which was fine with her, and since she was also eating, she couldn't have been more content. She did take the time, though, to leap from her feed against the wire of the pen and communicate something nasty to a passing filly from another barn. "She can't stand that one," said Alexis. "I don't know why."

Though irritable, Wowie did seem calm in his stall. Soon enough, he was tied to an eyebolt in the back wall, waiting to be cleaned off and led to the test barn. He stood, as always, with his hind legs crossed. In her office, Alexis tied a length of string around each of two pieces of cotton. She would stuff these into his ears, and the jockey would pull on the strings as they left the starting gate, letting the cottons fall to the ground. This was a perfectly legal trick I had seen used on all kinds of horses in exciting situations, a way of stifling the noises that might frighten them. Each time I passed the stall door, he looked at me over his shoulder, then moved around so that he could look at me with the other eye. Alexis tied a bow around his upper lip, which would focus his attention on his lip and increase his production of happy-making endorphins. An hour before the race, two grooms attached their leadshanks and led him out of the stall and down the road. We followed in the car.

The receiving barn at Del Mar is actually a large white tent. Inside, the horses for the sixth race were following each other around a dirt track. In the far corner, two officials stopped each one and lifted his upper lip to check his tattoo against the official tattoo listed for that horse on a clipboard one of them carried. "He's being pretty good," said Alexis.

"He's still dry," I said.

We saw horses we had seen before. In fact, I realized later, they were horses who had beaten us before. Alexis said, "There's a lot of speed in the race. More than I'd like, maybe. But we'll see." There were six three-year-olds and four four-year-olds in the race, a younger group than we had seen lately, and Wowie was carrying the highest weight—123 pounds compared with 121 for the other four-year-olds, 116 for five of the three-year-olds, and 118 for the three-year-old who had won most recently. Since a pound supposedly equals a length, he was giving seven lengths, or one and two-fifths seconds, to the three-year-olds. The paddock looked like regular Del Mar, not leftover Del Mar— the fans were numerous and well dressed, the flowers looked colorful and fresh. Almeida came striding from the jocks' room, and he looked colorful and fresh, too, visible from the moon in the bright blue and yellow of my silks, with his yellow cap. I began to get excited. It always made me happy to have the best-looking dappled-gray horse carrying the best-looking lean and smiling jockey in the jolliest silks. The horse continued well behaved—not relaxed, but restrained, the best he'd ever been.

The two speed-horses, the five and the nine, broke sharp and ran out ahead of the rest. Wowie was third by about two lengths, running safely alone, showing off Almeida and my silks. The next six ran in a pack behind. The speed-horses were indeed speedy. They did a quarter-mile in twenty-three seconds, and Wowie was about two-fifths of a second behind them, fast for him. They were still zipping at the half, in just under forty-seven seconds, and he was closer to them. Into the second turn, he started to move forward, and, coming into the stretch, he was second by a head. Almeida was whipping him, we were yelling, but I still didn't have that driving sense that he was going to win, and there in the stretch, right below us, the stalkers, who had been running fourth, sixth, and ninth all the way around, came up and overtook the front-runners, as they so often do. The horse who had led all the way finished fourth, and the horse who had run second all the way finished seventh, and Wowie finished fifth by a nose, enough for 2 percent of the purse and some self-respect. The time at the mile was 1:36.12, a time Wowie was just a hair behind, and a fast time for him.

We went down onto the track to welcome him back, and he was the same as always—sound, excited, his eyes big, and his nostrils flaring. Almeida shook his head. "I asked for a little more, you know, but he doesn't have it. He's a one-paced horse. That's how fast he goes." He shrugged. Not fast enough for Del Mar, I thought. Or Santa Anita. I knew Alexis was thinking that along with me.

On the way back to the barn, we ran into the vet. He asked how the horse had done. I said, "He did fine. He's a pure plodder. Can't speed up, can't vary his rhythm."

The vet smiled. He said, "Those are the ones that last forever," and I saw that it was true. He would never tweak or jolt his joints and tendons. His stride was always the same length, and always the same tempo. His strategy was to grind the others down if they could be ground down, not to laze around in the back and kick into gear at the end. We were not exultant as we went back to the barn, but we had a sense of well-being, as if the race were our own private demonstration of what a good boy we had in the barn, a baby who had learned in seven months how to be a racehorse. I said, "He got fifth, Alexis. That's a toehold."

And, in fact, the details of the race showed how good a boy he was—a couple of three-year-olds had beaten him, but he had beaten all the four-year-olds, two of the three-year-olds, and all three of the horses who had beaten him earlier in the year. Hopso, the one he had battled with at Bay Meadows, only to concede at the wire, had run tenth all the way around. Alexis was happy because he had behaved himself. Wowie's regular exercise rider, who later saw the tape of the race, was happy because he had dug in and tried every step of the way. We were

Hornblower training at Santa Anita Racetrack. Andy Durnin up.

happy the way parents and teachers are when the late-blooming child graduates from high school, not with honors, but with a solid B average, and heads off, not to Harvard, but to a good state university. Most of the worries of the child's development have been resolved; he is healthy and happy and satisfied with himself, and lightning can still strike.

Four days later, Wowie got on the van again for Bay Meadows, and I said goodbye to my dual-career fantasy for Wowie and Waterwheel and their son, Triple Crown winner Waterblower, and settled down to hoping only that the two of them would start earning a living.

TWELVE

Five Senses and More

A WOMAN I KNEW had come home from the racetrack some years ago and stopped by the barn to check on her horses. The barn was a shedrow, located in the lee of a steep hill. After checking the last one, she crossed the courtyard and went into the feed room. While in the feed room, she heard a tremendous crack, followed by a crash. When she looked out, she saw that a huge limb had broken away from the tree overhanging the barn where the horses were, and had fallen directly on top of the spot in the stall where she had been standing not ten minutes before. The happy end to the story was that the horse in the stall managed to escape injury by pressing himself against the wall, and that most of the limb fell on the tack room. What she remembered afterward, though, was that, of the four horses in that barn, two had been looking uneasily out their windows toward the hillside and the tree, and two of them had not. She always wondered if they had heard something or maybe felt something—a creaking in the tree or a movement in the ground. She had heard and felt nothing, though.

Another woman, living in Minnesota at the time, borrowed an expensive mare from a friend of hers for the foxhunting season. The mare lived with my friend's gelding for about six months, and then the hunting season ended, and she went back to her original owner. The gelding, and, it was reported, the mare called for each other for several days—longer than usual—but then settled down. Some four or five months later, my friend loaded her gelding into her trailer and drove him over to the farm where the mare lived. As soon as she drove in the driveway, before the mare had seen the gelding and before he had made a sound, the mare began staring at the closed-up trailer, whinnying and calling. The way in which the mare sensed her buddy was not apparent to any of the humans.

My trainer Ray's uncle Lawrence, who lived and worked his entire life on a ranch in California, was riding his best mare one day. This mare was a perfectly trained workhorse, and Lawrence had ridden her all over the ranch, through creeks and ponds and every kind of draw and gully. She was in the habit of doing everything he asked. One day, though, she balked at going through some water, and Lawrence actually had to battle with her to get her through. Given the conviction that every equine disobedience must be dealt with, he thought he would be doing neither of them a favor to give in. But a few steps into the pond, the mare began to sink (yes, quicksand), and it was only with great effort that Lawrence and the men with him managed to save her. The interesting thing is that the mare began to balk before her feet even touched the water. Smell? Something about the feel of the ground? Lawrence had no idea whether the mare had ever seen quicksand before.

When Jackie was a yearling at the ranch, I saw him and the other four colts he was pastured with chase a calf that had gotten into the field. They ran after the calf as a group, turning, wheeling, stopping. Their best maneuver was a line-of-skaters move: As they approached the calf at a gallop, he stopped, pivoted, and ran around one end of the line of colts. As one horse, the whole line turned, with the inside colt pivoting and the outside colts running to keep even. It did not occur to even one colt to do an independent spin; they stayed together like a school of fish. Whose idea was that? How did they do it? By sight, or by the feel of each other?

A friend of mine once watched an experienced cowboy take his Thoroughbred/quarter-horse mare into an arena with several cows. After he chose the one for her to work, he reached forward and removed the horse's bridle. For the next eight to ten minutes, he sat quietly on her back while she anticipated every move the cow made. When the two were done, and my friend was complimenting him, he said, "You should've seen her last week. It took me twenty minutes to get her out of there."

At the racetrack, a horse accident rarely involves more than one or two horses, even if the horses are bunched together. The jockeys are quick to see trouble, but the horses are quicker. No fifty-car pileups for them. If you consider that a horse in a race is running about fifty-five feet per second, and might be only a fifth or two-fifths of a second behind the accident, you can get some sense of how quickly they react. How do they do that?

The key to the incidents cited above might simply be that horses are better equipped to take in fine sensations than humans are. Their ears work like mobile satellite dishes, catching sounds even when they are dozing. Their eyes are large and set so that they have a much wider range of vision than human eyes. Their nostrils, too, are wide, and their nasal passages are long. The four hooves on the ground don't work exactly like human feet—they are hard and convex, capable of picking up vibrations the way a cup against a closed door picks up sounds in the next room. I knew a woman whose horse would not cross a certain piece of ground without bucking and rearing. The woman later found out that there were electrical cables set underground in that spot. Horses have sensitive skin—when flies land, horses feel them and quiver their skin to shake them off, even though the skin is covered with a haircoat.

But the differences between horses and humans encompass more than sensitivity. Humans' senses are directed forward; the way horses' ears, eyes, and nostrils are set indicate that their senses are longitudinal. The equivalent to "behind" a human is "above" a horse. We may imagine a person, at least a normal modern civilized person, as being two-dimensional—a being with a front and a back whose awareness of up, down, left, and right is minimal. He or she is most alive in the head, the eyes, and the hands. By contrast, I think it is instructive to visualize the horse as a creature who is three-dimensional, with six planes of awareness—in front of the head and chest, behind the tail, along each side, beneath the feet, and along the neck and back. Five of those planes are engaged at all times. A horse is alive all over, from his lip, which can investigate grasses or open a latch, to his back heels, which can whip around in a split second and lash out. If humans have smarter brains, then horses have smarter bodies, bodies where the parts can be smart independent of one another. Every vet has a story of how the owner stood by the horse's head and soothed and petted him, and the horse gave every sign of being entirely relaxed, but then kicked the vet anyway—the hind end didn't require permission from, or the attention of, the front end to react to an insult. The man on horseback is powerful because the man's sensory awareness and the horse's sensory awareness complement each other. The sector of least awareness for the horse is reduced in size by the presence of the man on the horse's back, and the vulnerability of the man to what is behind him is reduced by the horse's agile back feet. The original purpose of certain movements taught by the traditional cavalry schools in Vienna and France, the "capriole," where the horse leaps into the air and kicks out (knocking the block off any nearby infantrymen), and the "croupade," where the horse achieves an even higher kick by throwing his weight onto his forelegs and kicking up (perhaps knocking other cavalry officers off their mounts), shows that horses were not considered mere armored vehicles in war, but active participants. Their trainers expected to enlist their innate bravery and aggression in doing battle. And new horses weren't trained afresh for every engagement—a good warhorse proved himself in many battles.

A horse's five active planes of awareness stimulate the development of his mind and body. A human's one active plane of awareness is slower to learn physical things. Perhaps this is why it takes people much longer to learn to ride high-level dressage horses and grand-prix jumpers than it takes horses to become high-level dressage horses and grand-prix jumpers.

Much is always made of the horse's natural role as a prey animal rather than a predator, and certainly prey animals are required to be more alert than predators. In the course of a day, a horse not only receives more sensory input than a dog or a human (in terms of sleep alone, for example, horses actually lie down and sleep only about an hour in twenty-four, whereas humans require eight hours, and dogs can sleep all the time if they feel like it), he pays more attention to it. It is not impossible to surprise a horse, but it is hard to do. Equestrian Native American tribes posted their horses as sentries, not their dogs. A group of domestic horses sleeps in the same way that a group of feral horses does—some lie down and some remain on guard, facing the more open direction. I sometimes amuse myself by trying to sneak up on my pastured horses. The sound of my car, the sound of my footstep, perhaps my scent—one of the five of them always looks up within seconds of my arrival. More often than not, a second or two after the first horse turns her head to look at me, one of the others, eating maybe ten yards from the first one, looks up, too. One of the existential challenges of owning horses is how attentive they are. Every time a horseman is in his barn or in his pasture, horses are regarding him. It can be gratifying or disconcerting, but there is nothing to be done about it—once you have made yourself important to them, they watch you.

A herd of fifty feral horses galloping over rough ground is an almost clichéd image of western America or wild Australia. It is so natural that we hardly think about it, but in fact it is more like a school of fish or a flock of geese than a field of humans in a marathon. They run as a herd, not as a group of individuals—that is, they move in harmony with one another, at speed and in close quarters. In order to do so, they must have heightened awareness all over their bodies, including in their feet, because their feet have to react to holes and declivities and rocks without consulting the head. Fish, geese, and bees have sensory powers that humans do not. Horses undoubtedly do, too. One of the things that we have repeatedly noticed about Cheerful, blind in his left eye, is that he senses things to his left. He seems no more likely to bump into something on the left than to bump into something on the right. He moves away from stimulus on the left even when it could not possibly be seen by the right. My guess is that he is using whatever sense or combination of senses that horses use to know their position in a galloping herd, and that one of these senses is allied to that skin sensitivity that they show with flies. Perhaps this expands into a larger field, like some sort of energy field. What the herd is aware of, the individual becomes aware of through some disturbance in the field. When one of them notices me, the others sense the noticing as distinctly as if she told them about it.

LATE IN THE SPRING of 2002, when Jackie was recovering all too slowly from two abscesses and an inflamed tendon, I asked a local energy healer to come out and visit the horses. Numerous people in California believe in and like energy healers. They describe a sensation of waves of electricity moving up or down their limbs, causing them to tremble and cry out. One guy I knew fell off the table, his convulsions got so violent. Afterward, these people report a feeling of relaxation and well-being. But, of course, this could all be, not a hoax, but an effect of expectation, a version of the panacea effect. At any rate, it is not possible to enlist a horse's expectations. We brought Jackie and Essie some carrots, and the energy healer showed up a few minutes later.

Essie was the first to approach. She had a small swollen lymph node on the underside of her jaw that we had thought might be an infected tooth or the result of a tiny puncture wound, but X-rays had shown nothing, and antibiotics and draining had had no effect. It was simply a hard lump. Natasha, the energy healer, stood still while Essie came up to her with her ears pricked, and then put her left hand up to the horse's head, almost but not quite touching her just below the right ear. She then put her right hand on the left side of her head, down by the filly's mouth. They stood still like that for about five to seven seconds; suddenly the filly threw her head and jumped back in surprise, as if stung. She ran to the other side of the pen.

Natasha came over to where I was standing with Jackie, and

we began to talk about his leg and all the problems he had had with it over the spring—he had kicked himself in the tendon, then gotten a painful abscess, blah blah. Behind Natasha, Essie turned and came in our direction, her ears pricked again. She walked over, positioned herself right behind Natasha, and gave her a complete investigation. She didn't touch her, but she sniffed and looked at everything, from her short brown hair down to her waist, slowly and carefully and with curiosity, not fear. Natasha did not turn her head, but let the filly do as she pleased. After about two minutes, the filly came around Natasha and rejoined our group. In the meantime, Natasha began on Jackie. Once again, she did not touch him. She bent down in front of his right leg and began making wavelike motions with her hands, down, down, down, never up. Within seconds, he was staring at this leg, and then he stretched it toward her, lifting his foot off the ground. They did this for about thirty to forty-five seconds, he presenting his leg and staring at it, she making wavelike motions. When she stood up, he moved toward her after about two seconds, and investigated everything she was wearing, but more aggressively than Essie—not only by smell or sight, but with his lips, he touched her necklace, each of her buttons, the buckle of her belt, the rivets on her jeans. He was systematic, moving from her throat to her waist. Like Essie, he wasn't fearful, only very curious. When Natasha bent down to pick something up, he nosed the elastic of her underwear.

I had been hoping for a miraculous healing—all evidence of swelling and pain instantly gone—and that did not happen. But I found myself at least as interested in the horses' reactions to what was done to them. They clearly felt something that intrigued and attracted them, they associated it with the energy healer, and, judging by how closely they stood to us and how they watched us, they were perfectly ready for more, in the same way they are always perfectly ready for more carrots, though they are sometimes indifferent to petting or caressing.

Six months later, I asked Natasha to come back. Essie, in particular, had suffered a couple of injuries when mares from the next pasture broke down the fence and invaded, trapping Essie against a tree and kicking her several times. Mostly, though, I wanted to see what the horses would do if Natasha showed up a second time.

They were dispersed along the fence of the pasture as we walked toward the gate, and all their ears were up. Essie let out an eager whinny, and then two more, and she and Jackie met us at the gate. I had a halter in case we needed to lead anyone out, and a friend who had come along to watch had a bag of apples. We went in. Essie went straight up to Natasha and stretched her nose out to Natasha's mouth. She spent about a minute sniffing Natasha's breath. Persey and Cheerful stood nearby, attentive to Natasha, while Jackie and Kiss Me crowded my friend, attentive to the apples. Natasha lifted her right hand and lowered her left. Her posture indicated to me that she was feeling an energy flow. Essie now stretched out her neck and head, pointing her nose toward Natasha's chest and then turning her head slowly to the right. After about fifteen seconds, she pulled her head back, then stretched it out again and turned it slowly to the left. It looked very ritualized. The two of them sustained this posture for some thirty to forty seconds altogether. Essie's ears were "offline"–that is, neither pricked forward nor pinned back, but out of the way. Her eyes were open, but her eyelids were a tad droopy. Twice Essie acted like she was getting a little shock and jumped away: once when Natasha touched her neck, and once when she touched the hind fetlock where the horse's more severe injury was healing. Both times, Essie jumped and then came right back, her nose out, curious and attracted. When the two, filly and woman, were standing there looking at one another again, Natasha took off her sweater, folded it, and set it on the top of a fence post. She then turned to Persey. Essie immediately went over to the sweater and sniffed it carefully for about thirty seconds.

The reactions of the other horses were not so evident. Persey and Cheerful continued to watch Natasha and pay no attention to the apples. Kiss Me and Jackie stayed with my friend until the apples were gone, though they were not quite as pushy as usual. When Natasha began to work with Cheerful, Kiss Me interfered after about five seconds. Natasha said, "Well, she says that's enough for him." Cheerful went off about ten yards and stood looking at us. Then Jackie got interested in Natasha and insisted on having her to himself. Once again, he investigated everything she was wearing, and finally became so interested in her metal watch that he would not leave it alone, even though she waved him off four or five times.

I have to say that I have no idea what this is for. I don't see any evidence of miraculous knitting of tissues or relief of pain (though, an hour or so later, when my friend Cheri and I had Persey at a horse show, I asked Cheri how Persey, who had been stiff and uncooperative, was feeling without telling her that Natasha had worked with her earlier in the day, and she said, "Better"). What I do see is that the horses like it—they pay attention and are interested in what is going on. They behave with Natasha in ways that they do not behave with other humans, including Hali. They just can't get enough of her, even though they've only seen her twice. Useful? Who knows? But indicative of something about how horses' senses work? I think so. Fact is, they are different from us. We have powers that they do not possess, but they have powers that we do not and maybe cannot experience.

THROUGHOUT THE PRESENT BOOK, of course, I have reported on the inner lives of my horses as retailed through Hali. F. Scott Fitzgerald once remarked that it is a sign of intelligence to be able to entertain two contradictory ideas at the same time, so I could leave it at that. I talk to the horses and try to get them to talk to me, but I also behave around them as if they have no language. These ideas alternate in my practice, but they do not mesh. I am still content to be amazed at what Hali reports and at the very fact that she reports it. For one thing, the entertainment value is high for me—my horses are funny, and there is something delightful about being criticized as a namer of horses by a four-year-old colt. For another thing, that they should have ideas and idiosyncrasies meshes with my pleasure in characters—my novel-writer's pleasure in being surrounded by narratives and points of view. I don't mind fictions—fictions are always illuminating in some way. If these tales are somehow only conceits, well, so are most things. Much of what the horses say makes perfect sense given what we already know of them—but where does what we already know of them end and what we are hearing of them begin?

One of my favorite books about horses is *Talking with Horses,* by Henry Blake. Blake's credentials as an unsentimental English horseman of the old school are pretty sound. His father broke horses by roping them to the ground and then sitting on their heads and reciting such poems as "Mandalay" while smoking a cheroot. Blake himself broke or retrained hundreds of horses, while also riding in steeplechases, foxhunts, polo matches, and countless other reckless horsey English sports. What motivated Blake to write his book, which is a priceless relic of traditional English country life now that foxhunting is endangered by animal-rights activists, was his growing conviction that he could communicate with some of his horses telepathically.

Blake's book sets out to explore all forms of horse/human communication, and the first thing he does is analyze the context of horse/human interaction, moving from the most obvious—the human directing the horse with reins and spurs—to the more subtle—horses and humans making things known through the sounds they use. He explores how intentions are communicated more through tone than language (a point that reinforces the idea that mammals are quite able to communicate across species boundaries with emotional signals but have little luck with cerebral "ideas" like words). In two lengthy chapters, Blake categorizes and "translates" horse body language into discrete, intended communications, coming up with forty-seven "ideas" that horses understand and convey. Some of these ideas, such as "I am frightened" (number twenty-eight), are both expressions and communications. Blake writes, "This can be shown by a snort or a neigh, and if they are in a confined area the horses will lean against one another and gain reassurance from the group." Others are definite communications: "Is anybody about? A loud neigh repeated several times. This has an enquiring note and is used with the head and tail held high. . . ." And "Gangway! This is said by a boss horse by pushing through a herd and laying about the others with his head" (pp. 71–82). He points out a whole set of communications directed toward humans but not toward other horses—some having to do with feeding and watering (I had a horse once who communicated to me very clearly that his watering trough had been cleaned but not refilled; when I came into his stall, he walked straight out the back door and down the hill to the trough, where he stood over it and bobbed his head until I came down the hill to look) and others having to do with riding, such as "Come on then, said by whickering and dancing around a little to show his desire to go out and enjoy himself" (p. 84).

Blake was an enthusiastic and observant horseman, who was interested in the history and lore of horsemanship and familiar with stories of "horse-whisperers" in England and Ireland, men who were reputed to have a magical way with horses. He rejected the rough-and-ready methods of his father and devised a method of his own not unlike the methods my trainer Ray and other Dorrance-influenced cowboys use, though he moved the horse around a large square enclosure rather than a round pen. He called his method "gentling," and by his own testimony, it was successful in reforming "BAD'NS AND MAD'NS." But his real revelation came when he realized that he could communicate with some of his horses from a distance, through ESP. His first experience of this form of communication came when he was observing two horses that he was trying to catch. He writes, "Countless times have I driven Beauty and Bill into the corner of the field to try to catch them. I would approach them and they would be standing quietly . . . until I got to within five or ten yards of them, and then, without any signal I could see at all, one would shoot to the left of me and the other, to the right of me. . . . They would always start at exactly the same instant, so that there was no possible way of stopping them. I used to spend hours and hours trying to work out the signals they were giving, so that I could stop them beforehand, but I never could" (p. 90).

Blake came to believe that certain pairs of horses, usually horses of the same breed or type, were what he called "empathic pairs," and that people could also become half of an empathic pair with particular horses. He says, "A truly empathic pair is a pair of horses who literally think as one" (p. 89). Sometimes, they recognize each other immediately. Blake points out that horses at an auction usually keep to themselves, but occasionally he would see two horses that had never seen each other acting friendly. Other times, long association brings out the empathy. People, Blake felt, do the same thing–he notes that most strangers on a train open up rarely and reluctantly (remember, this was England), but sometimes two people link up right away.

Being of an empirical turn of mind, Blake attempted to prove empathic connection between horses by setting up controlled situations in which the two horses could not see or hear each other, but responded identically and simultaneously to certain stimuli. The premise of the first experiment was that horse B would know when horse A was being fed and demand to be fed as well, even though the two horses were being fed outside of their usual feeding times and were not operating on any inner clock. The premise of the second experiment was that horse B would become excited if, out of sight and sound, horse A was stimulated by movement and activity. There were three other experiments, and also a control–an experiment in which two horses who were not an empathic pair, but rather, had expressed an antipathy to one another, were paired. In addition, Blake didn't like either one of the horses ("We were a very hostile trio!" [p. 119]). Although overall results for the empathic pairs were positive about two-thirds of the time, the results for the hostile pairs (and the hostile threesome) were positive only about a sixth of the time. Through these experiments, Blake identified who he thought was in especially close communication with whom, and then set up a sort of "Telephone" experiment, where he could trace the path of communication through various horses: "After a very long series of experiments, we discovered that if we fed the Welsh cob, the other three all asked for food. If we fed the Welsh cob and the Thoroughbred mare was not there, neither the half-Thoroughbred pony nor the section B stallion would ask for food" (p. 120). And so forth. Blake came to feel that "we can and do communicate vocally, orally, and mentally all the time with our horses" (though not perfectly—sometimes, he thought, the humans were guilty of misinterpreting the grammar).

Blake went on from ESP to what he called telepathy, distinguishing between the communication of emotion and the communication of ideas. Telepathy he defined as the "transfer of mental pictures," which had their origin in the intellect.

This phenomenon was not exclusive to his own experience—he knew one man who had awakened from a sound sleep, gotten on his boots and raincoat, stopped to picked up a flashlight and wire-cutters, and gone out into the rain to find his favorite mare floundering in a bog with wire wrapped around her legs. Another friend had fainted at the very moment that her horse was being put down, and still another had seen a painful flashing light when his horse was put down. Blake himself once saw what he was sure was a picture from the point of view of his favorite old horse, of his wife approaching the field with the two dogs, coming to bring the two mares (which Blake could see) and the "projecting" horse in out of the weather. But Blake was less interested in what the horses were projecting to him than in what he was able to project to them—he found he could direct some of his horses, both well trained and poorly trained—to choose paths and stalls and feeding containers entirely by concentrating on those he wanted the horses to choose. He came to the conclusion that "we can interpret what our horses are saying to us and to each other, and we can make our horses understand what we are saying to them" (p. 134). Even so, Blake readily admitted that "telepathy" was harder to understand and reproduce than "e.s.p." He points out, "Since telepathic communication is spontaneous, it is not repeatable under controlled circumstances, and accurate records are extremely difficult to assemble." He charac-

teristically kept track of his own telepathic communications by
jotting them down on the back of cigarette packets.

Several of Blake's observations have interesting practical possibilities. For example, he relates having taken on a very spooky
horse to redeem and retrain. Knowing that horses generally
spook when they see something that they don't understand, he
made a habit of staring with concentration at anything that the
horse might find strange, and then directing his thoughts to the
horse, who would then "use" Blake's knowledge of the object to
come to know it himself. The horse never spooked with Blake,
and no longer spooked when returned to his owner. Was the
horse able to read Blake's mind? Possibly yes. But it could also
be true that Blake's body communicated such calm certainty to
the horse that the horse simply ceded decisions about scary
things to him and then, well, to use Alcoholics Anonymous
terms, he faked it until he made it—he went without spooking
long enough that he forgot things could be spooky.

I have focused on Blake because I find his book, in part, a
charming relic of an equestrian world that has passed, where
people and horses and other animals lived in much more routine
proximity to one another than they do now, even in England,
but I also see it as the sincere testament of an experienced and
practical horseman to phenomena about horses that few other
horse books dare to discuss.

For Blake, the test of his observations was whether he could
use them to train his animals, and he claims that he could.
Horses that he trained by fully engaging his ability to direct
their behavior telepathically were trained more quickly and to a
higher level than horses he trained with conventional methods.
Even so, not all horses were equally trainable by such methods,
and he came to think that he could connect more easily to Thor-

oughbreds and Thoroughbred crosses than he could to other breeds.

For me, the test is only, Am I getting along with my horses, and are they improving in their performance and demeanor? Because I am a middle-aged, not very bold woman, I expect them to be cooperative, calm, and friendly at all times. I would have to say that they are always friendly—they never bite, kick, or threaten me, or anyone, and they are perennially interested in whatever I am doing when I show up in their pasture. They come running and hang around as long as I am there. They are generally cooperative, and mostly calm, but I have not repealed their equine natures. They still look at things and sometimes spook. Cheerful can buck from time to time, Persey has opinions, Essie and Jackie occasionally spook, but for their ages (three, five, and six) and their breed (Thoroughbreds, except for Persey) they do quite well. And so, really, I impose no Blake-like test. Perhaps, though, there is an *effect*. I treat them the way one would treat sentient beings. I am alert to their responses toward me, I expect them to learn and improve because they have minds, I consider that their relationships with me are ongoing, built on memory and expectation, like all relationships. I consider their points of view. Where I am not the primary caretaker, I observe the person who is, and I pay attention to whether that person is treating my horses with consideration. My relationships with my horses are not perfect, but they are positive and apparently satisfactory to all parties. This is the effect of imagining them in the way I have described in this volume, partly as a result of talking to them.

But am I talking to them? Are they talking to me? And what about the dogs? Hali and I once asked my Great Dane why he stood on the hillside and barked furiously at dogs and owners passing on the road. He replied that those dogs were on leashes and he was not, and they required to know that therefore he was the boss. Then we asked the Jack Russell terrier the same question—why did she run down the driveway barking at those dogs? She said, "I don't know, it just happens." That is a good story, and I did not make it up. In this regard, I may be a fool, and I may not be reporting the truth, but I am truthfully reporting my experience. Is Hali tricking me? With all sincerity, I say I don't think so. She has no motive, and the communications by now have become so consistent and so elaborate that I can't see how she could be.

I still communicate with my horses in parts, and partially. I have not integrated all the aspects of riding into a smooth package, and may be too old to ever do so. Likewise, lazy mental habits have been hard to overcome. My horses have to give me more leeway than I would like, but, fortunately, they are kind enough and calm enough to do so. Even so, I sometimes get a glimpse of the sensory lives of the horses around me. It is more complex, more sensitive, and more continuous than my own. It is made up of a constant awareness of the landscape—what is moving, what is still, what smells strange, what sounds unusual, what is vibrating (like the electrical wires Persey encountered once at a horse show). Humans have been trained by paintings, photos, windows, and their own binocular vision to see things two-dimensionally. To get a really good look at the world, we have to turn our heads side to side, up and down. Always the lines of perspective recede like a railroad track, heading toward that vanishing point in the distance. What we don't sense, we supply mentally, in the same way that we fill in the blanks between the rods and cones in our retinas with what should be there. If the human in the world is at a window, looking out, then the horse in the world is at a multi-dimensional intersection, sensing all kinds of crosscurrents, checking what he hears by looking toward it, getting more evidence for what he feels in his hooves by putting his head down and sniffing, searching with his senses for reasons to take seriously his more ineffable awareness. In the end, we don't know what horses can do. We only know that when, over the past thousands of years, we have asked something more of them, at least some of them have readily supplied it.

THIRTEEN

What If

In mid-September, Alexis and I have one of those talks. Those talks are about how unforgiving horse racing is, and people who own horses or train horses or ride horses at the track have those talks from time to time. Fortunately, this talk has nothing to do with either of my horses. Wowie is happy and sound at Bay Meadows with Allen, waiting for a starter allowance that will be run at the beginning of October. Waterwheel is kicking up her heels in her usual fashion. She works a half in forty-eight seconds, then gallops out five-eighths in 1:02 and change. Alexis says, "She wasn't trying. She was perfectly in hand. I have horses who work in the time that she galloped out in." The reason this makes me happy is that another trainer I know once told me about a filly he had who could run four and a half furlongs as quick as a rabbit, but could not get five furlongs to save her life. The shortest regular race that Thoroughbreds run after the beginning of their two-year-old year is five and a half furlongs. To have a promising filly stop dead at four and a half would be heartbreaking.

But, then, there are all sorts of ways they can break your heart—this is the general category that those talks fall into.

One of the great unlearnable lessons about horse racing and horses as a whole is the lesson that money doesn't really mean anything. A yearling that costs a million dollars is unproved and unprovable. He may never win a good race, never even get to the races. "You should have seen one filly we got from the sale," says Alexis. "The weight just fell off her. At the end of a month, she didn't look like the same horse. We knew she'd been pumped up for the sale, but what can you do? She had great breeding." When people spend a lot of money on a horse, perhaps they are thinking that a horse is like a car, because the eighty-thousand-dollar car is so evidently more luxurious than the twenty-thousand-dollar car. The two-million-dollar house is so evidently of better quality than the fifty-thousand-dollar house. But a Thoroughbred costing ten or twenty thousand dollars has all the parts that one costing a million dollars has. People pay because they are trying to buy a winner, and they think that the investment in bloodlines will pay off in the end. Sometimes it does. The winner of the 2000 Kentucky Derby, Fusaichi Pegasus, cost four million dollars at the Keeneland sale of 1998, earned a couple million on the track, and was syndicated to stud for sixty to seventy million. He was by Mr. Prospector, the most valuable sire ever, who had recently died. He was big, beautiful, and of course had the look of eagles, whatever that is. But only one person in the world would take the gamble, a Japanese businessman named Fusao Sekiguchi. His gamble paid off. Most big gambles don't pay off. The main thing to know about horses, especially Thoroughbred horses, is that they are so closely inbred that the gene pool can mix up a winner or a loser anytime a conception takes place. The odds of getting a winner rise with the price, but they don't rise in proportion to the price. A million-dollar yearling doesn't have twenty times the chance of being a winner that a fifty-thousand-dollar yearling has (nor is a $275,000 hunter going to be fourteen times the horse a twenty-thousand-dollar hunter is). For that extra $950,000, the buyer has to be paying for something else, something besides the chance of getting a winner.

"Sometimes I think you're doing it the right way," says Alexis, still warm all over from watching Waterwheel work. I say, "Did she work with a partner?"

"No. No one can keep up with her."

I preen myself about her speed a bit, and of course I feel I am doing it right, because I fit my own criteria for doing it right—spend as little money as possible, be grateful for whatever good things happen, take good care of the horses, have the conviction that sentiment trumps economic interest every time. Lately I have been rereading *Pride and Prejudice,* one of the central texts of my adolescence, a novel that formed my world-view. The characters in *Pride and Prejudice* talk about money maybe as much as any characters ever in the history of the novel, but what they believe in is love—feelings of sympathy, kinship, and admiration all rolled up in a lifetime of quiet attachment and pleasure. In the end, because they are honorable and sincere, not to mention charming, the impoverished Jane Bennet and the impoverished Elizabeth Bennet get to marry the wealthy Bingley and the even wealthier Darcy, and they get to be cherished—dare I say, Elizabeth gets to have the upper hand all the days of her life. Forty years of female existence has been unable to eradicate my faith in the promise of *Pride and Prejudice.* Somehow I still believe that the honest Alexis and the well-meaning Jane will get to the Breeders' Cup, or to a stakes race, or to solvency. If my last forty years had been founded upon *Madame Bovary,* perhaps I would think differently.

We continue the talk. Alexis is worked up, a rare state for her. One of her owners is frustrated. She says, "He's been getting bad advice."

"From whom? Surely not from you."

"From people he knows. He goes to the sales, and they get all enthusiastic over some horse, and then they bid on it, and what am I supposed to say? That I don't like the horse? I don't think they would listen to me."

I imagine them all sitting around, several wealthy, boisterous men in their fifties and sixties and Alexis, still a bit girlish-looking, and by nature respectful. I imagine the money burning a hole in the client's pocket, the way it does at a sale, where the odor of masculinity is strong and exciting and bidding is a competitive sport. I don't think they would listen to her, either. She goes on, "They buy classic lines. Those are expensive."

They are. Stud fees in the $200,000 to $500,000 range mean yearling prices in the $600,000 to $1.5 million range. I tut-tut the way people do who don't have that kind of money to spend. She says, "You know what Baffert said to me once? He said, 'I used to buy those classic lines so that I could be sure the horse would get the distance, but it wasn't worth it. Now I just look for speed, and when I've got some of that, I hope the horse can stay.' " I nod and file this bit of wisdom away for when I can afford to buy some speed.

The other unlearnable lesson about horses is that lucky is better than good, and though I may preen myself, in the end there is no taking credit for how the gene pool mixes itself up in any given foal. Horse racing and Thoroughbred breeding are as statistical and mathematical as any endeavor in the world—so many horses are conceived, so many horses are born, so many get to the track, so many win, so many last, so many get back to breeding. Since almost every exploit of every Thoroughbred of the last 250 years has been recorded, analyzed, and interpreted, the studied population is huge and studies are revealing. The history of racing and breeding has a majestic design and, as a bonus, is adorned with superbly entertaining anecdotes. But it is because every horseman spends much of his or her life doing the very thing that statisticians are always warning us against—extrapolating from broad trends to individual cases—that we get into those talks, that heartbreak. We thought there was a promise when really there was hardly a chance.

On the morning of Wowie's race, I woke up thinking of Prince Ahmed bin Salman, especially famous in 2002 for buying a horse of iffy soundness from Chicago, named War Emblem, and then winning the Kentucky Derby and the Preakness with him. At one point, the Prince told reporters that before every race he prowled around, saying to himself, "Why am I in this business? What a terrible business this is!" And then, after every race, he knew. He knew, of course, the thrill of winning big races. But, I reflected, why was I in this business? I drove north to Bay Meadows in a blue mood.

I linked up with my sister and the boys. This time, the almost-two-year-old, Alex, was going along in addition to Will, now four, and there was no Raffi as we sped up the 101. I had two errands—to renew my owner's license and to deliver the lucky silks to the jocks' room. In the jocks' room, the boys got up on the scale. Will weighed thirty-five pounds and Alex weighed twenty-eight pounds. One more boy and we would have had a jockey. For the next hour, we availed ourselves of the facilities provided for children at Bay Meadows—popcorn, candy bars, ice-cream sandwiches, and four of those machines where you put in fifty cents and manipulate a three-pronged grabber into picking up a stuffed toy. After four dollars, we had the head of Steve Young in a box.

We went out to the trackside seats to watch the fifth race. Allen came up. I introduced Allen to Alex, who said, "Hi, Allen." The boys were short. Alex was probably the shortest person at the track, which turned out to be a good thing, because, from where we were sitting, he could not see one of the horses in the fifth race break down and fall over, my old nightmare. Nor could he see the jockey roll under the infield rail and other horses leap over the down horse. Best of all, he couldn't see the stricken horse jump to his feet and fall down again and stay down, a sure sign of a fatally broken leg. My sister turned to me, and we spoke in low tones. She said, "Is he all right?"

I said, "I don't know about the jockey."

The ambulance came up.

"What about the horse?"

I shook my head.

"Is he going to be all right?"

I shook my head. The boys weren't listening, were arguing over Steve Young's head.

"How do you know?"

"He got up and fell down again. They probably can't save him."

"Is he in pain?"

"They say that the pumping adrenaline keeps them from feeling pain right away. For half an hour."

"What are they going to do?"

The boys were not listening.

"Put him down."

"Shoot him?"

"Not with a gun. They give him a shot of barbiturates. In the Sleeping Room."

We sighed.

Then I saw a brown horse near the ambulance, a horse being

led, and for a moment I thought there had been a miracle, that the down horse had gotten up and turned out to be okay, but the horse being led was actually the first horse to come over from the barns for Wowie's race, and soon there they all were. While we were watching them, the horse ambulance drove away.

Wowie was the last in line, but we could see him clearly, because his head was up and his eyes were wide with his usual pre-race excitement. He didn't know that his odds were fifteen to one, that the *Form* didn't give him a chance, that he had to run from way outside—the ten hole in a twelve-horse race. Once we had shepherded the boys into the saddling area, I could see that Allen had indeed worked hard. The horse walked with some measure of calmness around the saddling enclosure while Allen tacked him up. Others were more obstreperous for once. When he came our way, Alex, Will, and I chanted, "Wowie, you're the man! Wowie, you're the man!" but we weren't exuberant or hardly, even, hopeful.

How many horses break down while racing? In the summer of 1998, after Hollywood Park installed new footing on the dirt track that was quicker to drain in the winter, many more horses broke down at Del Mar, which had its same old footing, now contrasting much more sharply with the Hollywood Park footing. Seventeen was a shockingly high number, and there are several ways to look at it. In eight weeks of racing, Del Mar runs 560 races with average fields of nine. That means that, out of almost five thousand runs, seventeen, or just over a third of a percentage point, ended in tragedy. Or, since some of the breakdowns took place during morning training hours, you could say that there are approximately two thousand horses training and running at Del Mar, and if they are on the track seven days a week, doing something, then out of 112,000 exercise or race opportunities, of which four-fifths are galloping or jogging rather than working or racing, an even smaller percentage of those outings resulted in breakdown. Or you could say that seventeen out of two thousand horses, or not quite 1 percent, broke down in the course of the summer. Horse racing is a dangerous sport, and the participants are followed closely throughout the race by an ambulance, which travels down the track behind the field and arrives at the scene of any accident within seconds. Accidents happen when horses interfere with one another, when horses take a bad step and break something, when horses suffer pulmonary embolisms and fall in front of those running behind. Accidents happen when unscrupulous trainers mask injuries or unsoundness with drugs and send a horse into a race knowing he's not all there. Chris McCarron, who thrived in racing longer than most jockeys, had a reputation for scratching horses if they didn't seem right to him as he was riding them to the post, and he was wise to do so—a horse who is hurting even a little bit puts undue stress on the legs that are not hurting, and those are the ones that break under the strain. A trainer who knowingly puts an unsound horse into a race is cruel, but even the most careful, knowledgeable, and honest trainer can watch his horse fall victim to bad luck. The world of horse racing contains both danger and cruelty. If cruelty were entirely eliminated, danger would still exist. If danger were minimized (and it has been in modern racing, with things like forgiving rails and padded gates), accidents and bad luck would still exist. And it is worth pointing out that European horses, and other horses trained on grass rather than dirt, tend to break down less frequently. One friend of mine says, "If we were real racing men, we would send all our horses to Europe to train and race," and, I suppose, move there ourselves.

My feelings about the evils of racing don't shed much light upon the subject. I hope nothing happens to Wowie or Waterwheel. I believe Alexis is the most careful trainer at the track. I wish I lived in Chantilly, the center of racing in France, where the turf is perfect, or Cambridge, New Zealand, where the race-horses live in pastures rather than stalls. It comes into my mind when the horse breaks down in the fifth race that somehow this means that no one will break down in the sixth. Given the nature of horses, every horse can be a danger to himself at any time, at the track or away from the track. Finally, though, the world of horse racing is an irretrievably compromised world, a world where moral questions crop up every day, much more readily and consequentially than they do in most of the rest of life, and that makes horse racing interesting and compelling as well as fraught with risks of all kinds, and not only physical ones.

I followed Allen to the walking ring and met the jockey, who looked as good in the lucky silks as Goncarlino Almeida, Chris McCarron, P Val, and all the others had looked. The saddle cloth for our number, ten, was a rich violet that set off the dappling of Wowie's shining gray coat.

We placed our bets (forty dollars to win at sixteen to one would be a nice $680) and went to our places in the window of the Turf Club. I stood the boys in front of me. The head of Steve Young was disregarded for the moment. Wowie loaded and stood with his usual good manners—there had been no trembling in the gate for months. I told the boys to look at the number-ten gate, and then it opened.

All the horses poured toward the rail, and the favorite, number one, a three-year-old who had cost forty thousand dollars as a yearling and just broken his maiden seventeen days before, went out ahead. We could see Wowie's face, with his white blinkers, clearly behind the other horses, and as he ran past the grandstand and into the turn, he was in the sixth position. Around the turn, I could count the sets of haunches out from the rail, one, two, three, and then his, four. He was making a very long trip.

He stayed with the others halfway around the turn, then slipped back. On the far side, he was safely alone—five horses in a bunch ahead of him, six horses in a bunch behind him. I began to get gloomy again, but he was running beautifully—stretching out easily and smoothly, not laboring, just saving himself. Although the times were fast enough—forty-six and change at the half—the race seemed slow to me. Behind me, Allen was sitting down, saying, "What are you doing? What is he doing?" In front of me, both boys were watching intently. The race seemed slow because there was so much for the horse to accomplish—in my own body I could feel the horse and the jockey trying to find a way through the first five horses. But there was nowhere to go. Finally, just into the second turn, I saw my horse's head lift and move to the outside—the jockey had decided to go around. Allen continued to shake his head. Though the jockey was doing his best, this was a textbook bad trip. Out of the second turn, they were still wide—the fourth lane out and looking for a break. And then they got one. The first horse dropped back, and Wowie and the horse he had been running behind moved up, with Wowie moving just a little faster than his rival. In the last furlong, he made up almost three lengths on the other horse, and he was still gaining. Another hundred feet and we would have claimed third. Allen jumped up to go down and meet the jockey. He was disappointed, as I suppose it was his job to be, but I was exhilarated. I was as exhilarated at our fourth (a month's room and board) as maybe Prince Ahmed bin Salman was at his Derby win. What exhilarated me was how the horse kept trying, how he was blocked here and blocked there and had to brake and go outside, but he kept coming anyway, digging in and trying hard and performing like a dedicated racehorse.

When we got to the jockey, he shrugged. Allen said, "If you'd found a hole, you'd have been a genius. But you weren't."

We all nodded. True, he was not a genius. True, the horse was not a genius. True, none of us were geniuses, but we had the pleasure of a hard job well and safely done.

Safely done. When I spoke to Alexis on the phone, we cooed about his effort, his work ethic. She said, "Oh, he was five wide around the first turn. There was no one in the inside lane." Five wide! Might as well have run through Sacramento! Then she called back, astonished and upset. A famous horse, a horse being trained by someone we knew and liked, had keeled over in the test barn after the third race. Just called out, reared up, keeled over. "Probably a heart attack. And—" She paused. "No, I don't want to talk about it. What kind of business are we in? What are we doing to them?" She hung up.

Three days later, we were having dinner in a restaurant in Pasadena—Alexis and her friend Nikki, who was married to the jockey Gary Stevens, me and my two friends Jack and David. David was a writer and an experienced horseman, who was raised with a hundred or more horses on a legendary farm in Australia, whose antecedents had been hunting, jumping, playing polo, racing, and steeplechasing for generations. Now he rode from time to time, but only under the best circumstances—at the Barbizon in France, say, when the weather was perfect and the horses were light as feathers. Nikki had gotten into racing because of her father, who had changed his career in mid-life from computer programming and repair to bookmaking. She had been born and raised in Doncaster, the home of Doncaster Racecourse, in York, England, where they run the St. Leger, traditionally the third leg of the British Triple Crown. There she had learned to ride before going on to Newmarket. We were talking about risk-seeking behaviors, another version of the eternal conversation about horse racing and its dangers. I said, "But don't you think the real risk-seekers ride steeplechasers?" Nikki looked at me. She said, "Nah. You know, those fellows, they get to Newmarket when they're sixteen or seventeen, and they have a year or two riding the flat horses, and then they get too big for it. You've got to ride at nine pounds under your natural weight, and some of them can do it, but most of them can't, so they go try and be a jump jockey, or a National Hunt rider." She took a bite of her lamb. "I mean, have you ever been to Newmarket?" She was gesturing toward me. "You've never seen so many little people in one place. Little plumbers. Little window-washers. Little butchers. You'd be quite out of place there. I don't see how you'd hold a conversation."

We laughed.

The talk turned to Waterwheel. Alexis said, "You know, Alex Solis' agent called me over to his car as I was leaving the track. They never do that." Alex Solis, a well-known jockey, had worked Waterwheel that day, a possible dress rehearsal for her first race, at Santa Anita, eight days away.

My friend Jack said, "Why don't they ever do that?"

"Oh, God! Most of the time after they ride your horse, they won't look at you for days afterward." She put her hand to the side of her face, like a perp avoiding the press. " 'Don't make me ride that one again! Don't ask me to ride her in a race!' But the agent called me over and said, 'Alex really liked your filly.' "

"How'd she go?" asked Nikki.

"Six in one-twelve and change. Galloped out in twenty-seven."

"That's fast."

"Too fast," said Alexis. "I told him to take it easy. But, you know, they get on 'em the first time and they just go for it, just to try it out." She shook her head.

"Gunning the Ferrari," I said. We all looked at each other. I said, "She's been working with colts. Older colts. She's too fast for fillies."

"Now she's got to race with fillies," said David.

Alexis grunted and made a gesture of a bossy woman elbowing other women out of the way. She laughed. "That's what she'll be like with fillies." I began thinking again that we had a guarantee.

In the morning, when we got to the track, Waterwheel was shining darkly in the sun, walking around with the other horses outside the shedrow. Every moment or so, she tossed her head or stamped her foot, or a quiver passed through her body. Her groom, Jose, was a tall, strong, and impassive older man who just kept stepping forward. He didn't even look at her. He was exactly what she needed—any more response or stimulation and she would have been in the air. I went over to her and said, "Hey, little girl." She pinned her ears and tossed her head, to all appearances insulted at the diminutive. I laughed, but stepped back. Jack and Alexis and I watched her from a distance as she threw her head again. She was tucked up and fit now. The soft, round, small filly who had shown up suddenly at the end of April had bulked out with muscle at Del Mar, and now had trimmed down and looked taut like a greyhound. Her legs were long and her strides were lissome and strong. Sometimes the loss of fat reveals parts of a racehorse that are badly conformed or awkwardly put together, but she looked as good fit as she had fat. She was as riveting to look at as any small, glistening, quick animal—a mink, perhaps. Alexis said, "Now's the time when they get a little bananas. She's ready, but she doesn't know for what." She grinned. My heart was fluttering. I said, "I'm supposed to be prepared for this. Jackie's and Wowie's harrowing adventures are supposed to have inured me to everything." But the fact is, the brilliant energy of every horse is new and fresh and precious, and the potential it holds for beauty or disaster is also new and fresh.

FOURTEEN

Training

THE TASK OF the horse trainer is to make something of the horse; the task of the horse is to become useful. Life is cruel to useless or dangerous equines. One of the great debates among horsepeople is whether to outlaw slaughtering horses for food—there are two slaughterhouses in Texas that ship the meat to Germany. The side that wants to outlaw the slaughter maintains that horses are different from cattle in their relationship to humans, and to put them into double-bottomed trailers, like cattle, and send them down the slaughter chute is to betray every aspect of the human/horse relationship.* The other side (which includes many vets) maintains that, without the option of selling horses to slaughter, irresponsible or impoverished owners would simply abandon them to die of starvation or disease rather than support them or euthanize them (which runs three to five hundred dollars, including disposing of the car-

---

*Eating horsemeat is almost taboo in America and Britain, but fairly common in continental Europe. In France it is called *chevaline*.

cass). Slaughter or euthanization is the extreme version of the Hobson's choice that is always present with horses. Every year, the federal Bureau of Land Management has to round up feral horses on federal lands, because the herds are overtaxing the ecosystem. Many are adopted out (in fact, in some parts of the country the feral herds are prized types that trace to superb Spanish horses of the seventeenth and eighteenth centuries, and look much like Andalusians or Lippizaners), but the ones that don't find homes must be put down. In a simpler and more common circumstance, when an owner has a horse that doesn't suit, he might sell it; if it is dangerous, then it is unethical to sell it, though a well-trained and cooperative horse is likely to have a good home for life.

When horses and men were expendable, riders and their mounts were trained in a rough-and-ready manner. In her memoir of a life with horses, Barbara Worth Oakford, in *My Seventy Year Trip to the Show Jumping Hall of Fame,* recounts watching the methods used by the U.S. Cavalry at Fort Riley, Kansas, early in the 1940s. New recruits and unbroken horses were started together: "As soon as the order was given to curry the horse, all hell broke loose. The man holding the horse was struck at, might have been bitten, and was dragged all over the place; while the other man was stepped on, knocked down . . . and kicked into the middle of next week. . . . If a man was injured to the extent that he was incapacitated, he was put on a stretcher and carried off to the infirmary and another man was assigned to his place" (p. 179). The next day, when the men and horses went out to the arenas in the cold wind at 7 a.m., their only protection against bucking, shying, and running away was to jam the horses' noses as closely as possible into the tails of the horses ahead of them in line. Once they were in the arenas, at least for a few days, chaos reigned as the men attempted to follow orders to trot and canter in straight lines around the periphery of the arena for two and a half hours at a stretch. As with the grooming, if anyone was injured, he would be carried off and replaced. In about ten weeks, as a result of continual work and repetition (to learn to jump, the men took the horses over a line of thirty-two jumps twenty times, with their arms held out to the sides at shoulder level so that the men would not touch the reins and the horses would learn to negotiate the jumps on their own), the men knew how to ride and the horses knew how to be ridden. Oakford herself became a great proponent of the cavalry method, because it made riding correctly second nature to her. But those days are gone.

Most of the people who buy horses these days are adults with leisure and discretionary income. Our horses are companion animals, recreational vehicles, sports equipment, and, for some, spiritual mentors. Many of them are carefully bred for jumping or dressage or endurance. They are expensive. We want them safe but not broken. In *Talking with Horses,* Henry Blake remarks that in thirty years of buying, training, and retraining horses (from the early forties to the early seventies) he found that "these have been, generally, of two types. The first type are very intelligent horses who have been frightened and brutalized by ill-treatment. In the early days, these were much the largest group we got. Today, most of the horses we get are in the second group—strong horses spoiled by weak handling, often by women for whom the horses are too powerful and too strong" (p. 97). Thirty years later, his observation still obtains.

In his book *The Covenant of the Wild: Why Animals Chose Domestication,* Stephen Budiansky points out that all domesticated species exhibit "neoteny"—that is, the adult bodies and behaviors of domesticated species are more similar to the bodies and behaviors of young wild animals than they are to those of adult wild animals. With special regard to dogs, Budiansky maintains that wolf cubs go through four stages of learning to hunt, and that the development of various breeds of dogs is arrested at the stage that is most useful for that breed. Thus, sheep-herding dogs learn to follow the heels of the sheep as if they were prey, but they are bred not to attack the sheep and bring them down, as wolves would do. Neoteny in dogs means that "infantile" adult dogs are playful, friendly, and willing to accept the presence of other species, characteristics that wolf cubs have but adult wolves lose.

Horses show neoteny in their bodies—the legs and bodies of domesticated horses, especially Thoroughbreds, are longer and lither than those of true wild equines, like zebras and Przewalski's horses. Adult horses also accept humans and other species in a way that zebras do not. A case could be made as well for equine playfulness—many of the activities we ask of horses, from jumping and dressage to cutting cows and performing in the circus, might be seen by the horses themselves as forms of play. Like dogs, maybe horses are always up for a game, whereas zebras are not. But horses are not as highly specialized as dogs. Some breeds and lines of horses are better runners or better jumpers or better dressage horses than others, but a jumper is much more likely to turn up in any horse breed than a hyperactive, yapping, digging, killing terrier personality is to turn up in a Great Dane.

If we have bred domestic animals for their "infantile" qualities, then that means we have taken raw material that was more like us than other wild species, and bred it over the millennia to be even more like us—longer childhoods, sustained attachment to us, susceptibility to the requirements of culture rather than insistence upon those of nature. In this context, it is interesting to look at the idea of training horses and educating humans as two versions of the same process, a process that takes the bent twig (the bundle of genetic material that civilization, on the one hand, and breeders, on the other, have selected for over thousands of years) and prunes it into the useful tree. Training a horse, like rearing a child, is really teaching it to take responsibility. Every activity that horses and humans do together, from grooming and doctoring and shoeing to racing and competing and breeding, is a sequence of small actions that add up to a process. At any point in the process, a horse can panic or resist or balk or push—that is, put his goals ahead of the joint goal. A well-trained horse understands the joint goal and joins the human in achieving it. In the course of any part of the process, a horse looks to his human with a question: Do I really have to jump this new jump? Do I really have to get into the trailer? Do I really have to tease this mare and then walk away? Do I really have to go through that tiny hole between that horse and the rail? And the human says yes. The horse who takes responsibility then asks himself the next question: Can I do it? And he may take the responsibility of saying yes, but he also may take the responsibility of saying no. Training promotes the horse's submission, but it also educates his judgment. Ultimately, in horses and in humans, the goal is that the individual will take responsibility for his actions—that is, will understand how intentions, actions, and results are connected, and will reliably choose to act in a way that will hurt neither himself nor others, even if there is some motive or stimulus promoting irresponsibility.

IN EDUCATING HORSES, as with humans, we have several interrelated systems to work with—attachment (the limbic brain), personality (the way the inborn possibilities of the species are mixed together in each individual), intelligence, and physical talents. In horses, as in humans, we have several goals—conformity to societal norms of behavior, doing useful work, health and well-being, and the realization of particular talents.

Horses, dogs, and humans all share at least one trait that has its origins in mammalian life. If they are focused on another and that other turns away, the horse, dog, or human becomes more interested in that other rather than less. No doubt this begins as a survival instinct on the part of the young mammal—when Mom moves away, looking for food, Junior must follow. And then, when Mom is doing something Junior needs to learn, Junior is programmed to pay attention. The reverse seems to be true of all three species as well—the child, foal, or pup is put on the alert when the other that it is focusing on turns toward it in a confrontational (literally, "front to front") manner. It may pay more attention, out of fear, but it may pay less attention, also out of fear. Rather than approaching or accepting approach, it may back up, or turn and run away. The body language of confrontation is a biological signal to the foal, child, or pup that it is in danger. Learning is more difficult in the presence of fear, because the mind is too preoccupied to receive new impressions. At best, the learner may, in retrospect, compare the rewards and punishments of learning or not learning something. But the lesson learned will always be associated in the learner's mind with the experience of fear.

A foal who weighs ninety to a hundred pounds at birth and three hundred pounds six months later is free to express his opinion of how he is being handled by running off or fighting back. The shortcuts of impatient parents or dog owners don't work with horses, especially young horses. Good trainers—for example those of the Dorrance-Lyons-Parelli-Berta school—make constant use of the young horse's attachment instinct.

They begin by turning the horse into the round pen and using a flag on the end of a whip to wave the horse away and to require the horse to move. Because the round pen is a bounded, curving space, the horse ends up moving, usually at a pretty good clip, around the periphery of the space. As the horse moves, he gets tired, but he also gets curious about the trainer, and willing or eager to turn toward him and find out what he is doing. He flicks his inside ear toward the trainer or looks toward him. At this signal of interest, the trainer lowers his whip and his arms, and turns slightly away from the eye of the horse, or he steps to the right, toward the back end of the moving horse. The horse soon learns to follow his instinct and turn off the track and come in to the trainer, who then pets him lightly on the face or the neck, and encourages these tentative moves toward attachment. If the horse signals submission but then fails to come into the center, or bucks, kicks out, or tosses its head, the trainer simply urges it forward again. The only punishment for not submitting is to keep going forward. The reward for submission is appreciation, rest, and a change of activity. As new lessons are begun, they are added into the context of the previous lessons. What is important is that the horse is always encouraged to "hook on" to the trainer, and the training process becomes a way of developing the relationship between the horse and the trainer. A barnful of horses trained in this manner are happy to see the trainer when he shows up in the morning, interested in what he is doing, and affectionate toward him, even though he may never have brought any of them a single carrot or other treat.

No aspect of the horse's life is ignored by this method of training, and every horse's quirks are addressed. For example, it was evident from the beginning of his training that Cheerful did not like to have his feet picked up or held. Since most horses see

Roy Forzani with Waterwheel at one and a half years, training her to approach.

farriers every six weeks for most of their lives, they can't be touchy about their feet. Ray patiently roped each of Cheerful's feet, session after session, until the horse was trained to stand quietly as soon as he felt the loop of rope tighten around his ankle. The bonus reward of this technique was later demonstrated when Jackie, who had been trained in the same way, happened to lie down in a pipe corral and catch his foot under the bottom pipe. Instead of struggling and possibly breaking his leg, he simply lay there, waiting for someone to come and release him. Horses often get their feet or legs tangled in rope or wire (a client of Ray's had a horse who got tangled in seaweed). If they've been taught that a tightening rope means "stand still," they are more likely to avoid injury. As another example, it isn't natural to a horse to step backward. In stressful situations, they almost always try to escape by pushing or leaping forward; they also use their weight and power to establish dominance. Ray (and every other knowledgeable horse trainer) spends a lot of time teaching horses to back off at a touch or a signal, to move out of and stay out of the human's personal space, and to be aware of where the human is at all times.

Not every successful horse trainer uses the Dorrance-Lyons-Parelli-Berta method. European systems are often more rigid and require that the horse obey perfectly rather than ever think for himself,* but every responsible and successful horse-training scheme draws upon and develops the trainer's methodical side. Anger and impatience quickly rebound and work to the detriment of the trainer—either he gets hurt or he finds that a valuable piece of property has hurt itself. Cruel trainers,

---

*Horses imported from Germany, for example, who are trained to go forward with their chins tucked, are sometimes quite disconcerted when American trainers allow them to lift their eyes and look around. The disagreements between various European training systems and their American counterparts fill many volumes.

whose ways of handling horses are based on ignorance, anger, and fear, are, first and foremost, in danger. Good trainers, I have found, trainers who know how to handle horses and remain safe in their company, are calm and forbearing, observant and appreciative of progress, considerate of their animals, intuitive, and, of course, at least reasonably athletic (that is, if they want to perform a certain physical action, they can actually perform it).

Superior horse trainers, though, are backed by theories that give weight to the horse's desire to attach to the trainer (at the racetrack, the horse may attach to the exercise rider, the groom, and the trainer). And the trainer encourages the horse's attachment by being, above all, trustworthy. Trustworthy is not the same, of course, as consistent. A trainer can be consistently insensitive and mechanical. That is better than inconsistent, and trainers who are simply consistent can get pretty far. Their methods work pretty well with many horses, who at least learn what to expect and how to avoid pain. Most horses, given consistent handling, can make something or other of themselves. Trustworthy, though, is better than merely consistent. Trustworthy is consistently responsible, reliable, and possessed of good judgment. Anyone can be untrustworthy—even the most loving owner can be untrustworthy because she is ignorant or fearful—and everyone can become more trustworthy.

In the course of good training, all facets of the horse's being are developed together. The basis of the training is the horse's growing trust in his trainer and increasing willingness to do as the trainer asks him.

The next level of the pyramid is the horse's growing ability to understand what it is the trainer wants him to do. An example of this is the first time we tried jumping Essie at the end of the rope. We set the fence at about eighteen inches and trotted her through it. She kept trotting, knocking the poles every which way. We set the fence again. This time she trotted through just as willingly, but she tried picking each foot up higher at the trot. The third time through, it dawned on her to bend her front knees and lift them over the poles. She never had to go through that learning sequence again. Trust, willingness, and understanding reinforce one another.

The next level of the pyramid begins when the trainer asks the horse to do something that takes either a physical or a mental effort. Most horses are like most people, in that without discipline they condition their bodies in the most convenient way. Playful horses will play, horses that like to run and romp will do so, but most adult horses amble about not far from the pile of hay, or they nibble on the grass, or they stand together in the shade, dozing. An athletic horse, like an athletic human, has to develop his strength and wind systematically, pushing himself beyond comfort on a daily basis, so that his comfort range expands. Theories about horse conditioning differ, as theories about human conditioning differ, but they are essentially similar—bear weights, climb hills, raise heart and respiration rates, do stretching and suppling exercises, and practice skills. Much of training a horse has to do with teaching him to bend laterally, step the legs over, and supple the spine. As the horse does these exercises, he develops the muscles along his topline, from his ears to his tail, and his whole body becomes stronger. His gaits become more powerful, more rhythmic, and smoother, while his body changes shape and becomes more beautiful. But training a horse for athletic performance should be the last add-on— the level that trainers undertake after the horse has been emotionally and intellectually socialized.

At last, the well-trained horse is a thorough joy to be with. His body is soft and supple, he is relaxed, and his mind is at

ease. The rider can influence him with subtler and subtler signals: horse and rider communicate by shifts of weight and attention, the merest electrical impulses that pass between their
muscles and their minds. Their relationship is in some sense
unique in the animal kingdom, like a pair of skaters, for example,
but even faster and more delicate, because, however athletic any
human is, a horse is more athletic; however sensitive any person
is, a horse is more sensitive. As the horse becomes supple and the
rider becomes trustworthy and tactful, the rider becomes more
adept at communicating only his intentions rather than his
intentions mixed with other, unintended signals; the horse
becomes more trusting and therefore still more attentive. His
performance improves, his skills improve, his life improves.

Quite often, a horse who is being well trained will put in a
good, obedient session, then be turned out afterward to roll or
move around. The horse will discharge some mighty bucks and
kicks, will gallop about and even squeal. He is getting rid of
pent-up energy that he voluntarily controlled during the training session, when he tried hard to please the trainer and do what
was desired. Such post-lesson antics are a good sign that, in spite
of training, he retains his energy and sense of freedom.

Horses go at their training idiosyncratically. Some horses,
like Kiss Me, seem to understand from the beginning that new
activities are fun. They are energetic but patient, and not easily
distracted. Other horses, like Cheerful and Waterwheel, learn so
quickly that they need constant new forms of stimulation to
keep them interested. If Cheerful gets bored, he might turn his
newly acquired fitness and suppleness against the rider and buck
him off. When the program remains demanding, he remains
attentive. Essie, who is lazy and calm but basically eager to
please, needs to be revved up just a little—maybe required to put
out 15 percent more than she wants to—but the new level of fit-

ness and the habit of making an effort come readily to her. Horses like Jackie, who have strong agendas of their own, require more persuasion. They have to experience the insistence of the trainer over and over in order to accept it and to understand that forms of achievement prescribed by humans are worth working toward, because they are fun and because they are something that the horse and his human can do together. Easily intimidated horses like Wowie are actively looking for someone to trust. They do what they are told, but require patience in building their tolerance of novel situations.

Each of these horses could go the wrong direction and end up worthless or dangerous. Jackie could end up frightening his owner, gaining dominance bit by bit until he became utterly convinced that he owed nothing to anyone but himself. Wowie, though compliant, could become more and more panicky. Essie could turn off completely, and just refuse to do much of anything. Cheerful, an athletic and powerful bucker, could buck the wrong person off at the wrong moment, and be left alone to get into still more mischief. Even pretty good raw material, like Kiss Me, could be pushed too far too quickly, or consigned to a less-than-alert rider, who might offend or confuse without meaning to.

The natures of horses are dynamic. Their affections, their ambitions, their mental stability, and their intelligence, along with their physical conditioning, grow and develop together, or decline and deteriorate together. Their progress requires systematic intervention on the part of a human more than canine behavior does, not because they are less intelligent than dogs, but because horse breeders have not specialized their horses genetically as much as dog breeders have. Most horses are generalists; their specific talents need to be solicited. The growing number of "guide horses"—that is, miniature horses trained to

lead the blind—is evidence that a task once considered exceptional for a dog is well within the powers of the right-sized
horse.

HOW DO WE amateurs become more like superior horse trainers and less like ourselves—that is, more capable of reading our
horses and giving them what they need when they need it?

One thing we can do, of course, is become stronger, more
athletic, and more adept physically, simply to cope with the
unexpected. A spook or a buck that at one time would have
unseated me no longer does so. Someday, I hope, it won't even
startle me, because I will have seen it coming.

Another thing is to read about horses and systems of horse
training. Horsemen from all disciplines and all ages have plenty
of interest to communicate. If we adhere to one system in every
way—read only about German-dressage training, or only about
hunters and jumpers—we have no perspective on what our trainers are teaching us. I remember, when I was first eventing Mr. T.,
my trainer decided he was too strong for me and changed his bit
to a harsher one. He bucked and bolted—was obviously
unhappy. On the long drive home from an event where he'd
nearly pulled my arms out of the sockets, I remembered that
Mark Phillips had written that horses often run through the bit
when they are trying to escape pain, so when I got home I
informed my trainer that I was changing the horse to a gentler
bit. She said, "I take no responsibility for what might happen to
you at your next event." I was a beginner, but Phillips' logic
seemed valid to me, and at the next event the horse was much
more manageable. Many trainers are very good, but no trainer is
infallible. Reading books helps the rider learn more quickly.

Another obvious thing to do is to watch our horses and see

what they seem to be like. Not every behavior translates into a global personality trait. Mr. T. was deathly afraid of things like mane combings blowing over the ground at his feet, but a huge piece of farm machinery could rumble by without causing him to flick his ears. I came to know to be more wary of fluffy bits skating under his nose than of big noises or to-dos. Perhaps seven years at the racetrack inured him to certain kinds of chaos. The more time we spend with our horses, the more they present themselves to us as who they are, rather than who we think they are. If the horse lives in a stall, is groomed and prepared, is ridden by the trainer, and then cooled out by the groom and put away, we know nothing of him and he knows nothing of us (besides, horses like to be groomed, and like their grooms, because grooming is something they do to one another). A horse whose rider has observed him closely and earned his fondness might put himself out for her or take responsibility for her.

My favorite thing to do for my horses (and my own skills) is to not belittle their capabilities. I don't deny that they have predilections and opinions and desires and fears. I try to judge whether these qualities that they express are productive or not. Though I ride them and compete them, I try not to use them, or to think of them primarily in terms of utility. I admire their beauty and appreciate their friendliness. I hug them and kiss them and stroke them and talk to them. I compliment them and greet them. I try to understand the way they express themselves, and I give them the credit of thinking that they can come to understand the way I express myself. Every horse I've ever known has been interested in human lips. They want to smell or touch that part of one another's faces, and they also want to smell or touch that part of my face. Who's to say they don't appreciate a kiss? Likewise with a hug—horses curl their necks over one another in what appears to be an affectionate embrace.

When I put my arms around my horse's neck, he feels a similar pressure. He presses his head against my back sometimes. I also try to reward them for qualities I appreciate. The fact is, they are talking to us all the time, even when the animal communicator is nowhere around. The best thing we can do to train them is to listen.

FIFTEEN

Debutante

Two days before the all-important first race, Waterwheel worked three-eighths of a mile. The powers that be at the race-track, the folks who keep tabs on how the works go so they can be printed in the *Daily Racing Form,* gave her a (B), which means "breeze." Every word in the *Form* means something. "Handily" (which is always the word after Wowie's works) means "under some urging, putting out some effort." "Breezing" means "easy as you please, exerting no effort." But still she went three-eighths in thirty-six and two-fifths, a very fast time. "And she wasn't pulling on him," said Alexis, meaning Alex Solis, the jockey. "She did whatever he asked. She wasn't being head-strong." Alexis entered the filly in the race for Sunday. She drew the eighth post.

One of the charming aspects of horse racing in America is how many eyes are watching. I'm not referring to fans, but to hangers-about, workers, trainers, touts, denizens of the backside and the frontside. Since most American horses are trained at the track, they train in public. Not so in England, where they train on the downs gallops, or in France, where the training fields at Chantilly are huge, and grandly shaded by ancient trees. A stranger watching European horses train would quickly be recognized as an intruder. There are no official clockers to report work times, and, indeed, works are not often measured or timed—horses train against one another, and the result of their training is kept secret. The bettors and the bookies don't have much to go on when they place their bets. (And in England and Ireland, both the bettors and the bookies are betting—the bookies give more or less attractive odds, which the bettors take them up on or not. If the bookie feels that the bettors have an advantage, he "lays off" a portion of his bets with other bookies, in case he has given too long odds on a winner. Bookies and bettors can go bust. Thus, there is incentive for the trainers and the owners to keep training results secret, because owners and trainers frequently bet on their own horses, so they want the odds to remain as long as possible.) In America, with horses training at the track, training results are witnessed and published. A bettor who reads the *Form* knows about as much as everyone but the horse.

Successful American betting systems rely more on ever-elaborating statistical refinements than they do on tips from the barn. One set of numbers in the *Form,* for example, called Beyer Speed Figures, attempts to regularize how fast horses go over a single racecourse over a certain period of time, and then make these ratings comparable over all racetracks, thereby establishing how fast the horse was *really* going. The Ragozin System takes into account not only the surface of the track, but also the wind speed and direction during the race and the exact placement on the course of the turf rail (which is moved around to maintain the condition of the fragile grass). The available public information on all the horses running in any race gives the advantage to retention and interpretation of detail, and around every race-track there are dedicated interpreters of detail who have devoted as much time and energy to contemplation of their subject as any professor in any university in the country. And no doubt the two categories of scholars have been remunerated to about the same degree. Newcomers to the racetrack, especially on the weekdays, often view the regulars with pity and fear–here are smokers, here are men prematurely aged and impoverished by their addiction, here are people who seem to care nothing about the middle class and its values, here is the population to be stolen from, upon which the whole edifice rests–but I see the gambling differently. There are many easier ways of losing money gambling. The bookmakers in England are always threatening to withdraw from horse racing entirely, because it is more lucrative for them to take bets on simpler contests, like football. The gambling dollar flows and will flow–to lotteries and numbers games and sports bets and Wall Street and poker games and casinos. Gamblers everywhere will always feel that Heaven reached down and touched them personally if they win. And of course there are gamblers at the track who haven't looked at a horse in the flesh in sixty years–who never even step into the sunshine. But it is always available to them to go out and watch the animals and their jockeys on the track eight or ten times a day, five or six days a week, all year round. It is always available to them to recognize that, in addition to money, there are horses; in addition to greed, there is beauty and talent and effort and joy and heartbreak. Personally, I think the money is better spent supporting Santa Anita, with its gardens and flowers and Art Deco façade, than supporting any hotel and casino in Las Vegas, because every hotel in Vegas is a fake something, and Santa Anita is a real racetrack.

When I got to Santa Anita on the morning of Waterwheel's

race, I was eager to see whether the handicappers had really been paying attention and knew, as we knew, what a star-in-the-making our filly was. Alas, there was no evidence. Though she had worked as fast as one of Bob Baffert's fillies, and though her sire, Grindstone, had produced quite a few horses who had won in their first outing, the writers for the *Form* wasted no ink upon her. The track handicappers viewed her with indifference as well—the morning line on her was fifteen to one. Alexis had gone home to get ready for the afternoon, so I sat on a bench with the *Form* in my hand, looking at the topiaried hedges and the graceful walks and the flowers and statues, and indulged myself in a lonely moment. Here I was, a solitary toiler in the Thoroughbred vineyard, bearing my humble filly on my back, and what could be more pointless? It is easy to realize, in the end, that horse racing is pointless, because horse racing could disappear without a trace and only horse people would miss it. In this, it is not like politics or religion or agriculture, but more like French couture or formal gardens—what it adds to human culture is a flourish that people who had never known it would not miss. I was saved from this moment of existential despair by the ringing of my cell phone—friends were on their way, they were at gate eight, where was I?

Back in the barn, the filly was reposing herself in her bedding, lying curled up like a dog, a few straws in her tail and in her forelock. When I leaned over the stall door, she got up and came over to me, her ears friendly. I stroked her lightly on the face, but only twice—after that, she got that look that said, I can hardly resist; I do so want to bite you. She was elegant and charming. I did so want to hug her.

I was no longer thinking apocalyptically. It would be just another race, not a disaster. That my plane had not crashed, had actually been on time, was a good sign that life goes on, would go on. Still, twelve inexperienced two-year-old fillies were a daunting prospect. I wondered if the jockeys were trembling in their boots. But that was reassuring, too—many of the best jockeys in southern California were riding—Gary Stevens, Patrick Valenzuela, David Flores, Kent Desormeaux, our own Alex Solis, and a host of others, faithful enough in the continuation of Routine Good Fortune that they were willing to commit themselves to these scared little girls.

The fillies came over from the test barn and entered the saddling enclosure. Those who had started before were the wildest. Unlike Waterwheel, they knew what was coming—a crowd of people yelling was the least of it. About half of them pranced and reared and objected and kicked out. Some of the others rolled their eyes but didn't act up. Waterwheel walked along, said Alexis, in oblivion, lamb-to-the-slaughter-ish. She told my friends, "The second start is the worst. The second start, all the bad memories of the first start come flooding back but they don't have enough experience to relax." The filly was quiet but edgy while being saddled, and then walked around and around in front of the fans. Caroline came over. She said to me, "Don't you think she looks bigger?" I nodded. Caroline walked away. I said to my friend David-the-real-horseman, "That's what they always say to me, 'Don't you think she looks bigger?' I have no idea. I never ever register size until they get to chin level on me. She's still only chest high." Actually, there have been quite a few good little racehorses—Lyphard and his sire, Northern Dancer, were said to be fifteen hands two inches, but at least some of that was a gimme.

The pony led the fillies out of the saddling enclosure toward the walking ring, and we followed them. Behind us, the door to the jocks' room opened, and the jockeys came forth, adorned in brilliant colors. At Santa Anita, the two halves of the saddling enclosure form the wings of the stage that is the door to the jocks' room. It is always dramatic when the door opens and the jockeys come out, casually fit and genuinely athletic, as athletic as any humans on the face of the earth, and then it gets even better when they walk out into the sunlight and the green plants. They are the stars of the show, and everyone's eyes are on them. When they get to the walking ring and mount the glistening horses, it is a moment full of pleasure as well as potential.

Alexis threw Alex onto the horse. He fit her perfectly, evidence that she was still little, no matter how they viewed her in the barn. All around her, fillies jumped and skittered, edgy as cats, but she walked along. "Just wait," said Alexis.

As we were passing from the walking ring to the tunnel under the grandstand, I heard the woman beside me say, "Hornblower. She owns Hornblower, too." My head swiveled in this miraculous direction. Two women about my age or a little younger were consulting their programs. I didn't hear the next thing she said—possibly my mind had gone blank from wonderment—but I did hear her say "Hornblower" again. And she was smiling. It was as if this woman were my personal handicapper, blessing my filly with a thought, a hope. I said, "That's me. I own Hornblower." She looked at me in surprise, and then we introduced ourselves. She said, "We follow Hornblower. Good luck."

We ran up to the betting hall to place our bets. When we got to our box, all we could see of Waterwheel on the track was her bright-pink saddle cloth. I was distracted, and even when they showed her on the TV screen, I couldn't make anything of it. Fillies were putting up a fuss about going into the gate. That's all that I could discern. Then Waterwheel's haunches and luxuriant tail disappeared, nicely, with only a moment of reluctance, into the metal monster. The TV scene shifted around to the front of the gate, and they stood there for what seemed to me like a long time, and I was just beginning to remember famous bad times in the gate—fillies rearing and falling—when there they went. "Bad start," said Alexis. I hadn't seen it, but the evidence was obvious to all—instead of running ahead of them, as, according to Hali, the filly had always intended, she was alone in the rear, six lengths behind the trailers, and the leaders were stretching out their lead every fifth of a second. I put my chin in my hand and watched. After a quarter-mile, which was run in under twenty-two seconds, she was six lengths behind the tenth horse (the twelfth horse was still standing in the gate, and never did, in fact, leave it) and fifteen lengths, or three seconds, behind the leader. At the half-mile, just before they ran into the turn, she was a head behind the tenth horse, and about twelve off the leader. The time there was just over forty-four seconds, a time for a half that Wowie, for example, didn't know existed. There were two furlongs to go, and coming out of the turn, she was ninth, right between the eighth horse and the tenth horse. In the stretch, the filly boldly went where she had never gone before— into the pack, first one direction, then another, finding holes and filling them. She finished fifth, about ten lengths, or two seconds, behind the winner, who had run the six furlongs in under a minute and ten seconds, very fast for two-year-olds in their first starts. Alexis was pleased. I was excited. Wowie, too, had gotten lost in his first start as a two-year-old, but he had stayed lost, coming in dead last. But Waterwheel had learned the most important lesson—that if you run fast you can catch them after all.

We ran down to consult with Alex, who reported that in the gate she was scared of the other horses, and after the bad start he had decided just to let her do what she wanted rather than push her. Later, on the videotape, it was clear what she thought about the whole starting-gate experience. Her door opened, she jumped out, and then threw her head and nearly stopped, as if she was dumbstruck at where she found herself—out on the backstretch, surrounded by fillies, in the midst of banging and clanging and God knew what else. Only then had she thought to run.

However it went with Waterwheel, though, what was fine, more than fine, was the way the silly girls ran safely and steadily, the way the race played out with no accidents or disasters, a pattern as ritualized as a dance—almost deliberate, as I saw it in retrospect, some horses slipping back and others coming on and always the pounding stretching rhythm of their strides below and the smooth passing above of the jockeys' bright, quiet, curved backs. And the check! How joyful is the tiny check for fifth place that so easily could have been nothing!

The next day, Alex came by to say how much he liked the filly. Alexis said, "Wasn't she bold about going into the pack like that?"

"Oh, she could have run between their legs," replied Alex. So little, yes, but so quick, too. Here's what Alexis was proud of: the filly had run well, and without even Lasix (a diuretic used to control edema and "lung bleeding"), which every other horse had been given, and then she'd come back and eaten every crumb and thread of feed, and the next day she wasn't tired, wasn't hurt, and was ready for more. Alexis said to me on the phone, "But don't you think her body is longer? I do. That's why she gets those big strides. I think she's growing, really I do." I didn't care about her size, though. To me she looked like a ballerina, taut and strong, tiny and bold.

The filly communicated to Hali that she had come in

"almost third," which confirmed my feeling that horses can count to three.

WOWIE RAN AGAIN ten days after the filly, and he predicted, through Hali, that he would come in third. Yes, I was already counting the proceeds, which for the race he was in, a twenty-two-thousand-dollar starter allowance, would be a nice two grand or so, a good sum for getting through the month. AJ was home sick, so I did not feel comfortable winning the bad-mom-of-the-day award by driving two hours to the track, leaving him to the kindness of strangers in the form of the housekeeper. I went to the simulcast at the fairgrounds. I was already counting the proceeds in my head and applying them to the horses' feed bills. But he ran fifth, pretty much blocked by the front-runners until he lost his rhythm and couldn't find it again until too late to make a difference.

Why I should find this such a cause for discouragement was a mystery to me, but on the twenty-minute drive home, I began planning for his new career as a beautiful show hunter, all dappled gray and elegant and, of course, a gelding. If there is a show-hunter stallion in America, I've never heard of him. As usual, I consulted by cell phone with everyone I knew about the horse's imminent transition. I have to admit I was acting a little crazy, substituting a new fantasy for a failed one. Feeding my frenzy was the fabulous Jackie, who had suddenly grown up on the first of June, and since then been a daily pleasure as, I told myself, only a Thoroughbred could be. I had found something in the firstborn that I had never felt before. Surely there would be more of that in the second-born? Wasn't it better to be a fabulous riding horse than a mediocre racehorse?

Several interested parties had something to say about this.

My retired vet, who had known Wowie since he was a foal and seen the race, said, "That was very high-level company, and he had lots of bad luck. Don't give up now."

My friend David suggested that Wowie was a known quantity, whereas his two-year-old sister, Darlin' Corey, could prove much different and more ambitious. If we brought the male home now and turned him out, the sister could have her chance, and we could be playing with Wowie by the first of the year.

But, of course, the deciding vote was cast by the horse himself. At first he was angry about the race—balked at every turn, he had not achieved his goal of finishing third. By the day after, he was discouraged. It was always the same thing—he went out there, ran his tail off, got stuck behind some other horses, and couldn't get free. It wasn't like it had been at first, when he didn't know what was what. Did I remember that first race, where he thought he won just because he didn't have any idea what the finish line was? Indeed I did. Now he knew exactly where the finish line was and what he was supposed to do with it. With knowledge came new eagerness and self-confidence, but, even in a horse, I suppose, also the despair of knowing how challenging the real task could be. After Hali related these particulars, she looked at me and said, "If you take him off the track now, he'll feel humiliated. It won't matter to him how great a show hunter he gets to be. You need to let him go out a winner."

Alexis said, "You know what I think."

She thought I should geld him and leave him at the track.

She said, "He'll be back to the races in forty-five days."

And here came the Breeders' Cup, a whole day of races, full of favorites and long shots, rich owners and poor ones, million-dollar horses and five-thousand-dollar horses. You could take any revelation you wanted to out of this kaleidoscope of signs and omens. I chose the image of the almost white seven-year-old, With Anticipation, running like a cloud near the back of the pack in the mile-and-a-half Turf, kicking into gear at the beginning of the stretch, and nearly swiping the race from the best horse in Europe, a three-year-old named High Chaparral. The next morning, future white horse Wowie was gelded while he was eating his breakfast, in the usual racetrack manner, while standing, with a bit of a sedative and a nerve block to the genital area (away from the track, horses are usually given a general anesthetic and stretched out in the grass on their sides—when Jackie was gelded, at nine months, the vet tied his left hind leg up by his ear, an image of vulnerability that I've never forgotten). According to Allen, the horse didn't miss a bite of his breakfast.

"Did you see them?"

"Yeah."

"How big were they?"

"Oh, about the size of small limes."

"That's small."

"Well . . ." said Allen.

Yes, said my vet friends, that is small. Small normal, but small. Big for a Thoroughbred is grapefruits.

Alexis said, "I had a vet once who would take a few extra cuts with the scalpel and leave them for me looking like smiley-faces." No place like the racetrack.

Two days later, Allen called to say that Wowie still hadn't seemed to notice anything missing. All these men talked about this with a certain jaunty good humor. The deed was done. The horse could be integrated into normal horse/human society whenever I pleased. Wasn't that a relief?

It is true that there is something paradoxical about a gelding. Almost all male horses are geldings, and so geldings are utterly commonplace, and yet every gelding, having been reduced to just himself, is the paradigm of an individual whose accomplishments, such as they are, are all that he has. Geldings are made for humans, and are generally more suitable human companions than stallions or even mares, being less opinionated and easier to keep, maintaining their relationships as friendships rather than passions. Geldings are useful and good, and now the world contained another one.

I confided my regrets to Alexis. "Don't be crazy," she said. "I was crazy for you. Remember my two stallions that I took to horse shows? Everyone said they loved them! Everyone was going to breed to them, but no one ever did. Even the one I sold to the biggest horseman in Atherton. You don't need to give yourself endless trouble keeping a stallion. I already learned that lesson for you."

"I admit that." There was a moment of silence while our thoughts began to gather and turn in another direction. I said, "Have you talked to Mindy?" Mindy was in charge of Darlin' Corey.

"She's ready to come in," said Alexis. "She's ready to breeze."

"She's so big. She's made of muscle. Much bigger in every way than he is. And very observant. Observant without being hypervigilant, you know what I mean?"

I felt the acceleration of hope, fantasy, love, pleasure. I felt myself smiling.

Alexis said, "Mindy says we're going to love her."

I felt myself grinning.

SIXTEEN

Horse and Human

I WOULD HAVE to say that, when I wrote a check for thirty-seven hundred dollars to buy Mr. T. in 1993, I did not know I was going to embark upon a course of training that would change the way I looked, thought, felt, believed, and acted. I saw the horse as a dangerous but alluring pet, a mystery, an opportunity to revisit a childhood dream, a charity project, and a potential friend. I had been mostly away from horses for twenty-five years at that point. Kinesthetic memory meant that I could still sit up there pretty well, still walk, trot, canter, and jump. It didn't even take me that long to get fit. The fifteen pounds lingering from my last pregnancy fell off in a month; more important, I stopped caring about it. I was simultaneously so fascinated and so ignorant about my new endeavor that mere self-image ceased to interest me.

The first new thing I acquired after the horse was a new set of associates—riding instructors. They seemed necessary to mere survival, and so I signed up for many lessons in which I was told over and over to put my heels down, look up, go forward, sit up straight, square my shoulders, lift my hands, turn my thumbs up, close my fingers on the reins, loosen my elbows, and relax. Being told what to do was a sudden and shocking change for me, since I was a novelist, a teacher, a parent, and a taxpayer. I was used to telling others what to do. I probably hadn't been told what to do, except in the friendliest, most respectful manner, in twenty years.

Good riding instructors are usually polite, but they are always direct. They don't make requests and they don't say "please." They know they are responsible for the student and the horse, and they establish authority immediately. Riding students, already unsure of themselves, are usually willing to cede authority. So that was the first lesson—I didn't know what I was doing; I had been returned to childhood, to a "state of unknowing," as Buddhists say. I was prepared to experience incompetence all over again. But that turned out to be the least of it. Even though my instructors were kind and straightforward, I soon recognized in myself a roster of shortcomings that was long and detailed. "Weak" and "uncoordinated" I could handle—I had never pretended to be athletic—but add to that "fearful," "impatient," "distractible," "inconsistent," "garrulous," "undisciplined," "defensive," and "indecisive." And I knew these were global traits, not just horse-related ones. I knew I had been getting by for years without having to address these shortcomings— or, rather, I had been addressing them with what seemed to be my only balancing qualities, "well meaning," "well disposed," and "clever."

I did what I was supposed to do. I practiced keeping my heels down and my eyes up. The effect of this was to orient my body properly on the horse, and, indeed, properly on the planet, so that, as in walking upright, gravity would promote stability rather than undermine it. The second effect, never to be underestimated, was to keep my eyes and mind forward, into the immediate future. To look down is to enter into a trance of self-consciousness and, potentially, to fall. A rider looking down is already beginning to part from her horse, because her seat and thighs are already beginning to lift and tilt forward. Her horse is already beginning to react to her shift in weight by shifting his own weight. He is getting ready to stumble.

I settled my shoulders, loosened my elbows, turned my thumbs up, closed my fingers on the reins, and thereby entered into a conscious relationship with my horse. From my body orientation, he could infer whether I was balanced or frightened, tense or weak, but through my hands and arms and shoulders, I communicated to him. I could do so tactfully, considerately, knowledgeably, and self-confidently, or insensitively, tentatively, and unconsciously. Through my arms and hands I told him what to do, where to go, how to carry himself, but also whether I was aware of his responses. I discovered that quite often I "spoke" but then didn't listen to his reply, because my arms and hands tended to fix themselves. This was a global shortcoming, too—in my relationships with my family and friends, I realized, I frequently held my breath while they talked to me, just waiting to continue with what I had been going to say all along. A rider's hands and arms tell the horse how self-centered the rider is, and whether, in order to defend himself, the horse needs to become self-centered as well—to brace his jaw and his neck against the rider's unresponsive upper body.

With my lower legs, I urged the horse to go forward. Here was my motivation made manifest. Did I really want to go forward, and so squeeze or kick with resolution, or was I content with half-measures? I could be kind and sensitive with my hands, but also ambivalent with my heels, ceding my rightful decisions to the horse, letting him decide, not where to go, but how to get there, and even, over fences, whether to get there at all. Going forward took some actual courage, expressed moment by moment as the horse and I moved across the ground. It was a different sort of courage from what I was used to. By contrast, I had always been a bit impulsive, ready to try things and then make the best of the consequences. Whatever courage I had manifested before had a large component of luck and momentum, not much thought or resolution. But if I failed to urge the horse forward with conviction, stride by stride, all sorts of bad things would happen: stopping at fences was the most dangerous (the rider can always keep going, right off the horse), but looking graceless and helpless was nearly as humiliating, and sensing that the horse was fed up with me was upsetting, too. Every time I took a riding lesson, and every minute of that lesson (let's say three times a week, forty-five minutes each time), I was confronted with whether to live by conviction or not, just through the process of trying to stick on the horse and cause him to do things. My experience was not at all unique but, rather, the routine experience of any adult learning to ride a horse.

I COMMITTED SINS and errors. I hit the horse with my whip in frustration. I clumsily jerked him in the mouth without meaning to. I interpreted his misunderstandings as disobediences, and let disobedience turn into willful resistance by being intimidated by it. As I took over more and more of the care of the horse from those who knew what they were doing, I made different types of mistakes. Once, I opened the back of the trailer without untying the rope, so that he broke out of the trailer and ran down the driveway. I was often inattentive and got into danger, both from the horse and with the horse. This was my worst and most long-standing failing. All my life I had been more or less lost in the clouds. As a child at school, I stared out the window, not even daydreaming or forming thoughts. I had a wandery way of walking from one place to another, even when I was going directly from point A to point B. I had a wandery way of talking and writing, too, never minding an interesting digression. Family life and career posed a challenge that I met by always trying to do two things at once. While I cooked and cared for the children, I plotted novels and worked out character quirks. But such obliviousness was dangerous around Mr. T., who was a Thoroughbred after all, energetic, alert, and sometimes skittish. I often felt embarrassment and sometimes felt shame at the mistakes I made with him.

My athletic skills did not progress very fast. The body learns by repetition. The older body needs more repetition, and the older not very athletic body needs endless repetition. And, of course, my garrulousness led me to bombard my horsey friends with questions and to propound foolish theories (some of which, no doubt, have found their way into this book).*

But as John Lyons, the famous trainer, points out on his Web site, horses are forgiving, even of amateurs. He maintains that if the trainer or the rider stops doing the wrong thing, whether the wrong thing is intentional or simply a product of inexperience, the horse will stop doing the wrong thing, too. When Mr. T. and

---

*I once asked a group of trainers whether adult men and adult women differ in the lessons they learn when they come to horses in middle age. The answers, of course, were both predictable and illuminating. Women generally reproduce my experience. They are afraid of going fast, making decisions, and committing themselves to directing the animal. Their commonest and gravest sin is to urge the horse forward and pull him back at the same time, afraid both to go forward and to not go forward. Such techniques make the horse numb or crazy. If they overcome that hurdle, then, often, they still have difficulty with athletic focus—seeing the goal (the jump, the finish line, the letter at the end of the dressage court) and going straight there, undistracted by the process.

I came together, we both brought presuppositions to our new relationship. I see now that he was irritable and defensive. If any horse passed his stall while he was eating, for example, he would kick out a time or two, making a racket against the boards, probably warning others away from his food—this makes perfect sense given how thin and no doubt hungry he was after his hard time on the low end of the pecking order in his previous pasture. After he came to know his meals were going to be regular and satisfying, he stopped kicking out. He also found certain operations annoying—being groomed (perhaps because he had thin skin), being shod, being vetted. He was hard to handle, but I loved him and I hardly noticed. As the years passed, he became more patient, and there were some operations, like giving shots, that I could perform easily because he trusted me. He was always forgiving. Defensiveness and irritability, which had seemed to be fixed characteristics of his personality, faded away like the obliviousness that had seemed to be a fixed feature of my personality.

Life with Mr. T. gradually forced me to address my fears, or, rather, by forcing me to address myriad small fears—am I going to fall off, is he going to kick me, will he be hurt in some way when I get to the barn in the morning, have I done, am I doing, will I do the wrong thing, will it be the wrong thing even if it seems like the right thing, will I not recognize the wrong thing, omigod what's that noise, that sudden movement, that odd thing?—it forced me to address the feeling of fear itself. Horses are fearful by nature and are made more fearful by their companions. A fearful horsewoman puts herself in ever more danger as she infects her horse with fear. It was thus required that I practice stemming fear as systematically and effectively as possible—sitting with confidence and authority in the saddle, asking the horse to habituate himself to the fearful object, breathing evenly and deeply, remaining calm in any small crisis. Many crises were weathered without harm. But there were fears that were realized. I did fall off. I did break my leg. Once in a while, the horse was hurt or ill when I arrived at the barn. I learned symptoms and signs; I nursed horses through injuries and had to accept bad prognoses and death sentences. Mr. T. colicked after six years and could not be saved. Yukie, who had cost me a lot of money, got so broken down in the hind fetlocks that after only two years he could not walk well enough to get enough to eat, and had to be euthanized. A mare died foaling, along with her foal. A two-year-old was discovered to have a severe spinal defect. Persey contracted an incurable lung disease similar to asbestosis.

If I had known ten years ago what I know now about having lots of horses, I would have thought the experience would make me more anxious and more susceptible to despair, but it has made me less so. So many crises have been gotten through, so many accidents and griefs and worries have been survived, so many potentially painful misadventures averted. What about the time Jackie kicked up and missed my face by six inches? What about the time Essie slipped in her pipe corral and put her head through the bars, but got up without breaking her leg or her neck? What about the time Lucy, Persey's dam, caught her shoe in the ramp of the trailer as she was being driven down the road, and wrenched her leg so hard that she pulled the shoe off, but was fine the next day? Through these crises, griefs, and adventures I became what I had never envisioned before—philosophical.

To be philosophical is not to be cold or indifferent or even stoic. It is not to numbly endure the parade of misfortune while shaking your head and sighing and saying, Well, that's life. To be philosophical about horses is to recognize that, with horses as with Hamlet, character is fate and irony abounds. My first

Cheerful a few months into his serious dressage training, four years old. Barbro Ask-Upmark is his rider and trainer.

moment of being philosophical with Mr. T. must have occurred some two or three years into our life together, long after I had somehow transferred all my other fears (for my children, for the state of the nation, for my own safety) onto him. These ran the gamut: Was he getting enough to eat? Was he safe? Was he bored out in the paddock with nothing to do? (I actually envisioned myself going out and reading aloud to him.) And then it occurred to me that he had lived fourteen years before I knew him, all over this country and even the world; that he had survived; that he knew how to be a horse and to take care of himself. Given a modicum of good care and reasonable oversight, he could continue to take care of himself as he always had. This first calming insight led to others. I came to understand the "insurance effect" as applied to horses. There is, of course, no end to the efforts an owner can make to ensure her horses' safety–they can be wrapped and blanketed and never allowed to run around, even alone, one horse in a large paddock. You can buy a video camera for your trailer and watch the monitor as you're driving down the road. In Mr. T.'s case, it seemed to me that he could be protected from a habit he had that caused repeated injuries to his right eye. He loved to roll, especially in the mud, but he had very high withers. As he got older, he found it harder to roll from his left side to his right side and then back over, and he began to use his head and neck as a rather violent lever. Once in a while, maybe twice a year, he must have forgotten to close his right eye when he was levering himself from right to left, and he would poke his eye and reinjure it. I got tired of this rather dangerous injury, and so I bought him a hood that had a half-blinker on the right side, thinking it would at least protect the eye. It didn't occur to me that the hood itself would be a danger, but it was–it was made of polyester, and after several days of wear, the sharp fibers of the polyester had dug into his skin; when I went to take it off, it made wounds. Another time, I put a blanket on him, but the blanket caused rubs, so I bought another covering, like a ladies' slip, to go under the blanket. The morning after I put it on him (according to instructions), I went out to discover that he had tangled himself in the two coverings, and only his good sense had prevented panic and injury. The fact was, it was safer to keep it simple–doctor the eye when he injured it, let him grow his coat in the winter and keep himself warm. The "insurance" principle works geometrically with horses–the one thing you do to prevent a mishap often results in two smaller problems that must be dealt with, and whatever you do to deal with them results in four smaller but no less time-consuming procedures to deal with the results of those two. Insurance proliferates. You can prevent a horse from acting in accordance with his own nature only for a short time and with great effort. Better to understand his character and accept its contradictions and dangers, hoping that, with a little bit of luck, he will survive and learn. That is being philosophical, and it works no less well as an aid to rearing children and to accommodating spouses.

NO RIDING INSTRUCTOR or horse trainer ever asked me about or showed the slightest interest in the psychological sources of my difficulties in learning to ride. In this they were perfectly consistent with their approach to the horses they trained. The trainer attempts to carefully and systematically overlay the bad experiences with repeated good ones, to rehabituate the horse to the idea of doing his job by repeating an exercise, such as jumping low and inviting jumps, enough, but not so much that the horse becomes sour on it. The horse is required not to delve into his bad experiences and think about them, as, say, an analysand is, but to substitute good experiences for the bad ones until the good experiences become habitual. In doing this, the trainer also attempts to solicit the horse into a positive, calm, and trusting relationship, so that the horse will do what the trainer asks because he trusts the trainer not to ask more than he can perform. Trust in the trainer combined with a systematic approach gives the horse the relaxation to raise his level of performance bit by bit, until he realizes sometimes brilliant talents that he had not given much evidence of possessing.

The horse learning or relearning his task requires patience and repeated guidance through the task. He thrives on "discipline"—not in the sense of punishment, but in the sense of mastering a directed curriculum of training, of not being allowed to deviate from the curriculum, and of being enlisted by the trainer in the achievement of a series of clearly graduated goals. Once the horse is embarked upon his "discipline," it is counterproductive to return in any way to the state of mind that had originally prevailed. To allow the horse the opportunity to be afraid of jumping again, by asking for too much, is to undo everything the trainer has attempted to do. Likewise, it seems to me, encouraging a rider to talk about her fears or problems encourages her to focus upon them and waste time feeling shame or regret. The goal is to learn, not to undo. The metaphor of learning is not one of understanding why and then coming to terms with it, but one of forming new ways of thinking and acting. Even Persey, with her attachment problems, could be habituated to new experiences and helped to live a happier and more settled life. Horse trainers actually expect to have to return a horse to "the basics" of going forward, stepping over, bending right and left, and stepping backward over and over as it matures, just to make sure that the basics are confirmed in the horse's mind. They expect to do it, and so they are patient with it.

I began to wonder if maybe psychoanalysis is much like facing a horse with the same scary jump time after time and hoping he will get used to it and jump it in the end. I began to think of my horses and my trainers as coaches, who would patiently help me develop the sort of habits of thought and behavior that I desired. It's the rare horse who, when put into a jumping arena, jumps around on his or her own, or produces advanced dressage movements systematically when turned out to pasture (though many horses show just what sort of extended trot, passage, or croupade they might produce when they are free and feeling exuberant), but many horses have been brought through training to enjoy the sustained effort required to jump high, or go through seven minutes of complex movements set to music, or work a cow to a standstill. If the goals for the average horse and the average human are similar—good manners, useful work, health, well-being, and development of individual talents—I found through experience that practice goes a long way toward making perfect, especially if practice is combined with consistent and responsible trustworthiness on the part of the trainer.

IT IS an overcast Friday morning, late in October. My jumping trainer, Dick, is setting fences in the arena as Jackie and I amble through the gate. We greet each other, and Dick says, "So—how's Jackie this morning?"

"Alert. Very alert. Maybe too alert." His ears are up, and I can feel energy in his body even though he walked down the hill in a mannerly fashion. He is such an honest horse that he even misbehaves in an honest way—when he bucks, he warns me well in advance by trying to take his head away and then trying to take his shoulders away and then bucking. We pick up a trot. His stride is big, and after two or three steps, he relaxes. As we trot around the end of the arena, I change my mind. I say, "No. He's fine. He's perfect." He has focused that bit of extra energy into forward movement and readily yields to my hand and seat, which are, indeed, my will. My will, as a rule, isn't much, as my children will attest, but it is enough for this horse. Dick calls out, "Horses tend to slow down on the turn. I want you to push him a bit on the turn and ease him a bit on the straightaway." Of course. Into my mind comes a picture of how perfect this is, the horse elastic and vigorous in a smallish circle, then open and smooth down the long side. A moment later, Jackie lifts himself into a canter. It is analyzable—I have seen the picture of how he steps so far under with his supporting hind leg that he is placing it right beneath where I am sitting; his leg and body become a

U-shaped spring that lifts me forward—but it is not describable. It is neither floating nor springing. It is power without labor, thrust without force, the very opposite of any sort of aggression, the particular physics of his anatomy, the demonstration and the effect of his personality.

Nevertheless, he is not the same every day. On days when Dick is in the center of the ring, he is especially good, for lack of a better word. I mention this to Dick, knowing he will think I am flattering him, but I am not. Dick has a soothing voice and a quiet, though not impassive, demeanor. I enjoy taking lessons from him because the work is easy, or at least it seems easy until it is suddenly hard, and the confidence I'd built up from the easy bits takes me through the hard bits. He gives me that feeling that he has a long-term plan, and that these spaced poles we are cantering over will turn, with only the passage of time, into three-foot-six-inch fences that we will one day be cantering over as easily as this. It doesn't hurt that he likes Jackie. One of the things I have learned about horses over the years is that they should never be trained by someone, however expert, who does not think well of them. Dick thinks well of Jackie.

We begin by lengthening and shortening the canter. To shorten, I sit up and tighten my legs against his sides, then fix my hands slightly. His body becomes more erect and rounded, his steps become shorter but more elevated. After ten or twelve such strides, I release my hands and let him stretch out, and then, after twelve strides of that, I urge him with my legs to really move out. Then it is back to shortening. After three or four cycles of this, I bring him back to the trot, and he extends his head and neck downward and stretches all along his spine. When he is well warmed up, Dick has me trot over a trot pole followed by a small crossbar. Twice through that, then we are to trot down the line of four widely spaced poles in the center of the arena. Jackie, as always, does these things perfectly, especially the line of poles. Then he canters through, in even stride and rhythm, neither slowing down nor speeding up. His natural length of stride is just what it should be, twelve feet—just what horses in the show ring are expected to achieve. Once we are in the rhythm of jumping these poles, I notice that I don't have to instruct Jackie much at all. After each time through, we go to the center and Dick says something, then we go out to the rail again. Jackie canters without being asked, turns toward the poles on his own.

But once Dick has set up jumps rather than poles on the ground, Jackie is more cautious. Some horses are willing from the first attempt to jump anything—Persey is one of these. Life spooks her, but jumping relaxes her. She tosses her head and goes for it, a defined task that she can focus on and accomplish. Jackie likes to approach each new jump more slowly, at a trot, and get a good look at it. Once he has been over it one time, he relaxes and is fine thereafter. This could become, however, an inconvenient preference: most of the time, a show horse has to jump fences he has never seen before, and he is supposed to jump them willingly, in good rhythm, from the canter.

A couple of months ago, when we were only cantering over poles on the ground, I noticed that Jackie had his eye on things. We had cantered over a single pole, maybe three inches in diameter, lying on the ground. He cocked his ear when Dick set another pole right next to it, and when we cantered over it, two poles now three inches high and six inches across, he added more lift to his stride. I have never ridden another horse with such a refined awareness. Now it is the same. Whatever Dick does, Jackie pays attention to it and responds accordingly. Jackie's awareness of Dick is unusual, and surely comes from his years of being trained by Ray, the man in the center of the round pen. Ray's method promotes equine attentiveness and relationship. When Dick is teaching and I am riding, he has to be conscious of both of us, and every evidence indicates that he is. A few weeks ago, Dick leaned down and scratched a diagram in the sand with the toe of his boot, and Jackie went over two steps and put his nose down to it.

Today his hesitations are minimal. Everything I ask of him he produces, and soon I am oohing and aahing, what a horse, what a good, honest, well-behaved horse, and Dick agrees with me. But, cantering around from this exercise to that, I am dissatisfied. I have not expressed what I mean. He is not being obedient or without misbehavior. He is not like a child in school who is not at the moment causing a problem. He is something else, a horse giving gifts. I say, "It's not that he's good, it's that he's generous."

"Well," says Dick, "he's enjoying himself."

And so am I.

I AM AWARE, of course, that horse sports sometimes come under fire, as foxhunting has in England in the last five years. American equestrians may or may not support foxhunting, but they do recognize that foxhunting, steeplechasing, horse racing, three-day eventing, show jumping, rodeo, and all the other horse sports that take advantage of the horse's speed and athletic ability may seem suspect to nonhorsemen. Among horsemen themselves, there can be internecine squabbling about what sports are better or worse for the animals, and almost any horseman can make a case for his sport and against sports he doesn't like, for his own tender care of the horses and against the heartlessness of others. German-dressage trainers seem cruelly exacting to racing men, who seem reckless to fans of cutting horses, who seem cold and bloody, with all that roping and branding, to hunter riders. What all of these people share is a love of their horses. Even if that love has been dulled by temptations of money or years of unrelenting work, every horseman is moved from time to time by the generosity of the animal.

Defenders of foxhunting in England have suggested that the first thing to happen should foxhunting be outlawed would be a mass slaughter of hounds and horses, now rendered useless. Maybe. But, however clumsily, they are making a point. Horses are too big and too expensive not to work for a living. If they do not serve a human use, they have no place in the human world. They cannot live like dogs do in third-world villages, taking care of themselves on the periphery of human society, wandering in packs and eating offal. They must be fed, confined, cared for, and trained. Humans must be motivated to do the work and take the responsibility. A horse can earn money, do work, or provide fun. He cannot just stand there.

But the economic burden of horses is only the beginning. It may be that there really are two types of people, and that those two types are horse-lovers and non-horse-lovers, who truly do not understand what the fuss is all about. Horse-lovers self-select early in life—they look at pictures of horses, they watch horse movies, read horse books, and plan and scheme to have a horse. They grow up, buy horses, and consider every expense a privilege. It is not horses in the abstract that draw them or delight them, it is horses in the flesh, a horse, the right horse, the particular horse with a name and a face and a personality. Horse sports of all kinds channel the desires and ambitions of those horse-lovers into a discipline and also into an intimacy. The intimacy cannot exist without a structure, and each discipline is a structure within which every horseman or horsewoman makes choices about how to care for and treat the horses. Most horses tend to the feral without regular handling. A horse in a herd whose owner never visits or cares for it comes to relate primarily to horses—it lets the other horses intervene between itself and humans, it lets what it has learned about riding or driving or being groomed be overlaid by suspicion or reluctance. Good horse/human relationships must be renewed every day or so—more when the horses are young, less when they are older. A horse's relationships to other horses and to humans are always dynamic. Horses present us with unique responsibilities compared with all other domesticated animals. They also present us with unique opportunities for relationships, pleasure, and, in my opinion, enlightenment. I used to see them as giant dogs, moving furniture, furry enigmas. Now I see them as individuals, with memories and intentions and desires, disabilities and talents, histories and temperaments, strangely beautiful feet and ankles, nostrils and lips and eyes, expressive faces, mobile ears, warm and solid bodies, existing within a host of connections, some that I can see and some that I cannot.

The lesson continues. The jumps get slightly larger—maybe two feet three inches, about as high as Jackie's knees. Some he goes over without a fuss, some that look odd stop him. My job is to sit up and be positive, which means to give him courage. Dick believes that it is easier and safer to maintain the momentum and get over the jump somehow, but I believe, deep down, that stopping, though a crisis for a moment, will at least bring relief to the fear. This is wrong, but it is hard to eradicate. Allowing the horse to stop, especially when he has jumped the jump before and is no longer justifiably cautious, solves no problems and creates many. Even so. When I was afraid of jumping before, I used to look fearfully at the jumps and get the image in my head of falling off and going peacefully to sleep in the sand, what a relief. My former trainer combated this by ordering me to kick Mr. T.

right in the sides. I gave a little squeeze. She came up to me. She looked me in the eye. She said, "Take your legs away from his sides and kick him! Two strides out!" I did. He jumped. I demonstrated conviction, and then got some. Like Mr. T., Jackie is sensitive to my state of mind in every way, as well as cautious on his own.

Dick is endlessly patient. Unlike many trainers, he is willing to admit that he has himself become more cautious over the years. He still has convictions, though, and one of these is that this horse's youthful anxieties are becoming a habit that is bad in every way—dangerous, inconvenient, and a bar to realizing his talents. He drops his gloves two strides out from a plank jump that he suspects Jackie will want to look at. As I pass the gloves, I am supposed to flick him with the whip and cluck to him. I do so. He jumps awkwardly and raps the fence with his hind foot. But I have forced him to do it, and he has done it. In my own body, I feel how high he arced over it, as high as if it were burning. That he can make this arc is good—it shows what his body is capable of. That he made it over such a small fence shows that he is still afraid. After the fence, on our turn past the bank, we almost run into another jump. This is one of Dick's principles—that every movement the horse makes, especially every jump, has subtle ramifications for subsequent exercises.

We come around the end of the arena at the canter and head for the jump again. Jackie's rhythm seems just right to me, and as we approach the gloves, I feel real conviction. The jump is there, not intimidating at all, just automatic. The horse lifts himself with the right degree of effort, and one stride afterward, we easily make the small turn and come back to the center, the sort of turn you can make only when you are balanced and moving freely forward. The jump was fun, but the turn was the reward— the bona-fide manifestation that we had done it correctly. I am

ecstatic. Jackie is relaxed. Here is the important point—the pleasure of accomplishment and the relief of fear can be felt in both
our bodies. It is a physical sensation in the muscles and the
nerves, and it is shared as soon as it is felt.

Another of Dick's students comes in on her big gray horse,
the sign that our lesson is almost over. Dick and I are laughing
and agreeing that Jackie has had enough, and it is a good thing,
because, really, *I* have had enough—certainly a sign that Jackie
and I will never get far, in the larger scheme of equestrian
accomplishment, but fine for now. The gate is open, and I ride
the horse past Dick toward it. "He was good," said Dick. And
just then, the horse turns his beautiful brown head and pushes it
gently but decidedly into Dick's chest, asking to be petted and
admired as clearly as if he had spoken. Dick laughs and strokes
and embraces Jackie's head and runs his hand appreciatively
down his sweaty brown neck.

That's Horses

WHEN I SET OUT to write my book about my year with Wowie and Alexis at the racetrack, it soon became clear to me that I had no control over whether the book would end happily or unhappily. I conceived it, of course, as a typical horse-racing story—average owner and average horse overcoming the odds and justifying themselves through winning. The scary part, though, turned out to be not that we might not win, but that I might have to write an unhappy ending. Statistically, in fact, it was more likely that I would have to write an unhappy ending: stakes winners amount to only about 1 percent of Thoroughbreds.

By the middle of February 2003, a year after Wowie's first start of 2002, both the lovely gelding and the lovely filly were finished with their careers at the racetrack, and I had plenty of leisure to ponder their fates. What happened to Waterwheel was the more sudden. After she ran fourth on the dirt in a race at Santa Anita on the first of January, we decided to try her on the turf, in a slightly longer race, which would allow her to make use of her closing speed. The race was to be run on the hill course—the horses start at the top of a half-mile-long hill that doglegs off the outside of the second turn. It joins the main turf course just at the top of the stretch. To do so, it crosses the dirt track. Sometimes horses are a little disconcerted when they cross the dirt track—they try to jump the boundary. For most racehorses, the hill course is a tad more complicated than the customary oval course, more like something you might find in Europe.* Though I didn't like the idea of my filly's crossing the main track at top speed—not because of the optical effect of the boundary but because of the change in the racing surface—absolutely no one at the racetrack that I had ever spoken to considered this a danger.

Nevertheless, on January 26, during the sixth race, when Waterwheel ran onto the dirt track in about the eighth position, the jockey felt her give slightly beneath him. By the time she was back on the turf, a second later, it was clear to Alexis and me in the stands that she was not going to make a move, and was in fact slowing down. Shortly after everyone crossed the finish line, the jockey jumped off her, and while the others turned and came back to their grooms, Waterwheel and her jockey were pacing around on the far side, waiting to be picked up by the horse ambulance.

An X-ray half an hour later disclosed that the filly had fractured the two sesamoid bones in her left ankle, in the back, just above the fetlock joint, though the fractures were not displaced and her tendons and ligaments were unaffected (the life-

---

*The course at Epsom, for example, where the Epsom Derby (the English equivalent of the Kentucky Derby) is run, is a U-shaped monster. The second leg of the U rises quite steeply to a corner; then the last leg runs downhill and also cants noticeably toward the left rail. And since horses in England train at training centers rather than at racecourses, a three-year-old might run on the Epsom course only once in his life.

threatening danger of a sesamoid fracture is that the whole suspensory apparatus that holds the hoof and the lower leg together will be destroyed). Waterwheel was lucky. She lived.

She stayed in her stall at the track for a month; then, when her fractures were stable enough and the pain eased enough, she went on a van back to the training farm, where she could rest and recover and go back to work in a year as a broodmare. Eventually, she would be sound and pain-free, but racing, the most taxing equine sport, would be out of the question. And she was too small, too energetic, and too well bred to make a good riding horse. The only rider who ever fit her was a jockey; the idea of the fiery Waterwheel submitting to the wishes of some affectionate little girl was laughable.

WOWIE CAME BACK from his post-castration layoff happy and full of go. Allen put him in a dirt race, and the oddsmakers dismissed him. The race was to be a tune-up, just something to see where he was and whether he remembered how to run. He did. He ran fourth in a fast field. We were elated. Three weeks later, he went back to the turf. I was blasé by this time—or maybe still a little shell-shocked by what had happened to Waterwheel. I hadn't gotten used to limiting myself to even modest hopes for her career, before suddenly there had to be no hope at all.

Wowie was working well in the mornings. Two thousand three was going to be his big year, because he was a year older and a year stronger. He was no longer going to be carrying the highest weights—six and eight pounds more than the three-year-olds. Now he and the four-year-olds were even. The handicappers agreed with me—he went off as the third favorite, and he looked good in the post parade. He was running at Golden Gate Fields, which is a lovely, green, old-fashioned racetrack. No giant video screen in the middle of the view. On the other side of the backstretch, the Oakland hills rise against the bright sky. I'm sure the owners of the track don't appreciate this, but there are so few people there that the place is practically contemplative.

Anyway, Wowie's final race was a whimper, not a bang. He was much different from the way he had been in January. He ran along in a relaxed gallop, for all the world like he didn't care that he was in a race, and crossed the finish line somewhere toward the back of the pack. I made up my mind, as usual, according to revelation. I decided that he had lost his competitive spirit, and that keeping him at the track was a waste of his talents and my money. Allen wanted me to throw the race out and try again, but I wanted the horse home, and a week later, he came home, back to Watsonville, California, where he'd been born and raised. Allen brought him. He looked fit and beautiful, lean and shining. As Allen drove away, he said, "I meant to have him shod. He's a little overdue." This turned out to be the understatement of the year.

In the ensuing five-month nightmare of Wowie's feet, I got a first-class education in laminitis, horseshoeing, and the paradox of hooves. Even after we figured out what was (probably) happening inside his feet, many mysteries remained that X-rays could not answer. However, my preliminary guess is that, contrary to my original feeling about his last race, painful feet accounted for his poor performance. Probably he ran fine on the dirt because it was soft, wet, and forgiving. When he moved over to the firmer turf, he felt it enough to be distracted, but he was accustomed to racing and competitive enough to try a little bit.

When he came home, his toes were so long and his heels so under-run that his feet didn't really work like they belonged to him anymore—they were just appendages that he had to do something with. He moved awkwardly, like a person wearing flippers. Normally, a horse's hoof is shaped like a wedge, and, depending upon conformation, the angle at which the toe meets the ground is about fifty-three to fifty-seven degrees. The architecture of the horse's leg above the hoof is very precise. The well-being of all the joints up to the shoulder depends on the cup of the horse's hoof meeting the flat of the land exactly balanced, right to left and front to back. Otherwise, the joints, the bones, and the soft tissues suffer repeated stresses as the hoof hits the ground and tilts out of alignment. "No foot, no horse" is about the oldest horseman's expression there is, and any horse owner or trainer who doesn't cater and kowtow to her skilled and knowledgeable farrier is a fool.

Nevertheless, racetrack shoers have their own traditions, and leaving the toes long is one of them. Although it has been proved over and over that long toes do not lengthen a horse's stride, racetrack shoers still shoe as if they do. In addition, daily galloping over the sand and grit of the racetrack wears away the horse's heels—there is nothing to be done about that. But not every trainer allows the usual to happen. Alexis, for example, is always careful to oversee her farrier very closely and to make sure she and he are in agreement about the angle of the horses' hooves. When Wowie was with her, his feet were good and he was happy. In addition, not every horse has a problem with long toes. It is never good to have overlong toes and under-run heels, but some horses' feet and limbs can accommodate it. Wowie's could not. As we discovered on the X-rays, the soles of his feet are thin and more flat than cupped. This meant that, as his toes got longer, his soles hit the ground with more and more impact. In San Francisco, he didn't wear the bright-yellow impact-cushioning pads between his hooves and his shoes that he had worn in southern California. The result was that the tissues holding the bones of his feet to the walls of his hooves, called "laminae" because they interlock in layers, became inflamed and bruised from the pounding, and then infected. This is called "laminitis." The infection ate away the front edges of his coffin bones where they touched the inflamed tissues. He was in a lot of pain. The only cure was long and grotesquely slow—to gradually reshape the hoof as it grew out, until all the parts, interior and exterior, were back in alignment, hoping against hope that the parts would not move or deteriorate permanently while the process was taking place.

I spent five months with Wowie, taking care of him and treating his feet. I would have preferred to be riding him and teaching him a new career, but I got to know him, and I think I came to understand his, yes, Pisces nature, and why his racetrack career went the way it did. First, the look on his face. It was the same look he had had as a young horse—serious and benign. He always greeted me with nickers and whinnies. He always crossed the paddock to meet me, omitting to do so only when his feet hurt so badly that he couldn't move. He was never irritable, never resisted treatment. He allowed himself to have bad-tasting painkillers put on his tongue without resistance, though afterward he might bend down and dig his nose into the dust to wipe it off his lips. He tolerated shots and stood for X-rays and held his feet up for treatment patiently and kindly. When the puppy walked under his feet and got into his feed tub, he sniffed the puppy calmly, neither annoyed nor hostile.

The brief and intermittent work that we were able to do with him showed that he was willing and eager, but easily intimidated. Though he was not brave about new sights and unaccustomed objects, he would go forward and experience them if I asked him to. I saw that this was how he had accommodated racing, that his measure of competitive spirit was balanced by

:ar, and that his mode of dealing with the fear was to get out in front and run by himself or with only one or two other horses. That way he felt safer, and in fact was safer. Having the other horses overtake him was easier than trying to overtake them, just as giving in is easier than attempting a bold move. His antics in the paddock were a kind of stage fright. Once he got out on the track, he knew how to get down to business, but he had to run the race in his own way. Many races are run at the same speeds, whether they are stakes races or claiming races—forty-five-to-forty-six-second half, three-quarters of a mile in 1:12–1:13, and a mile in 1:36 or 1:37. Charlie Whittingham famously remarked, "Time only matters when you're in jail." Wowie's experience agreed with the theories of Sylvan Tompkins that what dictates the outcome of the race is, in addition to good or bad luck, each horse's ability to withstand and make use of the social psychology of the field of runners. An astute jockey can strongly influence how a race is run, but he can't make an arrogant bastard out of a sweetheart. I came to understand that Wowie is by nature a sweetheart. He might have won more races eventually; experience might have overcome temperament; but the problems of his feet have closed off that possibility.

Waterwheel was like a promising high school athlete who has a style but not a technique. In her four starts, she never developed a habitual mode of running that suited her. Even though we had all sorts of hopes for her because of her ambition and energy—she was dominant, self-confident, energetic, and aloof—her eagerness, a mental quality, did turn out to be destructive to her body. It is almost certainly true that her sesamoid fractures resulted in some way from undetected stress fractures that were already present but not evident. Brian Nielson, quoted in an article in the *Thoroughbred Times,* maintains (as do other researchers), "The faster you go, the more strain you put on the legs and the greater likelihood of injury." She always wanted to go fast. She was never careful. Alexis understood the danger and tried to work with it and around it, but the accident intervened in spite of attention and care. Cautions, in horse racing, are general—"Don't race two-year-olds"—and there are thousands of counter-examples to every caution. Seabiscuit ran dozens of times as a two-year-old.

In Darlin' Corey, Wowie's younger sister, born the same year as Waterwheel, the qualities of personality and athleticism came up in yet another mix. She was much bigger than either of the other two—three or four inches taller than Wowie, and wider, with longer legs, bigger feet, sturdier bone. At two, she was tall and bulky, and also not very coordinated, so, instead of going to the racetrack, she stayed in Watsonville. She was also exceptionally sociable and relaxed. When she did get to the racetrack, in the December before her three-year-old year, nothing worried her. On her second day, there was a training accident that involved the horse ambulance and other noise and bustle. She stood quietly, watching, her ears pricked, but not shying or anxious. And nothing has since made her anxious—not racing or training or any other kind of event. She doesn't mind being in the middle of the pack, with other horses around her—she pushes them. With fitness, she has gotten bolder and more aggressive—she trots and bucks and pulls to get to her training sessions. In three starts, she has shown some talent and also had some bad luck. In her first start, she was the longest shot on the board. She showed confusion coming out of the gate and running down the hill, then crossing the main track, but she beat three other horses, and the handicappers, who had dismissed her so completely. In her second start, she ran last most of the way around, then went wide and came up to take second. In her third start, she was running about sixth when the horse right in front of her veered out, into her path, and Corey's jockey had to pull her up and turn her, interfering with her stride. She got going again before the end of the race, but didn't manage to overcome the bad trip. My intuition about her is that she is mentally suited to the life she leads. And she is gradually getting faster as she gets fitter.

Is this the one? That is the owner's perennial question, the question psychology asks of sociology, the question the individual asks the numbers. For Corey, the numbers say probably not. Her sire was a good racehorse, but hasn't produced many winners, and was sent from California to Mexico, a black hole as far as Thoroughbred breeding is concerned. Her dam, Emma, had a few winners, but more bad luck, and she was just a modest racehorse. Pedigree-wise, Corey would be bucking the odds. But her individual personality—dominant, self-confident, energetic, friendly—says maybe. Her physique—long legs, long stride, strong, sound—adds to the maybe. Her temperament—relaxation that revs into aggression rather than fear—adds again to the maybe. Into the mix we add luck, training technique, care, attention, timing, money, the world political situation, the state of horse racing in California, Alexis's health and luck, my health, luck, and impulsiveness, the march of time and fate. Maybe.

The fact is, I have written the unhappy ending now, as well as a hopeful beginning to the second volume (God forbid!), and what I was dreading—catharsis, the promise and threat of tragedy—has not come to pass. Waterwheel's injury was sobering, and gave me to think about two-year-old racing. Probably I won't race a two-year-old again. Wowie's hoof problems have been time-consuming and emotionally taxing, and they, too, have given me to think. Probably I won't send a horse to any trainer other than Alexis. Alexis is obsessively detail-oriented. Horses in southern California get the best care. Even when they aren't expensive enough to deserve it, they deserve it anyway, as creatures. More absolute, and possibly more moral, horsemen would swear off racing entirely. Alexis is always closer to swearing off than I am, even though it is her livelihood.

Five months after leaving the racetrack, when his feet were finally shaped normally and he was trotting soundly, I stood in the middle of the arena, watching Wowie taking his lesson with Ray. The horse was still something of a conundrum. Sometimes he acted like a frightened two-year-old who knew nothing; other times he acted ready to do anything he was asked. The week before, Ray had set out into the woods with Wowie on a loose rein, returning twenty minutes later with no problems. It wasn't until that evening that I realized that the horse had never been on the trail in his entire life, never away from the compound, never out and about with no equine companion, and yet had done beautifully. Now I had set up five trot poles in a grid, about six feet apart. Without taxing him too much, I wanted to see what Wowie thought about jumping, or at least stepping over poles. After walking through them a couple of times, Ray turned and came around in a large circle at a trot, aiming the horse for the center of the first pole of the grid. Wowie's ears were pricked; the look on his face was serious and attentive. He sparkled through the poles, lifting his feet quickly and elegantly, in perfect rhythm and form. I said his name, "Wow!" It wasn't as though he had accomplished anything fabulous in the larger scheme of things, or that I had not expected him to do such a thing. It was that his grace and beauty struck me anew, as they had over and over in his years at the racetrack. They did it again, as easily and brightly as before. Now Ray and I were both grinning.

Two days later, Hali called me. She said, "What did Wowie do Friday?"

"He trotted over some poles on the ground. He looked great."

"He loved it. He thinks this is the solution to the dilemma of his life."

"He does?"

"You know, he's fairly reserved as a rule. But he's been talking about it all weekend."

I babbled enthusiastically until she said, "Say, I'm seeing something like a tennis shoe with a pad in it. Is there some sort of padded shoe that horses can wear?"

"We put pads between his shoes and his hooves the last time he was shod."

"Well, he says that they prevent the sort of vibration in the bones of his legs that he used to have at the track. He likes them."

"Does he mind if I quote him in the *Thoroughbred Times*?"

She was silent for a moment. Then she said, "He doesn't know what the *Thoroughbred Times* is."

"A couple of years ago, they ran an article about how running in metal horseshoes causes a lot of vibration in horses' cannon bones. Think of bridge stress. I guess they should have asked the horses, huh?"

AND SO, the reward for me, and sometimes it is a bittersweet reward, is still in seeing how it all turns out—how character and events add up to the appropriate, always appropriate, denouement.

BIBLIOGRAPHY

Blake, Henry. *Talking with Horses.* E. P. Dutton, 1976.

Budiansky, Stephen. *The Covenant of the Wild: Why Animals Chose Domestication.* William Morrow, 1992.

———. *The World According to Horses: How They Run, See, and Think.* Henry Holt, 2000.

Chamberlain, Harry D. *Training Hunters, Jumpers, and Hacks.* D. Van Nostrand, 1952.

Diamond, Jared. *Guns, Germs, and Steel: The Fates of Human Societies.* W. W. Norton, 1999.

Gardner, Howard. *Frames of Mind: The Theory of Multiple Intelligences.* Tenth Anniversary Edition, Basic Books, 1993.

Keirsey, David. *Please Understand Me II.* Prometheus Nemesis Books, 1998.

Lewis, Thomas, M.D., Fari Amini, M.D., and Richard Lannon, M.D. *A General Theory of Love.* Random House, 2000.

Oadford, Barbara Worth. *My Seventy-Year Trip to the Show Jumping Hall of Fame.* Privately published.

Podhajsky, Alois. *My Horses, My Teachers.* Doubleday, 1968.

Sacks, Oliver. *The Man Who Mistook His Wife for a Hat.* HarperPerennial, 1987.

Tesio, Federico. *Breeding the Racehorse.* J. A. Allen, 1958.

Thomas, Elizabeth Marshall. *The Hidden Life of Dogs.* Houghton Mifflin, 1993.

———. *The Tribe of the Tiger: Cats and Their Culture.* Simon & Schuster, 1994.

Wright, Gordon. *The Cavalry Manual of Horsemanship and Horsemastership.* Doubleday, 1962.

DUPLICATE KEYS

Alice Ellis is a Midwestern refugee living in Manhattan. Still recovering from a painful divorce, she depends on the companionship and camaraderie of a tightly knit circle of friends. At the center of this circle is a rock band struggling to navigate New York's erratic music scene, and an apartment/practice space with approximately fifty key-holders. One day, Alice enters to find two of the band members shot dead. Then when she begins to notice things amiss in her own apartment, it occurs to her that she is not the only person with a key, and she may not get a chance to change the locks.

Fiction/Literature/1-4000-7602-1

GOOD FAITH

Forthright, likable Joe Stratford is the kind of local businessman everybody trusts, for good reason. But it's 1982, and even in Joe's small town, values are in upheaval: not just property values, either. Enter Marcus Burns, a would-be master of the universe whose years with the IRS have taught him which rules are meant to be broken. Before long he and Joe are new best friends—and partners in an investment venture so complex that no one may ever understand it. Add to this Joe's roller coaster affair with his mentor's married daughter. The result is as entertaining as any of Smiley's fiction.

Fiction/Literature/0-385-72105-6

THE AGE OF GRIEF

The Age of Grief captures moments of great intimacy with grace, clarity, and indelible emotional power. In "The Pleasure of Her Company," a lonely single woman befriends a married couple, hoping to learn the secret of their happiness. In "Long Distance," a man is relieved of the obligation to continue an affair that is no longer compelling to him, only to be waylaid by the guilt he feels at his easy escape. And in the wise and moving title novella, a dentist, aware that his wife has fallen in love with someone else, must comfort her when she is spurned, while enduring his own complicated sorrow.

Fiction/Literature/0-385-72187-0

A THOUSAND ACRES

When Larry Cook, the aging patriarch of a thriving farm in Iowa, decides to retire, he offers his land to his three daughters. For Ginny and Rose, who live on the farm with their husbands, the gift makes good sense—a reward for years of hard work and a challenge to make the farm even more successful. But Caroline, a Des Moines lawyer, flatly rejects the idea, and in anger her father cuts her out of the will. This sets off a chain of events that brings dark truths to light and explodes long-suppressed emotions. An ambitious reimagining of Shakespeare's *King Lear* cast upon a typical American community, this Pulitzer Prize–winning novel takes on themes of truth, justice, love, and pride and reveals the beautiful yet treacherous topography of humanity.

Fiction/Literature/1-4000-3383-7

ANCHOR BOOKS
Available at your local bookstore, or call toll-free to order:
1-800-793-2665 (credit cards only).